Study Guide

PSYCHOLOGY

Study Guide

Richard L. Leavy
Ohio Wesleyan University

PSYCHOLOGY

James D. Laird
Nicholas S. Thompson

Clark University

HOUGHTON MIFFLIN COMPANY   BOSTON   TORONTO
DALLAS   GENEVA, ILLINOIS   PALO ALTO   PRINCETON, NEW JERSEY

Senior Sponsoring Editor: Mike DeRocco
Senior Project Editor: Carol Newman
Assistant Design Manager: Karen Rappaport
Ancillary Coordinator: Tracy Theriault
Senior Manufacturing Specialist: Marie Barnes
Marketing Manager: Diane McOscar

Cover: Oskar Schlemmer, *Madchenkopf in Farbiger Karierung*, 1932. Private collection, © 1991, the Oskar Schlemmer family estate, Badenweiler, Germany. Photoarchive/C. Raman Schlemmer, Oggebbio, Italy.

Printed in the U.S.A.

Library of Congress Catalog Card Number: 91-71977

ISBN: 0-395-59231-3

ABCDEFGHIJ-PO-9987654321

CONTENTS

PREFACE

This *Study Guide* is designed to help you master the material in *Psychology* by James D. Laird and Nicholas S. Thompson. It is unwise to read the *Study Guide* in place of the textbook. If after reading a chapter in the textbook, however, you use the *Study Guide,* you will find your understanding and memory for information improved. The quizzes in the *Study Guide* will also help you gauge your mastery of the material before taking your professor's examinations.

Organization of the Study Guide

The *Study Guide* chapters correspond to chapters in the text. Each chapter of this book includes a list of learning objectives, a chapter outline, a quiz on key terms, and multiple-choice quizzes on text material.

- *Learning Objectives* The learning objectives are designed to focus your attention on the key concepts in each chapter. They ask you to define, describe, discuss, and differentiate among important ideas. Each learning objective is keyed to a section in the text. Page numbers for those sections are given in parentheses following each learning objective. Using the *Study Guide* and text interactively will help you achieve maximum benefit from both. If you can achieve all the listed objectives in a *Study Guide* chapter, you will have mastered a significant portion of the corresponding text material.

- *Chapter Outlines* The chapter outlines present the major topics in each chapter. Key terms are defined, and page numbers corresponding to the outline material are provided. Because they are condensed overviews of the text material, the outlines can help you review and assess your level of knowledge. They are excellent study aids and can help you organize material as you study for exams. They *cannot* and *should not* be used as substitutes for reading the chapter.

- *Key Terms* One of the challenges of introductory psychology is learning the terminology of each of the various subfields. To help you achieve this mastery, key terms are defined within each chapter of the text and italicized in the chapter outlines of the *Study Guide*. In addition, each *Study Guide* chapter contains a fill-in-the-blank quiz, designed to test and reinforce your mastery of the key terms and their definitions.

- *Multiple-Choice Quizzes* Once you have read a chapter in the text and worked your way through the learning objectives, chapter outline, and fill-in-the-blank quiz, you will be ready to test your knowledge of the chapter's content. There are thirty multiple-choice questions in each *Study Guide* chapter. Twenty fact-and-concept questions are designed to test your knowledge of specific facts, definitions, principles, and the relationships among them. Ten application questions test your ability to apply your learning in real-world contexts. Correct answers to the questions and explanations for why they are correct and the alternatives are wrong end each chapter of the *Study Guide*. Page numbers identifying supporting text material are given in parentheses.

A Final Word

The purpose of this *Study Guide* is to assist you in understanding and remembering the considerable amount of information presented in *Psychology*. Your active and persistent involvement in the learning process will help you achieve success in this, your first psychology course. Good luck in this class!

Carol Newman, my editor at Houghton Mifflin, provided ideas, freedom, and support as I developed this *Study Guide*. My wife, Chris, listened to my ideas, gave constructive feedback, and buffered me from family responsibilities so I could complete the book. My children, Aaron and Kate, also deserve thanks for their patience and good humor.

R. L. L.

Study Guide

PSYCHOLOGY

CHAPTER 1

PSYCHOLOGY: THE SCIENCE OF BEHAVIOR AND EXPERIENCE

Learning Objectives

1. Define psychology and explain the terms *science, behavior,* and *experience.* Describe the goals of the scientific method. (pp. 3–4)

2. Describe and discuss the characteristics of theories and hypotheses. Discuss how commonsense explanations make psychology a discipline that is both easy and hard to study. (pp. 4–6)

3. Describe the thinking in the prepsychology period, including Cartesian dualism and Darwin's contributions. Discuss the birth of psychology as a science. (pp. 7–8)

4. Describe and differentiate among the ideas and methods used by structuralism, Gestalt psychology, functionalism, Freudian psychology, behaviorism, humanistic psychology, and cognitive psychology. (pp. 8–11)

5. Describe the types of roles today's psychologists play—including clinical, counseling, physiological, sensory and perceptual, comparative, cognitive, developmental, personality, and social psychologists. (pp. 11–12)

6. Define and discuss the concepts *variable, naturalistic observation, comparison, case study, representative* and *random samples.* (pp. 13–14)

7. Discuss how psychological variables are quantitatively measured. Explain what *validity* and *reliability* mean. (pp. 15–16)

8. Describe the components of an experiment, including experimental and control groups, and independent and dependent variables. Explain how experiments clarify causal relationships. (pp. 16–18)

9. Describe what a research program is. Discuss how ethics constrain psychological research methods. (pp. 19–20)

10. Discuss how psychological knowledge affects our freedom of choice. Describe the general contents of the rest of the text. (pp. 21–23)

Chapter Outline

1. *Psychology,* **the** *science* (pp. 3–6)

   Psychology is the *science* of *behavior* and *experience*. A science is a discipline that uses systematic observation to describe, explain, and predict events. In psychology, we are interested in observable activities (behavior) and thoughts, feelings, and perceptions (experience). Psychology employs the *scientific method* to make observations objective, precise, and reliable. It also uses general explanations of behavior (*theories*) and specific expectations about how things will behave (*hypotheses*) based on theories to direct the investigation of behavior and experience. Theories use terms that have operational definitions so that they can be explicit. Scientists also attempt to create general and coherent theories.

   Although psychology's relevance to everyday living makes it an easy discipline to study, it can pose difficulties when commonsense explanations are violated.

2. **A history** (pp. 6–11)

   In the prepsychology period (before 1859), philosophers such as René Descartes dominated discussions about the mind and behavior. *Cartesian dualism,* the idea that the mind and body operate under different principles, gave encouragement to scientific investigation. By 1859, when Charles Darwin published *The Origin of Species,* the door was opened to the scientific study of the mind.

   Most psychologists trace the birth of the field to Wilhelm Wundt, who opened the first psychological laboratory in 1879. By the beginning of this century, psychologists had formed schools of thought. *Structuralism* was the school of psychology that analyzed experiences through a process called *introspection*. *Gestalt psychology* was a competing school that emphasized the whole, not the parts, of experience. Another school, called *functionalism,* maintained that instincts that helped the human being evolve and survive determined behavior. Sigmund Freud argued that unconscious motives explained our actions and developed a method called *psychoanalysis* to uncover these motives. *Behaviorism* is the school of psychology that holds that psychology should limit itself to the study of observable activity and that instincts play a very minor role in human beings. *Humanistic psychology,* developed in the 1950s, argues that people are free to shape their behavior. Finally, the school of thought that emphasizes mental processes and the means by which information is processed is called *cognitive psychology*.

3. **Psychology today: the subdisciplines** (pp. 11–12)

Rather than choosing one school or another, most psychologists today take an eclectic approach. Contemporary psychologists perform a wide range of tasks. *Clinical* psychologists help people with emotional problems and usually work in health settings. *Counseling psychologists* are more likely to help people with everyday living problems and work in educational settings. Other consulting psychologists work with schools, community organizations, and in government and business. Those who work in colleges and universities teach and can do research on the nervous system (physiological psychologists), sensory systems (sensation and perception psychologists), animal behavior (comparative psychologists), information processing (cognitive psychologists), changes in behavior across the life span (developmental psychologists), individual traits (personality psychologists), and interpersonal interactions (social psychologists).

4. **The research process: *naturalistic observation* and formal observation** (pp. 13–16)

Most psychological research examines the relationship between two or more *variables*. These variables can be examined in real-life situations through *naturalistic observation*. When formal observation is used to study some behavior or experience, we can look at one individual repeatedly in a *case study*. If we want to *generalize* about a whole *population*, however, it is important to have an adequate *sample* from the population. *Representative samples* have characteristics similar to the population from which they are drawn. Ideally, members of the sample are drawn purely by chance, a *random sample*, so that every member of the population has an equal chance of being included.

Variables must be measured in some quantifiable way. One means of doing this is the *rating scale:* an instrument by which behavior is scored numerically. For example, rating anxiety from 0 (none at all) to 10 (terrified) constitutes a rating scale. Ideally, the measuring instruments we use relate closely to the factor we seek to measure (they show *validity*) and are relatively absent of errors (they show *reliability*).

5. **The research process: experimentation, the research program, and ethics** (pp. 16–20)

When a relationship between two variables is found, a correlation exists, but this does not tell us anything about what causes what. An *experiment* in which a researcher manipulates the amount or presence of variables and then observes the effects can clarify cause-and-effect relationships. In an experiment, one group of subjects is exposed to the factor under study (the *experimental group*) and is compared with subjects who are not so treated (the *control group*). The *independent variable* is controlled by the experimenter; the *dependent variable* is the measure of behavior we anticipate the independent variable will affect. Because they involve artificial comparisons, results from experiments may have limited application to the real world.

Research programs are a series of investigations that may use different research approaches to test theory and explain and predict behavior. Because they study humans and animals, psychologists must be aware of the effect of research on their subjects. Ethical guidelines exist for research with both humans and animals.

6. **Science and behavioral control** (pp. 21–22)

Some fear that the scientific study of behavior will reduce our freedom. Psychologists believe that understanding increases freedom of choice.

7. **The plan of this book** (pp. 22–23)

This book opens with an examination of the nervous system. Then we look at sensation, perception, consciousness, and learning—basic processes for all people—followed by memory, thought, and language. The middle of the text discusses emotions, motivations, and development; then individual differences as well as psychological disorders. Finally, we investigate how society shapes people. Special features are interspersed to point out research method questions, provoke you to think, and help you master the material.

Fill-in-the-Blank Quiz

1. The school of psychology that believes that people control their own actions and thoughts is called _____ .

2. The school of psychology that believes that behavior is governed by instincts that help the individual adapt to the environment is called _____ .

3. Our feelings, thoughts, and perceptions are collectively called _____ .

4. In an experiment, the comparison group that receives no treatment is called the _____ .

5. A psychologist who diagnoses and treats emotional problems, usually in a health care setting, is called a _____ .

6. René Descartes' idea that the mind and the body operate under different principles is called _____ .

7. Any activity that can be observed is called _____ .

8. The school of psychology that believes that the study of psychology must be limited to the study of observable activity is called _____ .

9. The detailed examination of a single individual or instance of a psychological phenomenon is the research method called the _____ .

10. The school of psychology that emphasizes the mental processes by which people and animals come to understand the world is called _____ .

11. In an experiment, the subjects who are exposed to the factor being studied is called the _____ .

12. A variable that the experimenter controls or manipulates is called the _____ .

13. The process of watching subjects in real-life situations to see how they behave is called _____ .

14. The science of behavior and experience is called _____ .

15. An instrument that asks a subject to measure numerically the strength of a psychological variable is called a _____ .

16. A sample whose characteristics are similar to those of the population from which it was drawn is called a _____ .

17. The procedures that help make observations more precise, objective, and reliable are called collectively the _____ .

18. A characteristic or factor that can change is called a _____ .

19. A general explanation of how things work based on a number of systematic observations is called a _____ .

20. A discipline that uses systematic observation and experimentation to describe, explain, and predict events in the world is called a _____ .

21. The degree to which a measurement procedure makes few errors is called the procedure's _____ .

22. A sample whose members are selected purely by chance is called a _____ .

23. All the people or animals to which a theory applies is called a _____ .

24. The method used by structuralists that confronted subjects with a stimulus and asked them to describe it in detail is called _____ .

25. An expectation, based on theory, of how something will behave under specific circumstances is a definition of a _____ .

26. The school of psychology that believes that the whole, not its parts, is the fundamental experience is called _____ .

27. Drawing conclusions about a whole population from the study of a sample is called _____ .

28. A scientific procedure in which the researcher manipulates the amount or presence of one or more variables and then observes the effects on other variables is called an _____ .

29. The variable that is expected to change as a function of the independent variable is called _____ .

30. A psychologist who helps people with the practical problems of everyday life, often in an educational setting, is called a _____ .

31. The small part of a population that is studied in order to collect information about the whole population is called a _____ .

32. The school of psychology that analyzed experience by breaking it down into basic elements was called _____ .

33. The degree to which a measure relates to the factor it was supposed to be measuring is called the measure's _____ .

Fill-in-the-Blank Answers

1. humanistic psychology
2. functionalism
3. experience
4. control group
5. clinical psychologist
6. Cartesian dualism
7. behavior
8. behaviorism
9. case study
10. cognitive psychology
11. experimental group
12. independent variable
13. naturalistic observation
14. psychology
15. rating scale
16. representative sample
17. scientific method
18. variable
19. theory
20. science
21. reliability
22. random sample
23. population
24. introspection
25. hypothesis
26. Gestalt psychology
27. generalizing
28. experiment
29. dependent variable
30. counseling psychologist
31. sample
32. structuralism
33. validity

Fact and Concept Questions

1. Psychology is best defined as the
   a. science of the mind.
   b. science of behavior and experience.
   c. art of changing behavior.
   d. art of understanding the mind.

2. When psychologists are interested in the perceptions, thoughts, and feelings that people have, they say they are interested in
   a. behavior.
   b. the unconscious.
   c. common sense.
   d. experience.

3. _____ is designed to improve the precision, reliability, and objectivity of scientific observations.
   a. Correlation
   b. The scientific method
   c. Introspection
   d. The research program

4. Theory is to _____ as general is to specific.
   a. experiment
   b. operational definition
   c. hypothesis
   d. counterintuitive finding

5. The idea of Cartesian dualism argues that
   a. different principles guide the spiritual and physical worlds.
   b. there are unconscious motives that are separate from conscious thoughts and actions.
   c. observable behaviors are the only appropriate targets for study in psychology.
   d. the mind and the body are ruled by one set of principles.

6. Roughly speaking, when was psychology in its infancy?
   a. In Descartes' time—the 1600s.
   b. During the American Revolution—the 1770s.
   c. At the end of the 1800s.
   d. During the Great Depression—the 1930s.

7. Founded by E. B. Titchener, the school of psychology called _____ was most interested in consciousness, and studied it using _____ .
   a. structuralism; introspection
   b. Gestalt psychology; introspection
   c. structuralism; experiments with animals
   d. behaviorism; experiments with animals

8. Gestalt psychology was interested in _____ ; functionalism focused on
   _____ .
   a. the unconscious; the conscious
   b. analyzing the parts of consciousness; whole experience
   c. instincts; learned behaviors
   d. whole experience; instincts

9. Which school of psychology is most likely to use dreams and random thoughts to explain human behavior?
   a. Gestalt psychology
   b. functionalism
   c. Freudian psychology
   d. behaviorism

10. _____ psychologists are most likely to study the mental processes by which animals and humans understand and react to the world around them.
    a. Counseling
    b. Physiological
    c. Humanistic
    d. Cognitive

11. Which word best describes the way most psychologists think about their field today?
    a. eclectic
    b. Freudian
    c. clinical
    d. humanistic

12. What is an important difference between clinical psychologists and counseling psychologists?
    a. Clinical psychologists help people; counseling psychologists do not.
    b. Clinical psychologists often work in health care settings; counseling psychologists often work in educational ones.
    c. Clinical psychologists usually work with less serious problems; counseling psychologists usually work with more serious ones.
    d. Clinical psychologists cannot diagnose or treat people; counseling psychologists can.

13. One of the problems with naturalistic observation is that
    a. it does not allow us to see the relationship between two variables.
    b. it does not tell us what people are thinking or feeling.
    c. it manipulates the situation so much that it creates an artificial situation.
    d. it only looks at one person so we cannot generalize to others.

14. In order to generalize to an entire population, psychologists strive to form representative samples by
    a. asking interested people if they want to participate.
    b. studying only one very good subject.
    c. studying only those people whose behavior proves the theory.
    d. selecting participants by chance.

15. Psychologists use rating scales and other means to _____ psychological variables.
    a. quantify
    b. eliminate
    c. sample
    d. generalize

16. If a measurement procedure is very reliable, we know that
    a. there are very few errors in the way a variable is being measured.
    b. the dependent variable is equal to the independent variable.
    c. it is measuring the factor we want it to.
    d. the variable is being measured without using an operational definition.

17. If a research study employs an independent variable and a control group, we can assume that the study is
    a. a case study.
    b. a correlation.
    c. an experiment.
    d. an unethical one.

18. The dependent variable is the one
    a. the experimenter manipulates.
    b. found only in the control group.
    c. that is expected to change as a function of the independent variable.
    d. none of the above.

19. Which statement is true about animal research in psychology?
    a. Because psychologists are interested in human behavior, they do not use animals in research.
    b. Recent investigations show that animals are usually injured and mistreated by psychological research.
    c. The American Psychological Association has no regulations on the care and treatment of animals.
    d. Animals are used in research to increase our knowledge and help reduce human suffering.

20. Your textbook authors suggest that the value of learning psychology is to
    a. be able to control the behavior of other people.
    b. reduce the number of choices that a person can make.
    c. increase our freedom by understanding behavior better.
    d. expose people to ideas and feelings that they have never had before.

Application Questions

1. Mr. Rowlinson says, "Psychology is the science that studies the observable behavior of people by using systematic observations or experiments." Mr. Rowlinson's definition is not quite accurate because
   a. psychology is not a real science.
   b. psychologists cannot perform experiments.
   c. he left out the study of experience.
   d. psychology is not interested in observable behavior.

2. Dr. Erman is doing an experiment about human memory. When we ask him, "what do you predict will affect memory in your experiment?" he says, "I *have* no prediction." This research is missing something. What?
   a. a variable
   b. a hypothesis
   c. a sample
   d. a topic

3. Imagine you lived in the 1600s and you heard a philosopher say this: "The mind and the body are completely separate. They are governed by different principles. The body can be understood because it is physical; the mind is spiritual and can never be understood." These ideas reflect
   a. the school of thought called humanistic psychology.
   b. behaviorism.
   c. Freudian psychology.
   d. Cartesian dualism.

4. Dr. Willis says, "I am interested in the whole of our experience, not its parts. I think of music as a complete experience, not just a combination of notes." Dr. Willis's ideas most clearly reflect which school of psychology?
   a. Gestalt
   b. Freudian
   c. cognitive
   d. functionalism

5. A psychotherapist who stresses the ability of patients to control their own actions and thoughts and who believes that people are basically good is most likely to agree with the _____ school of psychology.
   a. humanistic
   b. structuralist
   c. behaviorist
   d. Freudian

6. Dr. Lawrence studies the changes that take place as people grow older. Dr. Lawrence's work identifies her as a _____ psychologist.
   a. cognitive
   b. physiological
   c. counseling
   d. developmental

7. Dr. Bingham is studying how boys and girls of different ages interact on the playground during recess at school. She collects data on this by standing on one side of the playground every day for three weeks. We can say that Dr. Bingham's research
   a. is an experiment.
   b. is using naturalistic observation.
   c. makes no comparisons.
   d. has no variables.

8. Which of the following is a representative sample of college students at a large university?
   a. All the male students at the school.
   b. Every fifth student in the school's directory.
   c. Students on the dean's list or honor roll.
   d. All psychology majors.

9. Dr. Parks is studying the effects of sleeplessness on creativity. Some research participants complete a creativity test after a normal night's sleep; others complete it after being deprived of a full night's sleep. The independent variable is
   a. performance on the creativity test.
   b. whether or not the person is creative.
   c. sleeplessness.
   d. There is no independent variable in this study.

10. Dr. Harvey started studying aggression by watching animals fight each other. Then he did a series of experiments in which crowding and other factors were varied to see their effect on aggression. Finally, he changed real-world settings to see if aggression could be reduced. This series of studies illustrates
    a. what a clinical psychologist does for a living.
    b. what a correlation is.
    c. what a research program is.
    d. the lack of ethical principles that plague psychology.

Fact and Concept Answers

1. * b. Psychology is the scientific study of both observable behavior and inner experience. (p. 3)

   a. Psychology is as interested in behavior as it is interested in the mind.

   c. Although psychologists may be interested in changing behavior, the foremost goal of the science is to understand behavior and experience.

   d. Psychology is a science, not an art.

2. * d. Experience is the internal world of people: their thoughts, feelings, and perceptions. (p. 3)

   a. Behavior is the observable actions of people and animals.

   b. The unconscious is a part of the internal experience, but so are conscious thought, perceptions, and feelings.

   c. Common sense is an explanation for behavior, not our feelings and perceptions.

3. * b. The scientific method is a system for making our observations of the world impartial, accurate, and consistent. (p. 4)

   a. A correlation is an association between two variables.

   c. Introspection is the not very scientific process used seventy-five years ago by structuralist psychologists to study the mind.

   d. A research program is a series of investigations, perhaps using different methods, to test a theory.

4. * c. A theory is a general set of expectations, whereas an hypothesis is an expectation about how something will behave in specific circumstances according to a theory. (p. 4)

   a. An experiment is one method for doing research involving an independent variable.

   b. An operational definition is a numerical way of defining a variable.

   d. Counterintuitive findings run against common sense; they are unrelated to the general-specific issue.

5. * a. René Descartes argued that the mind and body were governed by spiritual and physical rules, respectively. Based on his name, the idea is called Cartesian dualism. (p. 7)

   b. The idea of the unconscious is a contribution of Sigmund Freud.

   c. Behaviorists argue that observable behavior is the only appropriate target for study in psychology.

   d. This the opposite of Cartesian dualism.

6. * c. Wilhelm Wundt founded the first psychological laboratory in 1879. Most historians place the infancy of the field in the last twenty years of the 1800s. (p. 8)

   a. Descartes' time was in the pre-psychology period.

   b. The American Revolution was in the pre-psychology period.

   d. Most of the great schools of psychology were established by the 1930s: structuralism, functionalism, behaviorism, Gestalt and Freudian psychology.

7. * a. Structuralists like Titchener wanted to analyze the contents of consciousness. They did this by asking people to perceive the smallest possible unit of experience, a process called introspection. (p. 9)

   b. Gestalt psychology was interested in the whole, not the structuralism's parts; Kohler, Koffka, and Wertheimer were its founders, not Titchener.

   c. Structuralists were interested in human consciousness, so they did no animal research at all.

   d. Behaviorists took an opposite position from Titchener and the structuralists.

8. * d. Gestalt psychology investigated whole perceptions and experiences; functionalism was interested in instincts that developed through evolution and helped us adapt. (p. 9)

   a. Freud stressed the unconscious.

   b. Gestalt psychologists rebelled against the analysis of parts performed by structuralists.

   c. Functionalism looked at instincts rather than learned behaviors.

9. * c. Freudian psychology argues that the unconscious as expressed in dreams, slips of the tongue, and random thoughts controls what we do and feel. (p. 10)

   a. Gestalt psychology was interested in conscious, whole experience.

   b. Functionalism was interested in instincts, not dreams or random thoughts.

   d. Behaviorism has no use for dreams or thoughts because they cannot be objectively observed.

10. * d. Cognitive psychology emphasizes the methods by which animals and people take in and process information about the world. (p. 10)

    a. Counseling psychologists try to help people with daily living problems; they are not strictly interested in thought process.

    b. Physiological psychologists study the central nervous system.

    c. Humanistic psychologists are concerned with people's ability to control their actions and thoughts, but the interest in information processing is secondary.

11. * a. Most psychologists draw a little from many different points of view and use what works best. This is a definition of *eclectic*. (p. 11)

    b. Freudian psychology is one school of thought.

    c. Clinical psychologists can take many different perspectives, but they all seek to diagnose and treat people with serious emotional problems.

    d. Humanistic psychology is one school of thought.

12. * b. Clinical psychologists often work in health care settings because they deal with more seriously disturbed individuals; counseling psychologists more often work in educational settings such as university counseling centers. (p. 11)

    a. Both clinical and counseling psychologists are in the helping professions.

    c. The reverse of this statement is true.

    d. The major portion of the clinical psychologist's day is taken up with diagnosis and treatment.

13. * b. Because it can only investigate observable behavior, naturalistic observation cannot study thinking or feeling. (p. 13)

    a. All forms of observation allow us to see correlations between variables.

    c. Laboratory experiments have this weakness. One of the strengths of naturalistic observation is that it collects data in real-world situations.

    d. Only the case study looks at one person.

14. * d. When we select participants at random, with everyone having an equal chance, we produce a random sample that balances individual factors so well it is representative of the whole population. (p. 14)

    a. If people select themselves, there can be bias in the sample.

    b. A single person is not a sample; samples are groups of people who, we hope, represent many others.

    c. This would be a most unrepresentative sample and would bias all results.

15. * a. Rating scales such as thought that use a 10-point scale help psychologists quantify (define in terms of numbers) variables under study. (p. 16)

    b. Scales help measure variables; they do not eliminate them.

    c. People are sampled, not variables.

    d. Representative samples help us generalize to populations; rating scales are irrelevant to generalization.

16. * a. High reliability means few errors in measurement—it means we can trust the measurement we have made. (p. 16)

    b. The dependent variable is a measure of behavior that we expect to change as a function of the independent variable.

    c. Validity is defined as the ability of a measure to measure what we want it to.

    d. If a variable were not operationally defined, we would find it impossible to have a reliable measure of it.

17. * c. In an experiment, the researcher manipulates one variable (the independent variable) to see the effect on behavior (the dependent variable). In all experiments, there is a comparison made between, at a minimum, one experimental group and one control group. (p. 18)

   a. A case study uses only one person or animal, so no comparison can be made.

   b. A correlation is an association between variables where neither variable is manipulated, as in an experiment.

   d. Ethics is unrelated to this question.

18. * c. The dependent variable is a measure of behavior that is supposed to change in the presence of the independent variable. (p. 18)

   a. The independent variable is the one the experimenter can manipulate.

   b. The dependent variable is observed and recorded for both the experimental and control groups in an experiment.

   d. Because *c* is an accurate answer, this cannot be the best response.

19. * d. Animals are used because we cannot ethically perform some procedures on people in the quest for knowledge; policies ensure the ethical handling of animals. (p. 20)

   a. Animals are used in psychological research; a subdiscipline of psychology (comparative psychology) is directly interested in animal behavior.

   b. By and large, animals are not mistreated.

   c. The American Psychological Association has ethical guidelines for both human and animal research.

20. * c. Your authors argue that to know more about human behavior adds to our freedom of choice rather than reducing it (pp. 21–22)

   a. Fears of being controlled are groundless, say your authors.

   b. The opposite of this seems true, according to your textbook authors.

   d. Your authors suggest that most of us have thoughts and feelings that are shared by psychologists. The difference is that the psychologist uses scientific means to study these ideas.

Application Answers

1. * c. A full definition of psychology includes both behavior (the observable) and experience (unobservable thoughts and feelings). (p. 3)

   a. Psychology is a science.

   b. Psychologists can and do perform experiments.

   d. Psychology is interested in both the observable and the internal (unobservable) experience.

2. * b. A hypothesis is a theory-based expectation about how one factor will affect another; Dr. Erman has no clear expectation about what will affect memory. (p. 4)

   a. A variable is anything that can change, such as memory.

   c. A sample is a group that may represent a larger population; we have no information one way or the other about Dr. Erman's sample.

   d. Dr. Erman's topic is memory; that's just about all we know about his study.

3. * d. Cartesian dualism is the idea that the mind and body obey different rules; it was first voiced in the 1600s by the French philosopher, René Descartes. (p. 7)

   a. Humanistic psychology did not arrive until the middle of the 1900s.

   b. Behaviorism does not concern itself with the mind and did not emerge as a school of psychology until the early 1900s.

   c. Freudian psychology started at the turn of the twentieth century.

4. * a. Gestalt psychology investigated whole experiences: of music, visual perceptions, and creative problem solving. (p. 9)

   b. Freudian psychology emphasizes the unconscious motives for behavior.

   c. Cognitive psychology studies the mental processes by which animals and people come to understand the world.

   d. Functionalism focused on instincts developed through evolution that help us adapt.

5. * a. Humanistic psychology is interested in free will and the basic goodness of people. It sees people as being in personal control of their actions. (p. 10)

   b. Structuralism was interested in the components of consciousness and took no stand on the goodness of human nature.

   c. Behaviorism emphasizes the study of observable actions and took no stand on the goodness of human nature.

   d. Freudian psychology tends to see human behavior as caused by unconscious motives and views human nature as fairly negative.

6. * d. Developmental psychologists focus on the study of changes in people through the life span. (p. 12)

   a. Cognitive psychologists are interested in mental processes that help us interpret and react to the world.

   b. Physiological psychologists study the nervous system.

   c. Counseling psychologists help people solve daily problems such as marital conflicts or career choices.

7. * b. Since Dr. Bingham is observing the children's behavior in a natural setting, she is using naturalistic observation. (p. 13)

   a. In an experiment, an independent variable would be manipulated by the experimenter so that only certain children would be exposed to it.

   c. Dr. Bingham is making comparisons: boys versus girls and, perhaps, different age groups.

   d. Anything that can change is a variable, so the changes in age, gender, and play behavior are all variables.

8. * b. Picking every fifth student in a directory would select people randomly. Random samples are representative samples. (p. 14)

   a. This sample would not represent female students.

   c. This sample would not represent students at the middle or lower range of academic performance.

   d. This sample would not represent students from all the other majors.

9. * c. The independent variable is the factor the experimenter manipulates. It is also the one that is expected to produce an effect in a dependent variable. In this case, whether or not subjects have suffered sleeplessness is the independent variable. (p. 42)

   a. Performance on the creativity test is the dependent variable—it is what we expect to change as a function of sleeplessness.

   b. We may never know how creative people are ultimately. All we can do is measure their creativity in the experiment, and that measure is the dependent variable.

   d. Sleeplessness is being manipulated, so this is not true.

10. * c. A research program is a series of studies, often using a range of methods, to investigate a particular set of hypotheses. (p. 19)

   a. Clinical psychologists may do research, but more frequently they diagnose and treat people with significant problems.

   b. A correlation is an association between variables.

   d. There is no evidence here that Dr. Harvey failed to treat his research participants ethically.

CHAPTER 2

THE BIOLOGICAL BASES
OF BEHAVIOR

Learning Objectives

1. Describe the components of the nervous system, including the central and peripheral nervous systems. Define neuroscience. (pp. 25–27)

2. Describe and discuss the anatomical methods for studying the nervous system, lesion studies and Broca's area, electrical stimulation and monitoring methods, and computer-assisted techniques. (pp. 27–29)

3. Describe what neurons and glial cells do. Discuss the functions of the cell body, dendrites, axon, myelin, and anon terminals. Describe the various types of neurons. (p. 30)

4. Describe how an action potential moves information within the neuron. Discuss the role of the sodium-potassium pump, how depolarization and repolarization work, and the meaning of the all-or-none principle. (pp. 31–32)

5. Describe how neurotransmitters influence the movement of information across the synapse. Discuss the main neurotransmitters and their functions, including information about prescription and street drugs. Explain what white and gray matter are. (pp. 33–35)

6. Discuss the role of the peripheral nervous system. Describe the functions of the spinal cord. Identify the four lobes of the cerebral cortex. Give the location and function of the cerebellum, medulla oblongata, pons, midbrain, hypothalamus, and thalamus. (pp. 35–40)

7. Describe and discuss the motor functions of the nervous system. Describe and discuss the sympathetic and parasympathetic divisions of the autonomic nervous system. (pp. 40–42)

8. Discuss how hormones affect the pituitary, thyroid, and adrenal glands, as well as the pancreas and gonads. (pp. 42–44)

9. Describe the principles that apply to sensory functions including crossing over, visual fields, the role of the thalamus, and primary projection areas in the brain. (pp. 44–46)

10. Discuss the integration of neural information in the spinal cord, the reticular formation, and the limbic system. (pp. 47–49)

11. Explain why lesions that impair functions do not prove that brain "centers" exist. (pp. 49–50)

12. Describe and discuss the evidence for the brain having functions that are localized. (pp. 50–52)

13. Describe and discuss the evidence for the brain having functions distributed in different locations. Explain what is meant by a "distributed parallel system." (pp. 52–53)

14. Discuss the evidence that language is a lateralized function, including information about aphasias and Broca's and Wernicke's areas. Describe the method and results of split-brain experiments (pp. 54–55)

Chapter Outline

1. **The *nervous system* and how it is studied** (pp. 25–29)

   The *nervous system* consists of the spinal cord, the brain, and all the nerves that connect these structures to the muscles, glands, and sense organs. The *central nervous system* consists of the brain and spinal cord. The *peripheral nervous system* is the rest of the nervous system. Bundles of fibers called *nerves* carry information through this incredibly complex communication network.

   Neuroscience is the scientific study of the components and processes of the nervous system. It investigates nervous tissue with light microscopes, electron microscopes, and tracking methods using chemicals and immune system antibodies. Damage to an area of tissue (*lesions*) may cause a loss of function (*deficit*) and reveal how parts of the nervous system work. Electrodes can be used to monitor brain activity (*electroencephalographs*) or stimulate and record activity in individual cells (microelectrodes). Computer-assisted techniques such as *computerized axial tomography (CAT)* scans, *positron emission tomography (PET)* scans, and *magnetic resonance imaging (MRI)* help record the structure and activity of living neural tissue.

2. **Nerve cells** (pp. 30–35)

   Neurons are the cells that carry information in the form of electrochemical impulses. *Glial cells* support and protect neurons. Neurons are composed of cell bodies, *dendrites*, and *axons*, which end in *axon terminals*. Many axons are covered with *myelin*, a substance that speeds conduction. Sensory neurons transport information from sense organs, motor neurons carry information to muscles and glands, and interneurons connect sensory and motor neurons.

Nerve impulses move from dendrites to cell body to axon in a series of mini-events in which ions move into and out of the cell. When sodium ions get inside, the cell depolarizes, producing an *action potential*. Neurons either fire completely or they don't fire at all.

The junction between neurons is the *synapse*, the *synaptic cleft* being only 2 millionths of an inch wide. When the nerve impulse reaches the axon terminal, chemicals called *neurotransmitters* are released into the synaptic cleft. Some increase the likelihood of the next neuron firing (excitatory neurotransmitters), whereas others decrease the likelihood (inhibitory neurotransmitters). Many prescription drugs and street drugs have their effect on behavior because they influence neurotransmitters.

Bundles of neurons with myelin sheaths are called *white matter*. White matter is found in places where information must travel great distances. Gray matter, made of unmyelinated axons, dendrites, and cell bodies, is found in the integrative centers of the nervous system.

3. Divisions of the nervous system (pp. 35–40)

The peripheral nervous system is all the nerves outside the spinal cord and brain. The central nervous system includes the spinal cord, which receives messages from the peripheral system and sends them to the brain or processes information itself in the form of *reflexes*. The *cerebral cortex* is the gray matter that covers the top of the brain. It is divided into the frontal, temporal, parietal, and occipital lobes. The *cerebellum*, located at the rear of the brain, coordinates movements and maintains balance. Closest to the spinal cord are the structures of the *brain stem*, including the *medulla oblongata*, the *pons*, and the *midbrain*. The *hypothalamus*, working with the *pituitary gland*, regulates many of the body's automatic responses. The *thalamus*, located deep within the cerebral hemispheres, processes sensory information.

4. Controlling the muscular and endocrine systems (pp. 40–44)

The *voluntary nervous system* carries information to the striated muscles that move the major parts of the body. The *autonomic nervous system* controls the smooth muscles that make up the walls of glands, intestines, and other organs. There is a motor area in each hemisphere of the cortex. The right hemisphere controls the left side of the body and the left hemisphere the right side. The autonomic nervous system, made up of the *sympathetic* and *parasympathetic divisions*, controls a wide range of organs so that *homeostasis* is maintained.

One of the autonomic nervous system's chief functions is to control the *endocrine glands*, which secrete chemicals called *hormones* into the bloodstream. Hormones from the pituitary gland affect growth, sexuality, stress, and, by affecting the hypothalamus, many other physical and psychological functions. The *thyroid gland*'s hormones regulate metabolism, growth, and the nervous system's activity. The *adrenal glands* secrete hormones that play major roles in stress reactions. The *pancreas* produces insulin and glucagon, which control blood sugar in the body. The *gonads* are sex glands that secrete hormones that influence male and female characteristics.

5. **Sensory functions: Gathering information** (pp. 44–49)

Messages from sensory organs get to the brain along pathways that are organized according to certain principles. One principle is that each side of the body sends sensory nerves to the same side of the spinal cord, but most cross over to the opposite side. Therefore, information that receptors respond to on the left side of the body is relayed to the right side of the brain. All information from the right visual fields of both eyes crosses over at the *optic chiasma*, as does information from the left visual fields. Sensory information goes to the thalamus and then to primary projection areas in the cortex that are specialized to process types of sensory messages. In general, the space in the cortex devoted to a specific organ corresponds to the number of receptors in the organ, not its size. For example, the lips and thumb are very sensitive, so greater space is devoted in the brain to them than to the legs.

When information is integrated in the spinal cord, we see a spinal reflex: sensory neurons connect with interneurons, which, in turn, activate motor neurons. The brain is not involved. Within the brain, the reticular formation screens sensory information and regulates the activity level of the cortex. The limbic system, including such structures as the amygdala and hippocampus, plays a role in emotional responses and memory.

6. **The cerebral cortex: The great integrator** (pp. 49–57)

Complex integration of such functions as perception, learning, and memory occurs in the cerebral cortex. It is no longer clear that a portion of the cortex controls a function when damage to that area impairs the function. Other explanations are possible: the damaged part of the cortex could be part of the sensory or motor system carrying information or could be a region that links different functions. Each cortical area probably contributes to many functions.

The human cortex appears to operate on two contradictory premises—functions are localized in certain regions and functions are distributed in different regions. Evidence for localization comes from the finding that different layers of the cortex are wired to different areas. Lesions can produce specific deficits, and stimulation to certain areas can produce specific responses. Computerized images of the brain show neural activity in specific areas of the brain when certain thoughts or actions occur.

When some areas of the brain are damaged, however, lost functions later return. Particularly when it occurs early in life, brain damage can be completely overcome. Apparently, brain tissue can take over the function of damaged areas. A combination of the two hypotheses—distributed parallel processing—argues that there are certain cortical areas but that different areas are organized in different ways and may be influenced by the individual's experience.

In many ways the two sides of the cortex perform identical functions, just for different sides of the body. Language, however, appears to be a *lateralized function*, one performed on the left side of the brain only. *Broca's area* is essential for normal speech and is located in the left frontal lobe. *Wernicke's area*, in the left temporal lobe, is necessary for understanding speech. Damage to the area between these two produces conduction aphasia, the inability to connect the understanding and expression of language. Split-brain experiments by Roger Sperry involved severing the corpus callosum so that the two hemispheres could not communicate. He found that the left hemisphere is more competent at language and the right hemisphere is better at solving spatial problems.

Neuroscientists emphasize the unity of the brain: most functions require large areas of both sides of the cortex for their execution.

Fill-in-the-Blank Questions

1. The relative stability of the body's internal environment is called _____ .

2. A device that monitors and records the electrical activity of the brain on a moving paper chart or computer screen is called an _____ .

3. The method that uses a computer-driven X-ray machine to map the internal structures is called a _____ .

4. The portion of the brain that controls coordinated movement and maintains balance is called the _____ .

5. The portion of the brain close to the spinal cord composed of the medulla oblongata, pons, and midbrain is called the _____ .

6. The fine fiber at the end of an axon that connects the neuron to other neurons, glands, or muscles is called the _____ .

7. The electrochemical impulse that travels down a neuron is called an _____ .

8. An area of tissue that has been damaged is called a _____ .

9. A process that uses the brain's magnetic fields to trace the cellular activity and chemical makeup of brain tissue is called _____ .

10. Bundles of nerve fibers that carry information throughout the nervous system are collectively called _____ .

11. A nerve cell that carries information in the form of electrochemical impulses is called a _____ .

12. The part of the autonomic nervous system that conserves energy is called the _____ .

13. The process that uses radioactive tracers and computer-driven X-ray machines to study the activity of internal organs is called _____ .

14. The part of the autonomic nervous system that mobilizes the body for vigorous action is called the _____ .

15. The submicroscopic space that separates the axon terminals of the presynaptic neuron from the dendrites of the postsynaptic neuron is called the _____ .

16. The gland in your throat that secretes hormones that regulate metabolism, growth, and the activity of the nervous system is called the _____ .

17. The area in the left temporal lobe that is necessary for understanding speech is called _____ .

18. The small structure in the limbic system that monitors the body's internal environment, controls hunger and thirst, and receives information from the sense organs about the external environment is called the _____ .

19. The nerve cell that supports and protects neurons is called a _____ .

20. A specific inability to perform tasks such as walking or to perceive stimuli such as hearing is called a _____ .

21. Taken together, the spinal cord and the brain are called the _____ .

22. The part of the neuron that carries information away from the cell body is called the _____ .

23. The pair of glands located on top of the kidneys that secrete hormones involved in long- and short-term reactions to stress are called the _____ .

24. Located in the lower part of the brain stem, the structure that controls heart rate, respiration, and the diameter of blood vessels is called the _____ .

25. The spinal cord, the brain, and the nerves that connect these structures to the body's muscles, glands, and sense organs are collectively called the _____ .

26. A chemical produced in the presynaptic axon terminal that moves across the synaptic cleft and binds with postsynaptic neuron receptor sites is called a _____ .

27. The pealike gland in the brain that secretes hormones that control almost every system of the body is called the _____ .

28. Automatic responses that involve the spinal cord but not the brain are called _____ .

29. Two masses of gray matter in the brain that relay all sensory impulses except smell and that interpret pain, temperature, and pressure messages are collectively called the _____ .

30. The part of the peripheral nervous system that controls striated (striped) muscles is called the _____ .

31. The part of the peripheral nervous system that controls the smooth muscles of the body's organs and glands is called the _____ .

32. The part of the left frontal lobe of the cortex that is necessary for the production of speech is called _____ .

33. The wrinkled six layers of tissue that cover the top of the brain are collectively called the _____ .

34. The thick band of nerve fibers that connect one cerebral hemisphere to another is called the _____ .

35. The part of the nerve cell that carries information from other neurons to the cell body is called the _____ .

36. A gland that delivers its secretions to the bloodstream is called an _____ .

37. The male (testes) and female (ovaries) sex glands are called the _____ .

38. The substance secreted into the bloodstream by endocrine glands that has broad effects on physiology is called a _____ .

39. A function that is performed by just one side of the brain is called a _____ .

40. The junction between two neurons is called a _____ .

41. The place in the brain where fibers from the right and left visual fields of both eyes cross to the opposite side of the brain is called the _____ .

42. The portion of the nervous system that connects the brain and spinal cord to the rest of the body is called the _____ .

43. The gland that produces insulin and glucagon is called the _____ .

44. The study of the components and processes of the nervous system is called _____ .

45. The shiny white fatty substance that often coats the outside of axons and speeds conduction is called _____ .

46. The group of structures in the brain that help to control emotional behavior and memory is collectively called the _____ .

Fill-in-the-Blank Answers

1. homeostasis
2. electroencephalograph
3. computerized axial tomography (CAT)
4. cerebellum
5. brain stem
6. axon terminal
7. action potential
8. lesion
9. magnetic resonance imaging (MRI)
10. nerves
11. neuron
12. parasympathetic division
13. positron emission tomography (PET)
14. sympathetic division
15. synaptic cleft
16. thyroid gland
17. Wernicke's area
18. hypothalamus
19. glial cell
20. deficit
21. central nervous system
22. axon
23. adrenal glands
24. medulla oblongata
25. nervous system
26. neurotransmitter
27. pituitary gland
28. reflex
29. thalamus
30. voluntary nervous system
31. autonomic nervous system
32. Broca's area
33. cerebral cortex
34. corpus callosum
35. dendrite
36. endocrine gland
37. gonads
38. hormone
39. lateralized function
40. synapse
41. optic chiasma
42. peripheral nervous system
43. pancreas
44. neuroscience
45. myelin
46. limbic system

Fact and Concept Questions

1. The _____ connects the central nervous system to the rest of the body.
   a. spinal cord
   b. glial cells
   c. peripheral nervous system
   d. parasympathetic nervous system

2. One way of studying the brain is to see if a particular function is lost or impaired if a portion of the brain is damaged. The damage is called a(n)
   a. lesion.
   b. deficit.
   c. action potential.
   d. electrode.

3. The imaging technique that uses radioactive tracers and computer-driven X-ray machines is called
   a. computerized axial tomography (CAT).
   b. magnetic resonance imaging (MRI).
   c. electroencephalogram (EEG).
   d. positron emission tomography (PET).

4. Which statement about neurons is true?
   a. Neurons are only found in the brain.
   b. Neurons consist of dendrites, a cell body, and an axon.
   c. Neurons are cells that support and protect glial cells.
   d. Most neurons have myelin covering their dendrites.

5. When a neuron is stimulated, the membrane around it opens so that
   a. all positively charged ions can be pushed out.
   b. the synaptic cleft is closed up.
   c. blood can get inside.
   d. positively charged sodium ions can get in.

6. When a nerve impulse reaches the axon terminal, what happens?
   a. The impulse dies.
   b. Neurotransmitters are released into the synaptic cleft.
   c. Hormones from the postsynaptic neuron flood into the synaptic cleft.
   d. The sodium-potassium pump keeps the impulse alive.

7. Which statement about neurotransmitters is true?
   a. Neurotransmitters only increase the likelihood that the next neuron will fire.
   b. Neurotransmitters are only found in the synapses of the brain.
   c. Some neurotransmitters decrease the likelihood that the next neuron will fire.
   d. Prescription and street drugs cannot affect the functioning of neurotransmitters.

8. The white matter of the nervous system
   a. is found in places where information must travel long distances.
   b. is that color because it consists of axons covered with white myelin.
   c. Both *a* and *b*.
   d. Neither *a* nor *b*.

9. The frontal, temporal, occipital, and parietal lobes are all portions of the
   a. cerebral cortex.
   b. limbic system.
   c. brain stem.
   d. cerebellum.

10. The cerebellum is mostly responsible for
    a. the coordination of movements and the maintenance of balance.
    b. controlling emotional behavior and memory.
    c. governing the body's internal environment and regulating thirst and hunger.
    d. controlling heart rate, respiration, and digestion.

11. The striated muscles that connect bones and move the major parts of the body are controlled by the
    a. spinal cord.
    b. autonomic nervous system.
    c. hypothalamus.
    d. voluntary nervous system.

12. It is sometimes called the master gland because the hormones it secretes affect growth, reproduction, stress responses and other important body functions. It is located next to the hypothalamus. What is "it"?
    a. the thalamus
    b. the thyroid gland
    c. the gonads
    d. the pituitary gland

13. The pancreas is to _____ as the adrenal glands are to _____ .
    a. metabolism; growth
    b. blood sugar; stress response
    c. sexual reproduction; stress response
    d. growth; metabolism

14. The nerves from the eyes meet at a place where some fibers cross over to the other side of the brain and some remain on the same side. The place where this occurs is called the
    a. occipital lobe.
    b. receptor site.
    c. optic chiasma.
    d. visual field.

15. Which statement about sensory areas of the cortex is true?
    a. The bigger the body organ, the more space is devoted to it in the cortex.
    b. Touch and pain messages as well as sensory information from muscles are sent to the temporal lobe of the cortex.
    c. Sensory messages from the right side of the body go to the right side of the cortex.
    d. Because they are more sensitive, the fingers get more space in the sensory cortex than the legs.

16. Damage to the hippocampus is most likely to produce impairments in
    a. emotional control and memory.
    b. the ability to respond to stress.
    c. eating, drinking, and temperature regulation.
    d. All of the above.

17. Concerning the cerebral cortex, what does the distributed-function hypothesis predict?
    a. That every portion of the cortex has its specific function to perform.
    b. That different areas of the cortex can perform different functions at different times.
    c. That functions are controlled not only by the brain but by other organs in the body, too.
    d. That once a portion of the cortex is damaged or destroyed, the function it controlled is lost forever.

18. Distributed parallel processing combines two concepts. Which concepts?
    a. That one side of the brain controls the opposite side of the body and that the brain works as one integrated system.
    b. localization of function and distribution of function
    c. That the two hemispheres of the brain are identical and that the two hemispheres of the brain are different.
    d. autonomic function and voluntary function

19. Damage to Wernicke's area should produce problems in
    a. understanding other people's speech.
    b. being able to speak.
    c. connecting the process of understanding speech with the ability to speak.
    d. the ability to hear sounds.

20. What is the position of most neuroscientists on the results of split-brain experiments?
    a. They emphasize the unity of the brain and highlight the need for both sides of the cortex to perform most behaviors.
    b. They stress the fact that the two hemispheres are so different, we actually have two brains.
    c. They point out the poor quality of the experimental methods used and the questionable ethics of those experiments.
    d. They underscore the fact that the right side of the brain controls nearly all of language whereas the left controls visual-spatial abilities.

Application Questions

1. Lisa is seated in a doctor's office. A machine is monitoring and recording all her brain waves on a moving strip of paper. The technique being described is called
   a. an electroencephalograph (EEG).
   b. microelectrodes.
   c. computerized axial tomography (CAT).
   d. a lesion study.

2. Dirk said this about neurons: "They are composed of dendrites, a cell body, and an axon. The axon picks up stimulation and sends it to the axon terminal. Some axons are covered with myelin so they can send messages more quickly." Dirk was in error when he said that
   a. all neurons have dendrites and a cell body.
   b. axons pick up stimulation.
   c. axons are covered with myelin.
   d. myelin helps send messages more quickly.

3. Suppose drug X increases the effectiveness of an inhibitory neurotransmitter in the brain. We could reasonably expect that drug X
   a. makes the action potential of neurons more intense.
   b. increases the likelihood that postsynaptic neurons will fire.
   c. is a naturally occurring hormone.
   d. reduces the likelihood that postsynaptic neurons will fire.

4. Barry was in an auto accident in which the lowest portion of his spinal cord was severely damaged. We can expect that Barry will
   a. have limited use of his hands and arms.
   b. not be able to use the right side of his body.
   c. have limited use of his legs and feet.
   d. not be able to see or hear normally.

5. Alice cannot hear or see, but her ears and eyes work perfectly. There is nothing wrong with her temporal or occipital lobes. The reason for her being deaf and blind appears to be damage in a structure deep in the brain near the hypothalamus. What is the most likely damaged structure?
   a. the thalamus
   b. the cerebellum
   c. the pons
   d. the pituitary gland

6. After seeing an especially scary movie, Terry's heart rate and respiration rate slow down to normal. The _____ nervous system was responsible for *increasing* Terry's heart and respiration; the _____ nervous system was responsible for *decreasing* them.
   a. autonomic; voluntary
   b. voluntary; autonomic
   c. sympathetic division of the; parasympathetic division of the
   d. parasympathetic division of the; voluntary

7. Suppose there were a medical condition in which adult males began to take on the physical characteristics of females and adult females to take on the characteristics of males. We could predict that abnormal levels of hormones secreted by the _____ would be the cause of this condition.
   a. thyroid gland
   b. pancreas
   c. adrenal glands
   d. gonads

8. Vernon experiences severe damage to the occipital lobe of his brain. Which function is most likely to be impaired?
   a. hearing
   b. vision
   c. touch and sensations from the muscles
   d. reflexes

9. While awake during brain surgery, a patient moves his left hand when electrical stimulation is applied to a tiny portion of the brain. As soon as stimulation stops, so does the movement. This demonstration would argue
   a. against the idea that the two sides of the cortex control different functions.
   b. that there is localization of function in the brain.
   c. Both *a* and *b*.
   d. Neither *a* nor *b*.

10. A split-brain subject is shown a picture of a key in the right visual field and a picture of a chair in the left visual field. The subject would probably say he/she saw
    a. a key.
    b. a chair.
    c. both a key and a chair, since the brain works together.
    d. nothing.

Fact and Concept Answers

1. * c. The peripheral nervous system connects the brain and spinal cord (central nervous system) with the rest of the body. (p. 25)
   a. The spinal cord is part of the central nervous system.
   b. Glial cells provide support and protection to neurons.
   d. The parasympathetic division of the autonomic nervous system conserves energy and brings the body back to homeostasis after the sympathetic division has produced arousal.

2. * a. A lesion is damage to tissue that may cause a deficit in functioning. (p. 27)
   b. A deficit is an impairment in the ability to do or perceive something.
   c. Action potentials are the messages sent down an axon in a neuron.
   d. An electrode is a metal instrument that either records or stimulates brain activity.

3. * d. Positron emission tomography (PET) involves the injection of radioactive tracer substances that, once in the brain, can be detected by X-rays to show where brain activity is strong or weak. (p. 29)

a. Computerized axial tomography (CAT) makes no use of radioactive tracers.

b. Magnetic resonance imaging (MRI) uses neither radioactive tracers nor X-rays.

c. Electroencephalograms monitor and record on moving strips of paper or computer screens the general activity of large portions of the brain.

4. * b. All neurons have dendrite fibers that pick up stimulation, a cell body, and an axon that transmits the action potential to the axon terminals. (p. 30)

a. Neurons are found throughout the nervous system and, therefore, throughout the body.

c. The reverse of this is true: glial cells support and protect neurons.

d. Myelin covers axons, not dendrites.

5. * d. When a neuron membrane opens up, positively charged sodium ions get inside and change the electrochemical balance. This change is the action potential. (p. 32)

a. Sodium ions are pushed out after the action potential has left a specific portion of neural membrane.

b. The synaptic cleft is never closed.

c. Neurons have sodium and proteins entering and leaving; blood is unrelated to action potentials.

6. * b. When the nerve impulse gets to the axon terminal, vesicles release neurotransmitters into the synaptic cleft. (p. 33)

a. The impulse *may* end here if the postsynaptic neuron is not sufficiently stimulated, but also it is likely that sufficient stimulation *will* transmit the impulse to the next neuron.

c. Neurotransmitters flow from axon terminals to postsynaptic dendrites, not the other way around.

d. The sodium-potassium pump plays a role in moving the action potential down the axon; it is not involved in what happens at the axon terminal.

7. * c. There are both excitatory and inhibitory neurotransmitters; inhibitory ones reduce the stimulation of the postsynaptic neuron. (p. 33)

a. Both excitatory and inhibitory neurotransmitters exist.

b. Neurotransmitters are found in neurons throughout the body.

d. Drugs such as the tranquilizers Valium and Librium have their effect because they make the inhibitory neurotransmitter GABA work more effectively; cocaine activates excitatory neurotransmitters.

8. * c. White matter gets its color from white myelin coverings on axons. Myelin speeds the conduction of nerve impulses, a particularly important thing to have when messages have to travel long distances. Because all of this (both *a* and *b*) is true, *c* is the best answer. (p. 35)

   a. This is true, but so is *b*.

   b. This is true, but so is *a*.

   d. Since both *a* and *b* are true, this cannot be the best answer.

9. * a. The cerebral cortex is the wrinkled covering on the top of the brain. It is divided into four sections: the frontal, temporal, occipital, and parietal lobes. (Fig. 2.13)

   b. The limbic system is made up of the hypothalamus, amygdala, hippocampus, and other structures.

   c. The brain stem is made up of the medulla oblongata, pons, and midbrain.

   d. The cerebellum does not have four lobes.

10. * a. The cerebellum, located at the lower rear portion of the brain, coordinates movements and helps us maintain balance. (Fig. 2.14)

    b. The limbic system is most involved in emotional behavior and memory.

    c. The hypothalamus is responsible for maintaining an internal environment and regulating thirst and hunger.

    d. Heart rate, respiration, and digestion are controlled by the medulla oblongata.

11. * d. The voluntary nervous system sends signals to the striated muscles of the body that allow us to move. (p. 40)

    a. The spinal cord only controls reflexive actions.

    b. The autonomic nervous system sends messages to the smooth muscles that activate internal organs of the body.

    c. The hypothalamus regulates internal states and is unrelated to voluntary muscular movements.

12. * d. The pituitary gland secretes a variety of hormones that affect, directly or indirectly, a great number of physical and psychological functions. For that reason, it is called the "master gland." (p. 43)

    a. The thalamus is a switchboard for most of the sensory systems; it is not a gland at all.

    b. The thyroid is located in the neck and its hormones influence growth and metabolism.

    c. The gonads are the sex glands and are neither located in the brain nor involved in stress responses.

13. * b. The pancreas secretes insulin and glucagon, which regulate the level of sugar in the bloodstream; the adrenals secrete adrenaline and noradrenaline, which are important in stress reactions. (p. 44)

      a. The thyroid is most involved in metabolism and growth.

      c. The pituitary and the gonads are involved in reproduction, not the pancreas.

      d. The thyroid is most involved in metabolism and growth.

14. * c. The optic chiasm is an X-shaped structure deep in the brain where information from the right visual fields of both eyes is integrated and sent to the left side of the brain; left visual field information is sent to the right hemisphere. (p. 45)

      a. The occipital lobe is where messages about vision end up (after the crossing-over process).

      b. Receptors are specialized cells that respond to physical stimulation; receptor *sites* are located on the dendrites of postsynaptic neurons.

      d. Visual fields are what the two eyes see.

15. * d. The amount of space in the cortex devoted to sensory information from body organs is dependent on the sensitivity of the organ, not its size. Therefore, the face and fingers get much more space than the back and legs. (p. 46)

      a. Sensitivity determines the cortical space, not size.

      b. The sensory portion of the cortex is in the parietal lobe.

      c. Sensory information from the right side goes to the left side of the brain and vice versa.

16. * a. The hippocampus, a portion of the limbic system, is involved in both emotional reaction and the transfer of information from short-term to long-term memory. (p. 48)

      b. The hippocampus is unrelated to response to stress.

      c. Eating, drinking, and temperature regulation are controlled, in part, by the hypothalamus.

      d. Because the hippocampus is uninvolved with stress or internal regulation, this cannot be the best answer.

17. * b. The distributed-function hypothesis suggests that the whole brain works as an integrated system; different areas have different functions at different times. (p. 51)

      a. This idea is basic to the localization of function concept.

      c. The distributed-function hypothesis only pertains to the brain.

      d. The distributed-function hypothesis uses as evidence the fact that areas that are damaged do *not* necessarily result in lost function.

18. * b. Distributed parallel processing combines the idea that the brain has separate control centers (localization) with the idea that the brain works as a whole (distributed function). (p. 53)

      a. There is no debate about the fact that one side of the body is controlled by the other side of the brain.

    c. Cortical lateralization is unrelated to distributed parallel processing.

    d. Autonomic and voluntary functions are unrelated to distributed parallel processing.

19. * a. Wernicke's area must be intact for people to understand others' speech; damage to it produces receptive aphasia. (p. 54)

    b. The inability to speak (expressive aphasia) only occurs when Broca's area is damaged.

    c. When the tissue between Broca's and Wernicke's areas is damaged, this occurs.

    d. Hearing is not related to Wernicke's area.

20. * a. Most neuroscientists emphasize that large portions of both hemispheres are necessary to perform most behaviors. Furthermore, the overwhelming majority of us have our corpus callosum in one piece! (p. 56)

    b. Rather than two separate brains, we have an integration of somewhat different, but related, functions on the two sides.

    c. Few neuroscientists argue with the method or ethics of split-brain research.

    d. The left side of the brain is most involved in language; the right side is more competent at visual-spatial tasks.

Application Answers

1. * a. An electroencephalograph monitors and records on a moving strip of paper (or computer screen) the general activity level of the large portions of the brain. (p. 28)

    b. Microelectrodes are usually used in laboratory animals to stimulate single neurons.

    c. Computerized axial tomography (CAT) scans use X-rays and computers to examine structures inside the body.

    d. Lesion studies involve inflicting damage on tissue to see if deficits develop.

2. * b. Dendrites pick up stimulation; axons generate action potentials and send the message on to the axon terminals. (p. 30)

    a. Neurons *are* composed of dendrites, a cell body, and an axon.

    c. Axons *are* covered with myelin, particularly in portions of the body and brain where messages must traverse long distances.

    d. Myelin *does* serve to speed the conduction of impulses.

3. * d. Inhibitory neurotransmitters reduce the chances that postsynaptic neurons will fire; any drug that increases the effectiveness of an inhibitory neurotransmitter will further reduce that likelihood. (p. 33)

    a. Nothing can make an action potential more intense; the all-or-none principle prohibits that.

b. Excitatory neurotransmitters increase the likelihood that the postsynaptic neuron will fire.

c. Although some hormones are also neurotransmitters, there is no information here to suggest this is true of drug X.

4. * c. Sensory and motor nerves enter the spinal cord close to their origins; nerves from the legs enter at the lowest portion of the spinal cord. (p. 30)

a. Nerves from the hands and arms enter the spinal cord high up in the back.

b. If the spinal cord is damaged, impairment occurs on both sides of the body.

d. Nerves for sight and hearing get to the brain without ever getting down to the spinal cord.

5. * a. The thalamus is the sensory switchboard for hearing and vision. (Fig. 2.15)

b. The cerebellum controls balance and the coordination of movement.

c. The pons is the bridge between the two hemispheres of the cerebellum.

d. The pituitary gland is unrelated to vision.

6. * c. The sympathetic division of the autonomic nervous system arouses the body; the parasympathetic conserves energy and returns the body to a relaxed state. (p. 42)

a. The voluntary nervous system controls the muscles of the body that move us in the world.

b. The voluntary nervous system controls the muscles of the body that move us in the world.

d. The parasympathetic division reduces arousal; it is more or less quiet when you are scared.

7. * d. The gonads are sex glands (testes for men, ovaries for women) that secrete hormones that maintain sex characteristics. (p. 44)

a. The thyroid secretes thyroxin that is involved in metabolism and growth.

b. The pancreas secretes insulin and glucagon that are involved in blood sugar regulation.

c. The adrenals secrete hormones involved in short-term and long-term responses to stress.

8. * b. The primary projection area for vision is in the occipital lobe of the cortex. (p. 45)

a. The primary projection area for hearing is in the temporal lobe of the cortex.

c. The sensory cortex is in the parietal lobe of the cortex.

d. Reflexes do not involve the brain: sensory, interneuron, and motor neurons in the spinal cord produce reflexes.

9. * b. Work by Penfield and others has shown that stimulation of very small portions of the brain can produce movement, visual and auditory experiences, and other results that suggest a localization of function in the cortex. (p. 52)

  a. Cortical lateralization has been shown in split-brain research.

  c. Since *a* is not an accurate answer, this cannot be the best response.

  d. Since *b* is a correct answer, this cannot be the best response.

10. * a. Since the left hemisphere is superior at language and the right visual field's messages arrive at the left hemisphere, the person will be able to say the word "key," but only be able to point to a picture of a chair. (p. 55)

  b. Information about the chair will get to the right hemisphere, which has little capacity for language and speech.

  c. The split-brain subject cannot communicate across the hemispheres of the cortex because the corpus callosum has been severed. Such a person's brain cannot work together.

  d. Because language competence "resides" in the left hemisphere, the subject will report what that hemisphere sees.

CHAPTER 3

SENSATION

Learning Objectives

1. Describe what the sensory processes entail. Define and discuss transduction and the coding of sensory activity. (pp. 59–61)

2. Describe the characteristics of sound waves and how they relate to loudness, pitch, and timbre. Describe the structures of the outer, middle, and inner ear. (pp. 62–64)

3. Describe and discuss how transduction occurs in the ear. Know how a combination of frequency theory and place theory explains how information about sound is communicated to the brain. (pp. 64–66)

4. Know the wavelength range of visible radiation. Describe the structures of the eye and the role of accommodation. (pp. 68–69)

5. Describe and discuss how images are recorded by ganglion, bipolar, and photoreceptor cells. Know how rods and cones are different. (pp. 69–70)

6. Explain how transduction occurs in the eye. Discuss negative afterimages and adaptation. (pp. 71–72)

7. Describe the process of contour enhancement. (p. 72)

8. Describe and discuss the processes of color mixing and the tricolor and opponent process theories of color vision. Trace the path of neural information sent from the retina to the occipital lobe of the brain. (pp. 74–78)

9. Discuss the functions of smell and taste. Describe and discuss how we sense smells and tastes. (pp. 78–81)

10. Describe the skin senses of touch, temperature, and pain. Know how skin sensory information is coded and transmitted to the brain. Describe and discuss the gate theory of pain. (pp. 81–83)

11. Define the vestibular and kinesthetic senses. Describe how the semicircular canals monitor balance and how the receptors for the kinesthetic sense send information to the brain. (pp. 83–84)

12. Define and discuss absolute and difference thresholds. Describe and discuss Weber's Law. Discuss how sensitivity can vary. (pp. 84–86)

Chapter Outline

1. **The sensory processes** (pp. 59–61)

Sensation is the process of gathering information from the environment and the body, translating it by receptors into nerve impulses through the *transduction*, and carrying the message to the brain after *coding* it. Each sense is specialized for its own *sense* task.

2. **Hearing** (pp. 61–67)

Sound waves vary in *intensity* (loudness) measured by *amplitude* of wave (height in decibels), *pitch* (placement on musical scale) measured by *frequency* of wave crests in one second (Hertz or Hz), and complexity (*timbre*). The frequency range for human hearing is from about 20 Hz to about 20,000 Hz. The *outer ear* collects sound; the *middle ear* (consisting of the ossicles) transforms sound into mechanical vibrations and passes sound to the *inner ear*. In the *cochlea* vibrations are turned into nerve impulses. The *semicircular canals*, crucial for the sense of balance, are also located in the inner ear.

The receptor cells for hearing are *auditory hair cells* on the basilar membrane. *Frequency theory* suggests that hair cells reproduce the frequency of sound waves in the impulses they generate. *Place theory* argues that the location of hair cells governs how sounds are sensed. A combination of frequency theory and place theory explains how we hear both very low- and very high-frequency sounds.

3. **Vision: visible radiation, the eye, and transduction in the eye** (pp. 67–72)

We see visible radiation (light) in the narrow range of 380 nanometers to 760 nanometers. This visible radiation goes through the *cornea, iris, pupil,* and *lens* before hitting the *retina* at the back of the eye. Light is focused by the cornea, the watery aqueous humor, the lens, and the jellylike vitreous humor in a process called *accommodation*. Images on the retina are upside down and reversed from what occurs in the environment.

The retina is made up of ganglion cells, bipolar cells, and two photoreceptors called *cones* and *rods*. Cones, found mostly in the *fovea*, are responsible for color vision and visual *acuity* in bright light. Rods, in the *periphery*, are responsible for vision in dim light. Strong light can cause a *negative afterimage;* the eye has great powers of *adaptation* to bright or dim light.

4. **Vision: processing in the retina, color vision, and transmission to the brain** (pp. 72–78)

Light passes through the ganglion and bipolar layers of cells before stimulating photo-receptors in the retina. Nerve impulses travel to the bipolar and ganglion cells. The retina processes information so that images are not as fuzzy as they otherwise would be. In contour enhancement, ganglion cells, which work on a center-surround basis, increase the contrast between adjacent dark and light regions. This can produce optical illusions where black and white areas intersect.

The *brightness* of light is analogous to the amplitude of light waves, *saturation* has to do with purity of color wavelengths, and hue is analogous to wave length. Colors can be mixed with lights (additive) or pigments (subtractive). In additive mixing, the three primary colors are red, green, and blue. *Tricolor theory* argues that three receptor systems respond primarily to red, green, and blue wavelengths. Although this theory explains much of color vision, it fails to account for red-green color blindness or negative afterimages. *Opponent-process theory* explains these phenomena by suggesting that red-green, blue-yellow, and black-white systems exist in the retina.

Visual information from both eyes is conducted by the optic nerve to the optic chiasm and then the thalamus before arriving in the occipital lobe of the brain. *Feature detectors* in the brain assemble the images we see.

5. **The chemical senses: smell and taste** (pp. 78–81)

Smell and taste involve response to chemicals in the air and in the foods we eat. Odor and taste have important protective functions for all animals. Social messages are also communicated through odors called *pheromones*. Hair cells in the nasal epithelium are the receptor cells for smell. Information is sent to the olfactory bulbs in the brain and then to the cortex and limbic system. Taste buds are housed in papillae on the tongue. There are four basic tastes: sweet, sour, salty, and bitter.

6. **The skin senses: touch, temperature, and pain** (pp. 81–83)

Skin, the largest organ of the body, responds to touch, temperature, pressure, vibration, and stretch. There are many receptors. Free nerve endings sense pain among other stimuli. *Gate theory* suggests that pain can be reduced by stimulating an area near pain receptors or through chemicals in the brain called *enkephalins*, which close the pain gate.

7. **The body senses: balance and motion** (pp. 83–84)

Balance is experienced through the *vestibular sense*. Hair cells in the *semicircular canals* of the inner ear are the receptors for this sense. Information travels to the medulla and cerebellum and motor areas of the cortex, where messages tell muscles how to move to maintain balance. Motion is experienced through the *kinesthetic sense*. Receptors for this sense are located in the skin, joints, and muscles. The kinesthetic sense operates as a *feedback mechanism*.

8. **Sensitivity** (pp. 84–87)

Psychophysics is the field that focuses on the relationship between physical stimuli and our experience of them. The smallest amount of energy needed to sense a stimulus is the *absolute threshold* for that stimulus. The smallest noticeable difference between two stimuli is the *difference threshold,* or just noticeable difference. *Weber's Law* shows that there is a constant ratio for each sense by which the intensity of stimulation must be increased to detect a just noticeable difference. Sensory sensitivity varies from sense to sense and from situation to situation. Other animals have similar or superior sensitivity to humans.

Fill-in-the-Blank Quiz

1. The process of changing the shape of the lens to bring objects into focus on the retina is called _____ .

2. The placement of sound on the musical scale is called _____ .

3. The area surrounding the fovea, where rods are concentrated, is called the _____ .

4. The process of translating a physical or chemical stimulus into a nerve impulse is called _____ .

5. The purity of color waves—the number of waves that combine to form a color—is called _____ .

6. The intensity of light is called _____ .

7. The pinna, auditory canal, and tympanic membrane collect sounds and collectively are called the _____ .

8. The cochlea and semicircular canals are the two parts of the _____ .

9. The structures that detect the vestibular sense are called the _____ .

10. The awareness of conditions inside and outside the body is called _____ .

11. The round clear flexible material inside the eye that focuses images on the retina is called the _____ .

12. The transparent membrane that covers and protects the outside of the eye is called the _____ .

13. The receptor cells for audition are threadlike projections on the basilar membrane called
    _____ .

14. The psychological experience of color is called _____ .

15. The photoreceptor cells that respond to dim light are called _____ .

16. The intensity of a sound is measured by the height of the wave it makes and is called the
    sound's _____ .

17. The small dip in the center of the retina where cones are concentrated is called the
    _____ .

18. The photoreceptors that respond to bright light and color are called _____ .

19. A system that gathers information from the environment and communicates it to the
    brain is called a _____ .

20. The sense of balance is also called the _____ .

21. Cells in the visual cortex that respond to specific elements in the sensory impulses
    transmitted from the eyes are called _____ .

22. A chemical smell used to communicate among organisms is called a _____ .

23. The reverse visual image seen after exposure to a bright stimulus is called a
    _____ .

24. The systematic relationship between a stimulus and the output of a receptor cell is
    defined by the process called _____ .

25. The loudness of a sound is also called the sound's _____ .

26. The principle that states there is a constant, but specific, ratio between the difference
    threshold and the intensity of a stimulus for every sense is called _____ .

27. The smallest noticeable difference between two stimuli is called the _____ .

28. The smallest amount of physical stimulation necessary to detect the existence of a
    stimulus is called the _____ .

29. A mechanism that constantly reports information back to a control region is called a
    _____ .

30. The theory of hearing that proposes that hair cells respond at the same frequency as
    sound waves is called _____ .

31. The number of wave crests in a unit of time is called a wave's _____ .

32. The eye's ability to sense the environment in widely varying light levels is called _____ .

33. The sense of motion is also called the _____ .

34. The theory that a mechanism in the spinal cord can block pain messages to the brain is called _____ .

35. The theory of color vision that states that three types of cones account for all of color experience is called the _____ .

36. The part of the ear that contains the ossicles and links the outer ear with the cochlea is called the _____ .

37. The colored tissue in the eye that controls the size of the pupil is called the _____ .

38. The theory of color vision that states that all color experience is derived from three opponent color systems is called the _____ .

39. The opening in the eye behind the cornea that allows light through is called the _____ .

40. The thin layers of light-sensitive tissue at the back of the eyeball is called the _____ .

41. The complexity of sound waves that relates to the tone of sounds is called _____ .

42. The structure in the inner ear that houses the receptor cells for hearing is called the _____ .

43. The theory of hearing that states that different frequencies target different regions on the basilar membrane is called _____ .

44. The degree of sharpness in an image is called visual _____ .

Fill-in-the-Blank Answers

1. accommodation
2. pitch
3. periphery
4. transduction
5. saturation
6. brightness
7. outer ear
8. inner ear
9. semicircular canals
10. sensation
11. lens
12. cornea
13. hair cells
14. hue
15. rods
16. amplitude
17. fovea
18. cones
19. sense
20. vestibular sense
21. feature detectors
22. pheromone
23. negative afterimage
24. coding
25. intensity
26. Weber's Law
27. difference threshold
28. absolute threshold
29. feedback mechanism
30. frequency theory
31. frequency
32. adaptation
33. kinesthetic sense
34. gate theory
35. tricolor theory
36. middle ear
37. iris
38. opponent-process theory
39. pupil
40. retina
41. timbre
42. cochlea
43. place theory
44. acuity

Fact and Concept Questions

1. In every sensory system, an environmental stimulus is converted into a nerve impulse by a process called
   a. accommodation.
   b. transduction.
   c. synaptic transmission.
   d. adaptation.

2. Intensity is to the _____ of a sound as complexity is to a sound's
   _____ .
   a. loudness; timbre
   b. timbre; brightness
   c. pitch; loudness
   d. pitch; timbre

3. Which list accurately describes the path that sound takes to become a set of nerve impulses?
   a. eardrum, cochlea, ossicles, semicircular canals
   b. cochlea, hair cells, oval window, ossicles
   c. cochlea, eardrum, oval window, hair cells
   d. eardrum, ossicles, oval window, hair cells

4. The theory of hearing that assumes that auditory hair cells reproduce the frequency of sound waves in the nerve impulses they send is called
   a. place theory.
   b. opponent-process theory.
   c. pitch theory.
   d. frequency theory.

5. It is now generally assumed that hearing is best explained by
   a. place theory alone.
   b. frequency theory alone.
   c. a combination of place theory and frequency theory.
   d. neither place theory nor frequency theory.

6. Humans can hear in the range of _____ ; we can see in the range of _____ .
   a. 20 Hz to 100 Hz; 380 nanometers to 760 nanometers.
   b. 20 Hz to 20,000 Hz; 380 nanometers to 760 nanometers.
   c. 380 Hz to 760 Hz; 20,000 Hz to 250,000 Hz.
   d. 380 nanometers to 760 nanometers; 20 Hz to 20,000 Hz.

7. Which statement is true about images focused on the retina?
   a. Images are upside down but not reversed.
   b. Images are right side up but reversed.
   c. Images look exactly as they do in the external environment.
   d. Images are upside down and reversed.

8. At the back of the eyeball there are three thin layers of light-sensitive tissue including rods, cones, bipolar and ganglion cells. This structure is called the
   a. cornea.
   b. vitreous humor.
   c. retina.
   d. optic nerve.

9. The photoreceptors responsible for vision in dim light are
   a. rods.
   b. hair cells.
   c. cones.
   d. bipolar cells.

10. When a bright light temporarily uses up our light-sensitive pigment, we see a dark blotch in the same shape as the light. This is called
    a. a negative afterimage.
    b. color deficiency.
    c. contour enhancement.
    d. dark adaptation.

11. Because ganglion cells are more active when light falls on the center of its receptive field and *less* active when light falls on the surrounding area, we can experience greater contrast between dark and light areas because of
    a. opponent process.
    b. lens accommodation.
    c. contour enhancement.
    d. the olfactory process.

12. Helmholtz's tricolor theory of color vision argues that
    a. the primary colors are red, yellow, and blue.
    b. three kinds of color systems exist: yellow-blue, black-white, and red-green.
    c. red, white, and blue lights can be combined to make all the colors we can see.
    d. activity from red, green, and blue color systems combine to produce all the colors we see.

13. What phenomenon does opponent-process theory explain better than tricolor theory?
    a. how the color red is seen
    b. negative afterimages
    c. feature detectors in the cerebral cortex
    d. None of the above.

14. In what way are the sense of smell and taste different from audition and vision?
    a. Smell and taste do not require transduction.
    b. Smell and taste involve a response to chemicals.
    c. Smell and taste involve a response to wave phenomena.
    d. Smell and taste receptors respond to specific "primary" odors and tastes.

15. Compared to other mammals, the human sense of smell is
    a. not as important in daily life.
    b. much more important in daily life.
    c. unrelated to pheromones.
    d. unrelated to the sense of taste.

16. Gustatory cells are to taste as _____ are to smell.
    a. papillae in the nostrils
    b. free nerve endings
    c. hair cells in the nasal epithelium
    d. semicircular canals

17. Large neurons and smaller, unmyelinated neurons help to explain why
    a. we see a red, white, and blue flag after looking at a green, black, and yellow one.
    b. we are unable to taste foods when we have a stuffed-up nose.
    c. we experience immediate pain and delayed pain.
    d. rubbing the skin near an injury reduces the pain we experience.

18. The sense of balance, also called the _____ sense, is monitored in the
    _____ .
    a. kinesthetic; occipital lobe of the brain
    b. vestibular; semicircular canals
    c. vestibular; skin, joints, and muscles of the body
    d. kinesthetic; olfactory bulb

19. The smallest amount of stimulation we can detect, such as tasting one teaspoon of sugar
    in two gallons of water, is called the
    a. absolute threshold.
    b. adaptation gradient.
    c. psychophysics.
    d. difference threshold.

20. Which statement most accurately describes Weber's Law?
    a. All sensory systems show the same sensitivity to changes in stimulus intensity.
    b. The amount of increased stimulation necessary to produce a difference threshold
       cannot be predicted.
    c. Each sense has its own ratio between the difference threshold and the intensity of the
       stimulus.
    d. For each sense, humans have a higher difference threshold than other mammals.

Application Questions

1. Jenny listens to two sounds. The first has a high amplitude and low frequency. The
   second has a low amplitude and a high frequency. Which statement about the sounds is
   correct?
   a. The first is loud and high pitched.
   b. The first is loud and low pitched.
   c. The second is quiet and low pitched.
   d. The second is loud and low pitched.

2. Because of a severe infection, all the hair cells in Bart's cochlea are destroyed. This would
   lead to
   a. an inability to maintain balance.
   b. a decrease in his ability to hear only high-pitched sounds.
   c. an inability to hear anything.
   d. a decrease in his ability to see in dim light.

3. Dr. Thompson says, "A combination of place theory and frequency theory explains how human beings hear." What is an accurate assessment of Dr. Thompson's statement?
   a. It is incorrect because place theory is concerned with color vision.
   b. It is incorrect because place theory is superior to frequency theory.
   c. It is incorrect because frequency theory is concerned with color vision.
   d. It reflects how most psychologists view audition.

4. A creature from the planet Nebbish has the ability to see in ultraviolet wavelengths but not infrared. It has a band of colored muscles that control the opening that light passes through to get to the retina. The creature's retina consists of three layers. In what way is the creature different from humans?
   a. Humans cannot see in the ultraviolet range.
   b. Humans can see in the infrared range.
   c. Humans do not have muscles that control the light opening.
   d. Humans do not have a three-layer retina.

5. Dr. Earlham, an astronomer, wants to see very faint stars at night. He should let the image of the stars fall on the _____ in his eye so he has the best chance of seeing them.
   a. rods
   b. fovea
   c. ganglion cells
   d. cones

6. Oscar goes from a brightly lit room into his photographic darkroom. At first he can see virtually nothing in the darkroom, but over several minutes he can make out many things. This process is called
   a. accommodation.
   b. contour enhancement.
   c. the opponent process.
   d. adaptation.

7. Kerry says, "I think we see color because we have three color systems, one that responds most vigorously to red wave lengths, one to green wave lengths, and another to blue wave lengths." Kerry's ideas agree with
   a. Hering's opponent-process theory.
   b. Melzack's gate theory.
   c. Helmholtz's tricolor theory.
   d. von Bekesy's frequency theory.

8. A manufacturer markets a new product called "Pheromone." We can expect that the product
   a. increases one's sense of taste.
   b. reduces one's ability to detect obnoxious odors.
   c. increases one's kinesthetic sense.
   d. produces a sexually arousing smell.

9. Diners in a Tokyo restaurant may compliment the chef for tastes in the food they were served that Americans cannot sense. This is probably because
   a. there are no basic taste sensations.
   b. taste receptors respond to one and only one kind of substance.
   c. there are only four basic taste sensations.
   d. cultures differ in the number of basic tastes they recognize.

10. While doing lighting for a theater production, Kyle adds a 100-watt light bulb to a set of thirty 300-watt bulbs. The director of the show cannot see a change in light intensity. This is because
    a. according to Weber's Law, the extra light bulb was below the ratio needed to produce a difference threshold.
    b. some individuals, like this director, have the vision deficiency called adaptation.
    c. the 100-watt bulb was below the absolute threshold for vision.
    d. the director is probably missing the feature detector for light in his occipital lobe.

Fact and Concept Answers

1. * b. Transduction is the process of converting physical or chemical energy into a nerve impulse. (p. 60)

   a. Accommodation is the lens's ability to change shape so that images are focused on the retina.

   c. Synaptic transmission is the process by which information from any neuron is transmitted to another; this occurs in systems that have nothing to do with sensation.

   d. Adaptation is the process by which the eye can continue to see images despite greater changes in brightness.

2. * a. Intensity (the amplitude of a sound wave) is related to its loudness; the number of additional waves that add complexity to the fundamental frequency accounts for timbre. (p. 61)

   b. Brightness has to do with the visual sense.

   c. Pitch is related to the frequency of a sound wave and loudness is related to intensity.

   d. Pitch is related to the frequency of a sound wave.

3. * d. Sound waves make the eardrum vibrate, which puts the ossicles (tiny bones) in motion, which, in turn, push on the oval window, which sets up waves in the fluid of the cochlea that trigger hair cells to fire. (pp. 63–65)

   a. The semicircular canals, although in the inner ear, are responsible for the vestibular sense, not audition.

   b. Hair cells are the receptors for hearing so they must be last in the list.

   c. The cochlea houses the hair cells, so it must be near the end of the list.

4. * d. Frequency theory argues that hair cells fire in a pattern that mirrors the frequency of the sound waves that stimulate them. (pp. 64–65)

    a. Place theory suggests that certain regions on the basilar membrane respond to sounds of certain frequencies.

    b. Opponent process theory is concerned with color vision.

    c. Pitch theory is a made-up term.

5. * c. Place theory best explains audition for high frequencies, frequency theory explains low frequencies, and a combination accounts for mid-range frequencies. (p. 65)

    a. Place theory alone is unable to account for low-frequency hearing.

    b. Frequency theory alone is unable to account for high-frequency hearing.

    d. Both place and frequency theory are useful explanations for audition.

6. * b. The range of human hearing is from roughly 20 to 20,000 Hz (cycles per second); visible radiation is from roughly 380 to 760 nanometers (billionths of a meter). (pp. 62, 68)

    a. Our hearing range goes to much higher frequencies.

    c. Visible radiation is measured in nanometers, not Hertz.

    d. Visible radiation is measured in nanometers, not Hertz.

7. * d. The lens focuses images on the retina that are upside down and reversed from the way they are in nature. (p. 69)

    a. When images fail to be focused on the retina, we are either farsighted or near-sighted, depending on whether the focused image is short of or beyond the retina.

    b. Images are both upside down and reversed.

    c. Images are both upside down and reversed.

8. * c. The retina is made up of ganglion, bipolar, and photoreceptor cells called rods and cones. (p. 70)

    a. The cornea is the clear membrane on the front of the eyeball that provides protection and helps focus images.

    b. The vitreous humor is a jellylike substance between the lens and retina.

    d. The optic nerve carries nerve impulses from the ganglion cells to the optic chiasm and into the brain.

9. * a. Rods respond to dim light levels. (p. 70)

    b. Hair cells are the receptors for audition.

    c. Cones respond in bright light and are responsible for color vision.

    d. Bipolar cells organize information from rods and cones.

10. * a. Negative afterimages occur after photoreceptors fire intensely and are then unable to fire. (p. 71)

    b. Color deficiency such as red-green color blindness has nothing to do with after-images.

    c. Contour enhancement has to do with the exaggeration of contrast between dark and light areas, and not with afterimages.

    d. Dark adaptation concerns the eyes' ability to respond to changes in light levels, as when we begin to see well in a darkened movie theater.

11. * c. Contour enhancement occurs when ganglion cells exaggerate the differences between dark and light areas of objects because they fire more when the center of the receptive field is lit and the surrounding area is dark. (p. 72)

    a. Opponent process is a theory of color vision.

    b. Lens accommodation has to do with altering the focus of an image so it lands on the retina.

    d. The olfactory process has to do with smell.

12. * d. Tricolor theory says that combinations of red, green, and blue receptor systems (the primary colors for additive mixing) account for our experience of color. (pp. 75–76)

    a. The primary colors are red, yellow, and blue for subtractive mixing, which has little to do with color vision.

    b. These pairs of color receptors are central to Hering's opponent-process theory.

    c. In neither additive nor subtractive mixing are red, white, and blue primary colors.

13. * b. Negative afterimages are explained by opponent-process theory because, for example, after a bright yellow light is continuously viewed one automatically sees a blue afterimage. (p. 77)

    a. Seeing the color red is adequately explained by tricolor theory since that theory proposes there are red cones.

    c. Feature detectors "make sense" of coded neural messages that are sent from the retina.

    d. Because *b* is a satisfactory answer, this choice cannot be correct.

14. * b. Smell and taste are chemical senses, whereas audition and vision involve responses to wave forms. (p. 78)

    a. All senses require transduction.

    c. Audition and vision involve responses to waves.

    d. As far as we know, there are no specific primary odors.

15. * a. Compared to animals who mark territory and hunt prey by smell, humans rely on smell rather little. (p. 78)

    b. Smell is less important to human survival than it is to lower mammals.

    c.   Pheromones, smells that are social signals, seem to exist in humans, too.

    d.   The senses of smell and taste are interdependent.

16. * c.   Gustatory cells are the receptors for taste; hair cells in the nasal epithelium are the receptors for smell. (p. 80)

    a.   Papillae, the structures that house gustatory cells, are located on the tongue.

    b.   Free nerve endings in the skin are involved in the sensation of pain, among other skin senses.

    d.   The semicircular canals are involved in the vestibular sense.

17. * c.   Large neurons are responsible for the sensation of immediate pain while smaller, unmyelinated fibers are responsible for delayed pain that rolls in. (p. 82)

    a.   This description of a negative afterimage is unrelated to pain sensation.

    b.   Taste and smell are unrelated to pain sensation.

    d.   Rubbing an injured area is related to the gate theory of pain, a separate issue.

18. * b.   The vestibular sense involves balance; hair cells in the semicircular canals are the receptor cells for this sense. (p. 83)

    a.   The kinesthetic sense involves sensing movement.

    c.   Receptor cells in the skin, joints, and muscles help us sense movement.

    d.   The olfactory bulb is involved in the sense of smell.

19. * a.   The absolute threshold for any sense is the smallest amount of stimulation needed to first detect it. (p. 84)

    b.   Adaptation gradient is a made-up term.

    c.   Psychophysics is the whole subdiscipline of psychology concerned with sensation and physical stimuli.

    d.   A difference threshold (or just noticeable difference) is the amount of increased stimulation needed to see a change in something already sensed.

20. * c.   Weber's Law states that there are specific ratios for each sense. For example, the intensity of a light must increase by at least 8 percent for us to detect the change. (p. 85)

    a.   Weber's Law shows that each sense has its own sensitivity ratio.

    b.   Weber's Law makes very definite (and accurate) predictions of the amount of stimulation necessary to produce a difference threshold.

    d.   In some cases, animals have superior sensitivity. Dogs, for example, have much lower ratios for detecting changes in smell.

Application Answers

1. * b. High amplitude produces a loud sound; low frequency produces a low-pitched sound on the musical scale. (p. 61)

   a. Low frequency is related to low pitch.

   c. High frequency is related to high pitch.

   d. Low amplitude produces a low decibel sound.

2. * c. Because the hair cells are responsible for all hearing, Bart would be completely deaf. (p. 66)

   a. Balance is related to hair cells in the semicircular canals.

   b. This would be true only if hair cells at the high-frequency area of the basilar membrane were damaged.

   d. The cochlea has nothing to do with vision.

3. * d. Most psychologists believe that a combination of the two theories best explains how we hear. (p. 64)

   a. Place theory is only involved in audition.

   b. Both place theory and frequency theory have strengths and weaknesses.

   c. Frequency theory is only involved in audition.

4. * a. Humans can see in visible radiation (380 to 760 nanometers) and not in the ultraviolent range (less than 380 nanometers). (p. 68)

   b. Humans cannot see in the infrared range.

   c. Humans have such a muscle; it is called the iris.

   d. Our retina is made of three layers: photoreceptors (rods and cones), bipolar, and ganglion cells.

5. * a. The rods respond to dim light. Dr. Earlham would do well *not* to look directly at the stars so that their image will fall on the periphery of the retina, not the fovea, where cones are concentrated. (pp. 70–71)

   b. The fovea is packed with cones that can only respond to higher light levels.

   c. Ganglion cells are not photoreceptors.

   d. Cones respond to higher light levels.

6. * d. Adaptation is the process in which our visual sensitivity changes with light levels. (p. 72)

   a. Accommodation is the capacity of the lens to focus images on the retina by changing its shape.

   b. Contour enhancement involves the exaggeration of contrast between adjacent dark and light objects.

   c. The opponent-process theory deals only with color vision.

7. * c. Helmholtz's tricolor theory says that there are color systems that respond maximally to red, green, and blue wavelengths. (p. 76)

    a. Hering's opponent process theory proposes that there are red-green, blue-yellow, and black-white color systems that work as on-off pairs.

    b. Gate theory has to do with the sense of pain.

    d. Frequency theory has to do with audition.

8. * d. Pheromones are smells that send social signals, including sexually arousing ones. (p. 79)

    a. Pheromones are unrelated to the sense of taste.

    b. Pheromones do not alter one's sensitivity to odors.

    c. Pheromones are unrelated to the kinesthetic sense.

9. * d. In addition to salt, sour, bitter, and sweet, the Japanese recognize a fifth taste they call *umami*. Other cultures recognize fewer than the basic four Europeans do. (p. 80)

    a. There are basic taste sensations; cultures simply do not agree on how many there are.

    b. Taste receptors respond maximally to one stimulus type but respond somewhat to a wide range of stimuli.

    c. The Japanese recognize a fifth taste sensation.

10. * a. Weber's Law predicts that there must be a certain amount of increase in stimulation (8 percent, in the case of light) before a difference threshold occurs. In this case, 100 watts represents about 1 percent of the original 9000 watts of lighting. (p. 85)

    b. Adaptation has to do with increasing sensitivity in low light levels and is unrelated to color deficiency.

    c. The absolute threshold for light involves the lowest amount of stimulation needed to detect anything. For vision, we can make out a candle flame (much less than a 100-watt bulb) at 20 miles on a dark night.

    d. Feature detectors are unrelated to difference thresholds.

CHAPTER 4

PERCEPTION

Learning Objectives

1. Define perception and differentiate it from the sensory processes. Describe and discuss the constructionist approach to perception. (pp. 89–91)

2. Define and discuss perceptual cues, assumptions, and principles of inference. Define the term *percept*. (pp. 91–93)

3. Describe and discuss the sound shadow and arrival time cues for localizing sounds. Describe and discuss the assumptions and principles used to localize sounds. Discuss whether these principles are available to newborn infants. (pp. 94–97)

4. Discuss the concept of constancy and the visual cue of reflectance. Describe and discuss the principles of inference for brightness and color vision. (pp. 98–101)

5. Describe and discuss the Gestalt monocular pictorial depth cues of proximity, similarity, continuity, closure, and common fate. (pp. 102–104)

6. Describe and discuss the monocular depth cues of retinal size, texture, interposition, height in field, atmospheric (haze) cues, and perspective. (p. 104)

7. Discuss how convergence and binocular disparity are cues for depth perception. (p. 105)

8. Discuss the assumptions that account for the Ames room, inside-out doghouse, Ponzo, Müller-Lyer illusions. (pp. 106–108)

9. Know the major principles of inference for depth perception. Describe the visual cliff. (pp. 108–109)

10. Discuss how the origins of spatial perception are understood through research with infants, animals, and people from various cultures. (pp. 110–111)

11. Describe Gibson's ecological approach to perception and compare and contrast its basic concepts with those of the constructionist approach. (pp. 112–114)

12. Compare and contrast the constructionist and ecological approaches methods of studying perception. (pp. 114–116)

13. Discuss how constructionist theory is supported by research on feature detectors and how ecological theory is supported by research on spatial frequency perception. (pp. 114–116)

Chapter Outline

1. **The study of perception: traditional theory** (pp. 90–93)

   Perception is the process of organizing, interpreting, and integrating sensory information. The traditional or *constructionist* approach to perception assumes that the nervous system assembles fragments of sensory information called *perceptual cues* on the basis of assumptions and *expectancies*, which produces our experience of the world. When the assumptions are violated, our perceptions are distorted in the form of *illusions*. Principles of inference turn cues into perceptions. Whether these principles are present at birth—as *nativists* believe—or are learned through experience—as *empiricists* believe—is a complex question in psychology. We generally experience the products of perception (*percepts*) as facts.

2. **Localizing sound** (pp. 95–97)

   Auditory localization is the process of determining the source of a sound using cues from the sound itself. Differences in the direction or timing of sounds help to localize them. The perception of sound seems based on the assumption that the same sound never arrives at both ears from two different sources at virtually the same time. Principles of localization seem to develop before a baby is born but are elaborated on over the course of infancy.

3. **Perceiving brightness** (pp. 97–101)

   Despite changes of the image on the retina, objects do not appear to change in size or brightness because of *constancy*. Judging the relative reflectance of objects gives us the perception of brightness. Under experimental conditions, even black can appear white! Color constancy is affected by lighting conditions and context.

4. **Depth perception: Gestalt cues** (pp. 102–103)

Perception of a three-dimensional world requires that we distinguish the object of interest or *figure* from everything else we see, the *ground*. Monocular cues for depth can be seen with one eye and include *Gestalt cues* that help us see an image as a whole. *Proximity* is the tendency to see objects that are grouped as a whole. *Similarity* is the tendency to cluster similar objects and see them as a form. The tendency to create continuous lines out of broken ones is the cue called *continuity*. *Closure* involves seeing solid forms rather than broken ones. *Common fate* is the tendency to group objects that are parallel or move together.

5. **Depth perception: other monocular cues, cues from eye muscles, and binocular cues** (pp. 104–105)

The size of images on the retina give cues to the size and distance of objects. Texture, interposition, height in the field, atmospheric cues such as haze, and perspective are other monocular depth cues.

Convergence—the contraction of eye muscles to focus images on the retina—serves as a depth cue also. The nearer the image is, the stronger the contraction.

The slight difference between what the right and left eyes see produces a depth cue called *binocular disparity*. Computer-generated random dot stereograms can produce the illusion of depth.

6. **Assumptions violated: illusions** (pp. 106–108)

The Ames room produces a powerful illusion because the room is not square and the floor rises steeply to one side. The inside-out doghouse is an illusion based on violation of continuity, interposition, and perspective cues. False height and perspective cues help explain the Ponzo illusion. The Müller-Lyer illusion may be explained in terms of faulty distance cues.

To examine the origins of perceptual principles, psychologists have developed an apparatus called the *visual cliff*. Infants and very young animals tend to avoid the "deep" end of the visual cliff, showing that depth perception is based on little experience. Cultural experience also influences illusions.

7. **Heredity or environment?** (pp. 110–111)

Human developmental studies can give only inconclusive evidence for perceptual principles at birth. Animal developmental experiments allow definite conclusions, but generalization to humans is suspect. Cross-cultural studies have the advantage of varying experience in humans but have their own weaknesses, too.

8. **The study of perception: ecological theory** (pp. 112–114)

Ecological theory stems from the work of James Gibson. It argues that we perceive the world directly through our senses and that information takes the form of *environmental invariants*—properties of the world apparent to any observer. Unlike constructionism, the ecological approach assumes we create an *ambient flow*, a pattern of environmental cues created by our motion. Unlike constructionists, ecological perception researchers prefer studies held under natural conditions.

9. **Reconciling the traditional and ecological approaches** (pp. 114–116)

The conflict between the traditional and ecological approaches remains unresolved. Research by Hubel and Wiesel on feature detectors in the visual cortexes of cats tends to support the traditional approach to perception. However, the ability to recognize waves of dark and light—*spatial frequency perception*—supports the ecological assumption that we can perceive complex aspects of the world directly.

Fill-in-the-Blank Quiz

1. People who believe that principles of inference are learned through long experience with the environment are called _____ .

2. The Gestalt cue showing the tendency to create solids in the objects we see is called _____ .

3. The Gestalt cue showing the tendency to perceive items clustered in a group as a single element is called _____ .

4. An assumption based on experience that shapes our perceptions is called a(n) _____ .

5. The inward rotation of eye muscles to keep both eyes pointed at an image is called _____ .

6. An element of sensory information from which perceptions are constructed is called a(n) _____ .

7. The ability to recognize spatial waves is called _____ .

8. The part of the visual field that attracts our interest is called the _____ .

9. The Gestalt cue showing the tendency to cluster similar objects and perceive them as a single form is called _____ .

10. The process of organizing, interpreting, and integrating sensory information is called _____ .

11. According to the ecological approach, the complex properties of the environment that are apparent to any active observer are called _____ .

12. The process of determining the source of a sound using cues the sound itself provides is called _____ .

13. The differences in the images projected on the retinas of the eyes are called
    _____ .

14. Distorted perceptions, when perceptual assumptions are violated, are called
    _____ .

15. The Gestalt cue showing the tendency to group together objects that are parallel or that
    move together is called _____ .

16. Pictorial cues that help us see the different parts of an image as a whole are called
    _____ .

17. In ecological theory, the pattern of cues in the environment created by our motion is
    called _____ .

18. The perception that an object is not changing when its image on the retina is changing is
    called _____ .

19. The Gestalt cue showing the tendency to create continuous lines out of broken lines is
    called _____ .

20. The product of perception that we consider a fact is called a(n) _____ .

21. An apparatus that tests depth perception in infants and young animals by creating an
    illusion of depth with a checkerboard pattern is called a(n) _____ .

22. People who believe that principles of inference are present at birth are called
    _____ .

23. The theory of perception developed by James Gibson that states we perceive the world
    directly through our senses is called _____ .

24. Everything in the visual field that is not figure is considered _____ .

25. The traditional approach to perception that states we compile perceptions from frag-
    ments of sensory information is called _____ .

Fill-in-the-Blank Answers

1. empiricists
2. closure
3. proximity
4. expectancy
5. convergence
6. perceptual cue
7. spatial frequency perception
8. figure
9. similarity
10. perception
11. environmental invariants
12. auditory localization
13. binocular disparity
14. illusion
15. common fate
16. Gestalt cues
17. ambient flow
18. constancy

19.	continuity	23.	ecological theory
20.	percept	24.	ground
21.	visual cliff	25.	constructionist theory
22.	nativists		

Fact and Concept Questions

1. _____ processes transform environmental stimuli into nerve impulses; _____ processes turn nerve impulses into the world we actually experience.
   a. Physiological; sensory
   b. Sensory; ecological
   c. Perceptual; sensory
   d. Sensory; perceptual

2. Which statement about the constructionist approach is true?
   a. It was begun by James Gibson.
   b. It assumes that unconscious inference pieces sensory information into experience.
   c. It believes that we can study perception only in naturally occurring situations.
   d. It assumes that sensory information is more accurate than perception.

3. What happens when expectancies about the perceptual world are violated?
   a. We experience ambient flow.
   b. We experience illusions.
   c. There is support for the nativist approach.
   d. There is support for the empiricist approach.

4. The difference in intensity between the two sounds in your two ears
   a. is called a sound shadow cue.
   b. is information used in auditory localization.
   c. both *a* and *b*.
   d. neither *a* nor *b*.

5. Wallach, Newman, and Rosenzweig's experiment to make sound disappear worked because
   a. the sensory system of the ear became overloaded with loud sounds.
   b. there are no depth cues for hearing.
   c. our auditory system "assumes" that a second source for two identical sounds is an echo.
   d. the loudness of the sounds became so faint that they could not be perceived.

6. The reason that a white dress still looks white even when it reflects the green of a shade tree is because
   a. we perceive the world with object color constancy.
   b. our brain disregards the relative reflectance of objects.
   c. of the Gestalt cue called proximity.
   d. of the Gestalt cue called brightness constancy.

7. The visual system gets its cues to brightness from the
   a. relative amount of light coming from an object.
   b. absolute amount of nerve impulses the brain receives.
   c. size of the object on the retina.
   d. degree of proximity and continuity of the object in the visual field.

8. Which of the following plays an important role in color constancy?
   a. perspective
   b. ambient flow
   c. retinal size
   d. lighting conditions

9. Which statement about Gestalt cues is accurate?
   a. They all assume that we use two eyes to determine depth.
   b. They are all monocular pictorial cues.
   c. They are based on the ecological theory of perception.
   d. They help us see images as separate fragments.

10. Which of the following is not an optical illusion?
    a. Müller-Lyer
    b. Ponzo
    c. figure and ground
    d. inside-out doghouse

11. The design ** *** ** **** ** is seen as five groups of objects because of the Gestalt cue called
    a. continuity
    b. common fate
    c. binocular disparity
    d. proximity

12. When we look at objects that have gaps in them, we perceive a whole object anyway because of
    a. the monocular depth cue called perspective.
    b. the Gestalt cue called closure.
    c. a phenomenon called the Müller-Lyer illusion.
    d. the Gestalt cue called common sense.

13. We see depth when one object partially overlaps another. This is the depth cue called
    a. interposition.
    b. binocular disparity.
    c. unconscious inference.
    d. perspective.

14. Binocular disparity helps us perceive depth because
    a. the image of an object on one eye's retina is slightly different from the image on the other eye's retina.
    b. two eyes cannot process information from one object at exactly the same time.
    c. all objects reflect a different amount of light into one eye versus the other eye.
    d. All of the above.

15. Underneath one side of a thick sheet of glass there is a checkerboard pattern that goes down into a deep box, giving an illusion of depth. An infant is placed on the "shallow" side of the glass top and is coaxed to crawl to the "deep" side. What is the apparatus called?
    a. the ambient flow
    b. the Ames room
    c. the visual cliff
    d. the convergence chamber

16. The results of cross-cultural research on optical illusions show that
    a. illusions are based on genetically determined perceptual assumptions.
    b. only the Müller-Lyer illusion is affected by culture.
    c. culture plays no role in perceiving optical illusions.
    d. some illusions are affected by cultures, but not all.

17. What is the best way to determine whether heredity or experience account for the way humans perceive the world?
    a. human developmental studies
    b. animal experiments
    c. cross-cultural studies
    d. No one method can answer the question.

18. Ecological theory argues that we perceive
    a. a distorted version of what our sensory system detects.
    b. without needing sensory processes.
    c. the world directly through our senses.
    d. the world because the brain constructs images.

19. Unlike the constructionist approach, the ecological approach suggests that
    a. perception research be conducted in natural settings.
    b. we ignore the fact that our motion creates its own pattern of cues in the environment.
    c. optical illusions are the single best way to understand how we perceive the world.
    d. binocular depth cues are far less important than monocular depth cues.

20. Which research best supports the constructionist approach to perception?
    a. work on spatial frequency perception
    b. the discovery of feature detectors in the brain
    c. learning that fetuses cannot hear until they are born
    d. sound localization based on ambient flow

Application Questions

1. Dr. James says, "I believe that sensory systems gather pieces of information from the world. The raw information is processed and constructed into perceptions that we experience as facts." Dr. James's ideas best match the _____ theory of perception.
    a. constructionist
    b. Gestalt
    c. ecological
    d. gate

2. Imagine a person with excellent hearing who watches a person crash two cymbals together but hears no sound. Because this would violate _____ for hearing, we could say this was the equivalent of an auditory _____ .
    a. perceptual cues; localization
    b. expectancies; localization
    c. Gestalt cues; illusion
    d. expectancies; illusion

3. Suppose the results of a research study show that, before infants are born, they tend to see whole images based on their similarity. These results would
    a. support an empiricist view of perception.
    b. support a nativist view of perception.
    c. reject the constructionist view of perception
    d. reject the Gestalt view of perception

4. As the orchestra rehearses, the conductor can spot which of the four trumpeters playing before him has begun playing the notes of a passage too soon. The conductor is able to localize the sound by using
    a. binocular disparity cues.
    b. the arrival time cue.
    c. the Gestalt cue called shadowing.
    d. the shadow sound cue.

5. There are three objects before you colored black, white, and gray. How do you know that the gray object is not as light as the black one but darker than the white one?
   a. We know that gray objects absorb all colors.
   b. We see the gray object reflecting ultraviolet waves of radiation.
   c. Relative to the others, the gray object has a middle range of light reflectance.
   d. The lighting conditions changed the object into what we perceive as "gray."

6. In some printing styles, letters of the alphabet are drawn without the lines making up the letters completely touching one another. We have no trouble perceiving these letters because
   a. of the Gestalt cue called closure.
   b. we are born with the ability to perceive letters of the alphabet.
   c. we use the perceptual cue called perspective.
   d. of the Gestalt cue called common fate.

7. You are looking at a landscape painting that shows a tree in front of a barn. The details of the corn plants in the foreground are much clearer than those in the background. We perceive depth in this painting because of depth cues called
   a. interposition.
   b. texture.
   c. Both *a* and *b*.
   d. Neither *a* nor *b*.

8. Perhaps you have looked at pictures in a ViewMaster. This device uses two slightly different slide pictures to produce the perception of three-dimensional scenes. The depth cue called _____ is responsible.
   a. the visual cliff
   b. proximity
   c. the Müller-Lyer illusion
   d. binocular disparity

9. A woman from a rural African village where all the buildings are round is shown the Müller-Lyer illusion. She sees no illusion at all. This would support the view that this illusion is explained by
   a. inborn perceptual cues.
   b. cultural experience with ambient flow.
   c. inborn depth cues.
   d. cultural experience with perspective.

10. Dr. Ireland says, "We perceive the world directly through our senses. There is little to be learned from contrived illusions; instead we should study perception in naturally occurring situations." Dr. Ireland's remarks agree with
    a. a Gestalt approach to perception.
    b. an ecological approach to perception.
    c. an empiricist approach to perception.
    d. None of the above.

Fact and Concept Answers

1. * d. Sensory systems detect environmental stimuli and convert them to impulses. Perception is the process of organizing these impulses into an experience of the world. (p. 89)

   a. Physiological processes cover much more ground than just the transduction of impulses; perception is the process by which impulses become experience.

   b. The ecological approach is one of two theories about perception.

   c. These choices are reversed.

2. * b. Helmholtz, an early constructionist, argued that sensory fragments were constructed on the basis of unconscious inferences about the world. (p. 90)

   a. James Gibson was the founder of the ecological approach to perception.

   c. The ecological approach emphasizes the need for research in natural situations; constructionists set up experiments that control for various perceptual cues.

   d. Constructionists believe that sensory information is raw material and that perception is a construction built from these data. Sensory information cannot be more or less accurate.

3. * b. Illusions occur when expectancies or perceptual assumptions are violated. (p. 92)

   a. Ambient flow is an ecological term describing the environmental cues that we create by moving around in the world.

   c. The nativist approach is supported if we find characteristics present at birth. This is irrelevant to the violation of expectancies.

   d. The empiricist approach is supported if we find that characteristics develop only after learning and exposure to the environment. This is irrelevant to the violation of expectancies.

4. * c. The sound shadow cue helps us detect the location of sounds because we perceive the slight difference in intensity between the two sounds in our ears. Since sound shadow cues are involved in auditory localization, both *a* and *b* are correct. (p. 94)

   a. This choice is correct, but so is *b*.

   b. This choice is correct, but so is *a*.

   d. Because both *a* and *b* are correct, this cannot be the best choice.

5. * c. Wallach et al. reduced the time difference of two sounds reaching the ears to a period less than an echo. The result of violating the assumption that an echo was occurring made the sound in one ear disappear. (pp. 95–96)

   a. Wallach et al. presented clicks, not loud sounds.

   b. Depth cues are appropriate only in visual perception.

   d. Wallach et al. did not vary the intensity of sounds, just the timing of them.

6. * a. Color constancy produces a perception of continuing color despite changes occurring in the retina. (p. 98)

   b. Relative reflectance is important in perceiving brightness.

   c. The Gestalt cues are important in perceiving form, not color.

   d. There is no Gestalt cue for brightness.

7. * a. The relative reflectance of objects determines how bright we perceive them to be. (p. 99)

   b. The intensity of stimulation from objects is compared, so *relative* reflectance is important.

   c. Retinal size is important in depth perception, not brightness.

   d. Proximity and continuity are Gestalt cues related to form perception.

8. * d. Lighting conditions affect whether we see color constancy. (p. 98)

   a. Perspective is a depth perception cue.

   b. Ambient flow is an ecological term describing the environmental cues we create by moving around in the world.

   c. Retinal size is a depth perception cue.

9. * b. Gestalt cues are pictorial cues that can be seen with one eye (monocular). (p. 102)

   a. The use of two eyes to perceive depth relates to binocular disparity—the fact that slightly different images are seen in each eye.

   c. Gestalt cues are unrelated to the ecological approach.

   d. The opposite is true: Gestalt cues help us see whole forms rather than fragments.

10. * c. Figure and ground are basic perceptual cues: figure is the part of the visual field we are interested in, ground is everything else. (p. 102)

    a. Müller-Lyer is an illusion using lines of identical length with arrows at the ends pointed in opposite directions.

    b. Ponzo is an illusion that simulates railroad tracks and railroad ties.

    d. The inside-out doghouse illusion gives confusing information about whether a puppy is inside or outside the structure.

11. * d. Proximity, the clustering of objects, is the Gestalt cue at work in the example given. (p. 102)

    a. Continuity is the Gestalt cue related to seeing continuous lines even when they are broken up.

    b. Common fate is the Gestalt cue related to grouping things that are parallel or move together.

    c. Binocular disparity is a depth cue.

12. * b. Closure is the tendency to see forms as complete even when there are gaps in them. (p. 103)

    a. Perspective gives a sense of depth and is unrelated to the perception of form.

    c. The Müller-Lyer illusion involves violations of perceptual assumptions about length and depth.

    d. The Gestalt cue is called common fate, not common sense.

13. * a. Interposition is the depth cue based on the overlap of one object by another. (p. 104)

    b. Binocular disparity is the depth cue based on the difference in images projected into our two eyes when we view a scene.

    c. Unconscious inference is an information-processing phenomenon assumed in all perception, according to traditional theory.

    d. Perspective is a depth cue based on parallel lines converging at the horizon.

14. * a. The retinas of our two eyes see slightly different images when we view one scene; this difference produces the depth cue called binocular disparity. (p. 105)

    b. Our two eyes simultaneously process information all the time.

    c. The reflectance of light is the same in both eyes.

    d. Since *b* and *c* are not true, this cannot be the best answer.

15. * c. The visual cliff is the apparatus designed to study infants' perception of depth. (p. 109)

    a. Ambient flow is an ecological term describing the environmental stimuli we create by moving in the world.

    b. The Ames room is a structure of a steeply rising floor that produces a powerful illusion.

    d. Convergence chamber is a made-up term.

16. * d. The Müller-Lyer illusion is not seen so strongly by people who live their lives in round structures. They still do see the illusion, however. (p. 108)

    a. Because culture influences the recognition of illusions, they cannot be entirely due to genetics.

    b. Other illusions beside the Müller-Lyer are affected by culture; Uzbeks recognize almost none of them.

    c. Because illusions are influenced by culture, this cannot be the best answer.

17. * d. All methods of studying the origins of perceptual principles have weaknesses and strengths. Therefore, the results of work using all research methods are best able to answer this question. (pp. 110–111)

    a. Human development studies are weakened by the inability to ensure limited environmental experience.

b. Animal experiments have the weakness of using organisms with perceptual systems different from those of humans.

c. Cross-cultural studies are weakened by the fact that experimenters come from a specific culture themselves and may have biases.

18. * c. A basic assumption of the ecological approach is that sensory information is perceived directly and is not constructed, as assumed in traditional theory. (p. 112)

a. Ecological theory does not assume we see a distortion of the "real world."

b. Ecological theory includes sensory systems since all perception depends on detecting environmental stimuli and converting them to nerve impulses.

d. The construction of perception is the basic assumption of the traditional (constructionist) approach.

19. * a. Ecological theorists argue that the traditional approach studies contrived situations such as illusions. They support research "outdoors under the sky." (p. 114)

b. Ecological theorists coined the term *ambient flow*, meaning the stimuli we create by moving in the world.

c. Ecological theorists deemphasize illusions because they are seen as contrived.

d. Ecological theorists make no judgments about the value of various depth cues.

20. * b. Hubel and Weisel's work on feature detectors in the visual cortex supports the idea that sensory information is processed in ways predicted by constructionist theory. (p. 115)

a. Spatial frequency perception supports the ecological approach.

c. Fetuses *can* hear before birth, but this is irrelevant to an ecological approach.

d. Ambient flow is irrelevant to sound localization.

Application Answers

1. * a. The constructionist (traditional) approach to perception argues that fragments of information from sensory processes are constructed by perceptual processes. (p. 90)

b. Gestalt principles involve only perceptual cues that help us see whole images.

c. The ecological approach rejects the constructionist approach and says we perceive the world directly through our senses.

d. Gate theory is related to the sense of pain.

2. * d. We have an expectancy (assumption) that when cymbals crash there is a lot of noise; illusions occur when expectancies are violated. (p. 92)

a. Perceptual cues are the elements of sensory information, not our assumptions about how they are organized.

b. Failure to hear a sound is unrelated to locating it.

c. Gestalt cues are visual, not auditory.

3. * b. The nativist view argues that characteristics are present at birth. (p. 92)

a. The empiricist view takes the opposite side of the argument: it suggests that characteristics are learned through interaction with the environment.

c. The constructionist approach does not take a stand on the nativism vs. empiricism debate.

d. The Gestalt view of perception does not take a stand on the nativism vs. empiricism debate.

4. * b. The arrival time cue helps locate a sound by perceiving the slight time difference between sounds heard in both ears. The conductor hears one player's note just before another's. (p. 95)

a. Binocular disparity is a visual depth cue.

c. Shadowing is not a Gestalt cue and involves the intensity of sounds, not their timing.

d. The shadow sound cue involves intensity not timing.

5. * c. We perceive black, white, and gray because we examine the relative reflectance of objects. (pp. 98–99)

a. Black is perceived when an object absorbs all colors.

b. We cannot see reflected ultraviolet rays.

d. Lighting conditions change color perception; brightness is related to relative reflectance.

6. * a. Closure is the tendency to create solids in the objects we see. (p. 103)

b. Certainly letter recognition is not present at birth; we must learn the letters of the alphabet.

c. Perspective is a cue for depth perception.

d. Common fate is the cue for grouping objects that are parallel or move together.

7. * c. The tree obscures some of the barn, so there is interposition. The reduction of detail from front to back is the texture cue for depth. Because both cues are present, *c* is the best answer. (p. 104)

a. The tree overlaps the barn so there is interposition.

b. The reduction of detail in the corn indicates texture.

d. Because both *a* and *b* are correct, this cannot be the best answer.

8. * d. The ViewMaster mimics binocular disparity by presenting slightly different images so that depth is perceived. (p. 105)

a. The visual cliff is an apparatus to study depth perception.

b. Proximity is a Gestalt cue unrelated to depth.

c. The Müller-Lyer illusion involves identical lines appearing to be of different lengths; it is unrelated to depth.

9. * d. Lack of experience with square buildings seems to alter the recognition of this illusion, which is partially explained in terms of perspective cues. (p. 108)

a. If these cues were inborn, everyone would see the illusion regardless of culture.

b. Ambient flow has to do with environmental stimuli created by our movement; this is irrelevant to illusions.

c. If these cues were inborn, everyone would see the illusion regardless of culture.

10. * b. The ecological approach asserts that we experience the world directly through our senses and that the study of perception should take place in naturalistic settings. (p. 112)

a. The Gestalt approach only examines how we see images as wholes.

c. The empiricist approach only predicts that perceptions are based on exposure to the environment and learning.

d. Because *b* is correct, this cannot be the best answer.

CHAPTER 5

CONSCIOUSNESS

Learning Objectives

1. Define consciousness and discuss its three dimensions. (pp. 119–120)

2. Describe and discuss selective attention, daydreams, subliminal perception, and the functions of attention. (pp. 120–124)

3. Describe the human biological clock and the role of the environment in resetting it. (pp. 124–126)

4. Describe the stages of sleep and the brain waves that characterize each stage. Differentiate among wakefulness, non-REM, and REM sleep. (pp. 126–129)

5. Discuss sleep and dream deprivation. Describe and discuss theories of sleep and Freudian and information processing theories of dreaming. (pp. 130–134)

6. Describe the symptoms, and discuss the causes, of: insomnia, narcolepsy, night terrors, sleepwalking, bedwetting, and sleep apnea. (pp. 134–136)

7. Describe the characteristics of hypnosis and the dissociation and social role theories that attempt to explain it. (pp. 136–138)

8. Describe research on the relationship of hypnosis to suggestibility, coping with pain, the hidden observer phenomenon, memory, and forgetting. (pp. 138–142)

9. Describe the changes that occur when people meditate. (pp. 142–143)

10. Describe and discuss the symptoms of physical dependence and psychological dependence on psychoactive drugs. Discuss placebo effects and drug interactions. (pp. 144–146)

11. Describe the major drug stimulants and their effects on behavior. (pp. 146–147)

12. Describe the depressant drugs and their effects on behavior. (p. 147)

13. Describe the hallucinogens and their effect on behavior. (pp. 147–148)

Chapter Outline

1. **Consciousness** (pp. 119–120)

   Consciousness is the awareness of one's thoughts, feelings and surroundings. The key dimensions of consciousness are the focus of consciousness (what we are aware of), the degree of consciousness (the level of awareness), and the quality of consciousness (the kind of awareness experienced). Technological advances have helped in the scientific study of these subjective states.

2. **Attention: the changing focus of consciousness** (pp. 120–124)

   Attention, the mental function that makes us fully conscious of an element in the environment, can focus on only one thing at a time. Attention has many possible functions: as a way to block out irrelevant stimuli, as a limit on the mental energy needed to process more than one stream of thought, or as a biological limit in our bodies. Attention sometimes wanders from the task at hand in the form of daydreams. Some people daydream more than most and are easily hypnotized. We can also respond emotionally to stimuli we are not paying attention to, the phenomenon of *subliminal perception*.

3. **Rhythms of consciousness** (pp. 124–126)

   One of our *circadian rhythms* is a sleep-wake cycle lasting approximately 25 hours. Our *biological clock* helps adjust the circadian rhythm to the earth's 24-hour period. Jet lag occurs when our biological clock cannot adequately adjust our rhythms.

4. **Sleeping and dreaming** (pp. 126–136)

   When we are awake, electroencephalograms show that the cortex is producing mostly *beta waves*. As we relax and enter sleep, we produce *alpha waves*. *Sleep spindles* are bursts of neural activity that characterize Stage 2 sleep. As sleep becomes deeper, slow *delta waves* become more and more common. After a period of quiet sleep, we enter active or *REM sleep* when there are rapid eye movements and high levels of brain wave activity. Dreaming often occurs in REM sleep.

   People vary in their need for sleep, and sleep deprivation has the primary effect of making us sleep more when we can. REM sleep deprivation also makes us dream more when we can. There are a variety of theories about why we sleep, but only two major theories about why we dream. Sigmund Freud argued that dreams were symbolic expressions of aggressive and sexual impulses. There may be sex differences in the content of dreams. Freud differentiated the *manifest content* (recognizable parts of a dream) from the *latent content* (actual meaning) of a dream. Information processing theories of dreaming emphasize dreams' role in organizing information and assisting with memory. Finally, dreams may be random neural firings that, according to attribution theory, are made into coherent stories when we awaken.

One sleep disorder involves difficulty falling asleep or waking very early (*insomnia*). Insomnia can be caused by anxiety, depression, or drug use. Disorders of REM sleep include *narcolepsy*, a bizarre disorder in which people rapidly change from the waking state to REM sleep, frequently collapsing on the ground. Some disorders of non-REM sleep are night terrors, sleepwalking, bedwetting, and *sleep apnea* (a breathing disorder) that is associated with sudden infant death syndrome (SIDS) in babies and severe snoring in adults.

5. **Hypnosis: what it is and theories about it** (pp. 136–138)

Hypnosis is an induced state of relaxation that increases the suggestibility of a person to perform behaviors not usually performed when not hypnotized. *Posthypnotic suggestions* involve actions taken when the subject is no longer hypnotized. *Dissociation theory* maintains that hypnosis is a separate state of consciousness in which a subject's attention is divided into two streams. *Social role theories* emphasize the expectations the subject feels and explain hypnosis as an exaggerated form of role playing.

6. **Research evidence related to hypnosis** (pp. 138–144)

While some people are innately susceptible to hypnosis, the ability to be hypnotized can be learned, too. Hypnosis can help people cope with high levels of pain. It can also produce the *hidden observer* phenomenon, when one part of consciousness is free of pain while another is aware of the pain. Hypnosis appears to produce manufactured memories, as in age regression, more than it produces improved memories. One possible reason is *experimenter influence*, subtle effects that experimenters can have on subjects. Hypnosis can affect forgetting in the form of *source amnesia*, an inability to gain access to memories. *Meditation*, a means of inducing inner peace, may have no special effects over and above those of relaxation.

7. **Drugs and consciousness** (pp. 144–149)

Psychoactive drugs are substances that affect behavior or experience. Sustained use of drugs can produce the *physical dependence* symptoms of *tolerance* and *withdrawal*. When coupled with *psychological dependence* on the drug, these symptoms produce a reliance on the substance that is considered an *addiction*. Drugs have variable effects, partly because of the influence of expectations or placebo effects.

Stimulants are drugs that increase energy, endurance, and confidence. Examples include caffeine, nicotine, cocaine, and *amphetamines*. Use of stimulants can lead to addiction, damage to the brain and other organs, and death. *Depressants*, such as *opiates*, *barbiturates*, and alcohol, slow the nervous system and generate relaxation as well as helplessness. *Hallucinogens* produce sensory experiences in the absence of sensory stimuli. Hallucinogens include LSD and PCP. Both can cause flashbacks, unexpected recurrences of *hallucinations*. Marijuana is the most widely used illegal drug, and although it does not generate symptoms of physical addiction, it can impair perception and memory.

Fill-in-the-Blank Quiz

1. Cycles of activity over a period of roughly 24 hours are called _____ .

2. A substance that induces changes in behavior or experience is called a(n) _____ .

3. Intermittent bursts of neural activity that are associated with Stage 2 sleep are called _____ .

4. The unintentional influence a researcher exerts on a subject's responses is called _____ .

5. The active stage of sleep characterized by rapid eye movements and high levels of brain activity is called _____ .

6. The dissociated consciousness seen in hypnosis is called the _____ .

7. According to Sigmund Freud, the actual meaning of a dream is called the _____ .

8. The process of inducing inner peace by emptying one's mind of thoughts or focusing thoughts on one object is called _____ .

9. Brain waves with frequencies between fourteen and thirty cycles per second that are characteristic of wakefulness and high activity in the cortex are called _____ .

10. Physical and psychological reliance on an external stimulus to carry on everyday activities is called a(n) _____ .

11. According to Sigmund Freud, the part of a dream we immediately recognize is called the _____ .

12. An individual's awareness of his/her own thoughts, feelings, and surroundings is called _____ .

13. A class of drugs that slows the activity of the cortex and induces relaxation is called _____ .

14. A sleep disorder involving rapid change from wakefulness to REM sleep is called _____ .

15. A class of drugs that speeds the activity of the cortex and induces confidence, endurance, and energy is called _____ .

16. Chronic difficulty in falling asleep or awakening too early is called _____ .

17. The phenomenon of subjects performing posthypnotic suggestions without being able to explain why is called _____ .

18. The internal mechanism that helps maintain the body's circadian rhythms is called the _____ .

19. The body's inability to function normally without an external stimulus is called _____ .

20. The mental function that makes us fully conscious of an element of the environment is called _____ .

21. The inability to sustain normal emotional functioning without an external stimulus is called _____ .

22. The emotional response to stimuli of which we are not aware is called _____ .

23. A sensory experience in the absence of sensory stimuli is called a(n) _____ .

24. A state of consciousness related to hypnosis in which consciousness is divided is called _____ .

25. Powerful depressant drugs that are sometimes prescribed to help patients rest better are called _____ .

26. A breathing disorder that is associated with severe snoring and causes sleep deprivation is called _____ .

27. A type of powerful manufactured stimulant drug whose effects last for hours is called _____ .

28. Brain waves having a frequency between eight and thirteen cycles per second and that characterize Stage 1 sleep are called _____ .

29. The need to take more and more of a drug to get the same effect is called _____ .

30. Theories of hypnosis that stress social expectations and interpersonal relations in the explanation for the phenomenon are called _____ .

31. A type of depressant drug derived from or modeled on extracts of the opium poppy is called a(n) _____ .

32. A suggestion given during hypnosis that produces action when the subject is no longer hypnotized is called a(n) _____ .

33. Drugs that induce hallucinations are called _____ .

34. Brain waves with frequencies between one and five cycles per second and that are characteristic of deep sleep are called _____ .

35. The physical and psychological effects of stopping the use of a drug are collectively called _____ .

36. The process of inducing a state of relaxation in people and then suggesting behaviors that they may not ordinarily perform is called _____ .

Fill-in-the-Blank Answers

1. circadian rhythms
2. psychoactive drug
3. sleep spindles
4. experimenter influence
5. REM sleep
6. hidden observer
7. latent content
8. meditation
9. beta waves
10. addiction
11. manifest content
12. consciousness
13. depressants
14. narcolepsy
15. stimulants
16. insomnia
17. source amnesia
18. biological clock

19. physical dependence
20. attention
21. psychological dependence
22. subliminal perception
23. hallucination
24. dissociation
25. barbiturate
26. sleep apnea
27. amphetamines
28. alpha waves
29. tolerance
30. social role theories
31. opiate
32. posthypnotic suggestion
33. hallucinogens
34. delta waves
35. withdrawal
36. hypnotism

Fact and Concept Questions

1. Which statement about consciousness is accurate?
   a. States of consciousness consist of observable behaviors that can be measured objectively.
   b. The three dimensions of consciousness are duration, intensity, and negative consequences.
   c. There are only two states of consciousness: awake and asleep.
   d. Consciousness constantly changes in focus, degree, and quality.

2. Although attention is _____ , we can respond emotionally to stimuli below absolute threshold through a process called _____ .
   a. selective; subliminal perception
   b. objective; subjective reasoning
   c. subjective; daydreaming
   d. unconscious; conscious perception

3. A reasonable explanation for why we can concentrate only on one thing at a time is that
   a. we need to filter out irrelevant stimuli.
   b. we experience REM deprivation if we don't.
   c. the brain is limitless in its energy and resources.
   d. All of the above.

4. Research on biological clocks shows that
   a. when humans are deprived of environmental cues, their bodies still function on 24-hour clocks.
   b. it is much easier to overcome jet lag when traveling from west to east.
   c. each day we reset our biological clock to conform with a 24-hour day.
   d. humans are able to reset their biological clocks by as much as 10 hours in a single day.

5. How are alpha waves different than beta waves?
   a. Alpha waves occur when we are deeply asleep.
   b. Beta waves occur when we are deeply asleep.
   c. Alpha waves are associated with REM sleep.
   d. Beta waves can occur when one is nervous.

6. Which statement is true of REM sleep?
   a. It is the first stage of sleep.
   b. Our eyes move and our breathing is irregular during it.
   c. Our brain waves are at their slowest during it.
   d. It is also called quiet sleep.

7. If we deprived people of REM sleep, what would happen?
   a. They would probably dream less later on, when they could sleep uninterrupted.
   b. They would develop ulcers, internal hemorrhages, and damage to internal organs.
   c. They would dream longer and more intensely when they could sleep uninterrupted.
   d. They would be able to sleep for shorter periods and wake up more refreshed.

8. According to Sigmund Freud, dreams are
   a. random nerve cells firing that we construct into meaningful stories.
   b. the symbolic expression of unacceptable impulses.
   c. ways of organizing information so that it can be remembered when we are awake.
   d. All of the above.

9. According to Sigmund Freud, the latent content of a dream is
   a. the biochemical changes that take place in the brain.
   b. the parts of the dream that we automatically recognize.
   c. information from the previous day that is forgotten when we awaken.
   d. the real meaning of the dream.

10. Insomnia is a sleep disorder that is characterized by
    a. an inability to get REM sleep.
    b. severe snoring and an inability to breathe normally.
    c. difficulty getting to sleep or staying asleep.
    d. an inability to stay in the non-REM stages of sleep.

11. A person with narcolepsy is likely to
    a. have attacks triggered by emotional states.
    b. have great trouble experiencing REM.
    c. be treated with depressant medications.
    d. be elderly and snore vigorously.

12. Which of the following is a disorder of non-REM sleep?
    a. sleepwalking
    b. bedwetting
    c. sleep apnea
    d. All of the above.

13. What is the key characteristic of hypnosis?
    a. increased suggestibility
    b. a loss of control over impulses
    c. increased accuracy of memory
    d. decreased need for approval from others

14. According to Hilgard, hypnosis is a form of dissociation. This means that
    a. the sympathetic and parasympathetic nervous systems are unable to communicate.
    b. the hypnotized person is simply playing a role that is expected when a hypnotist makes suggestions.
    c. hypnosis is a drug-induced state of consciousness.
    d. when a person is hypnotized, one part of that person is fully conscious and the other is not.

15. According to social role theories of hypnosis, the _____ induces hypnotized behavior.
    a. medulla oblongata
    b. dream life of people
    c. situation
    d. skill of the hypnotist

16. In hypnosis research, what is the "hidden observer"?
    a. the ability to see and remember details from scenes witnessed long ago
    b. a person who sits behind one-way mirrors to observe hypnotized subjects
    c. the person who is easily hypnotized because he or she daydreams a great deal
    d. one part of a hypnotized person reporting experiences that the rest of the person cannot

17. Which statement about a person's memory while under hypnosis is true?
    a. People try to please the hypnotist by calling up imagined events.
    b. Because memory under hypnosis is much more accurate than normal memory, hypnosis is used in criminal court cases.
    c. Memory under hypnosis is accurate only if the hypnotized person is affected by "experimenter influence."
    d. Age regression is the most accurate of all memories under hypnosis.

18. A person who shows tolerance for a drug and whose physical functioning requires continued use for a drug is said to be
    a. psychologically dependent.
    b. going through withdrawal.
    c. experiencing a placebo effect.
    d. physically dependent.

19. Research on the effects of alcohol and soft drinks on erotic fantasies indicates that
    a. alcohol makes people have more fantasies.
    b. alcohol makes people have fewer fantasies.
    c. expectations have more effect than the alcohol itself.
    d. expectations have little effect on behavior when people have drunk alcohol.

20. Which drug is correctly paired with its description?
    a. Amphetamines—manufactured stimulants
    b. Opiates—hallucinogens
    c. LSD—manufactured stimulant
    d. Barbiturates—naturally occurring hallucinogens

Application Questions

1. Jerry listens to two tapes through earphones. In one ear he hears a man reciting poetry; in the other he hears a woman reading a list of names. Jerry will be unable to remember both things he heard because of
    a. subliminal perception.
    b. selective attention.
    c. the hidden observer.
    d. daydreaming.

2. Rhonda is easily hypnotized. She is creative and scores high on tests of vivid mental imagery. We can also expect that Rhonda
   a. suffers from narcolepsy.
   b. is excessively selective in her attention.
   c. has difficulty dreaming at night.
   d. daydreams a good deal.

3. Astronauts on the light side of the moon would have no cues for "day" or "night." Research predicts that their wake-sleep behavior would indicate a biological clock that is
   a. greater than 24 hours long.
   b. exactly 24 hours long.
   c. less than 24 hours long.
   d. completely irregular and unpredictable.

4. Harriet is hooked up to an electroencephalogram. Her brain waves are mostly those of the alpha pattern. What can be supposed about Harriet?
   a. She is taking stimulant drugs.
   b. She is in the deepest stage of sleep.
   c. She is fully awake and active.
   d. She is relaxed and ready to sleep.

5. Pat is asleep but her breathing is irregular and rapid. Her brain waves look as active as though she were awake. When we wake her up, she says, "Boy! what an interesting dream I had." In what stage of sleep was Pat before being awakened?
   a. Stage 1
   b. Stage 4
   c. REM sleep
   d. non-REM sleep

6. Dr. McGuire says, "No matter what you think your dream is about, the unconscious mind wants to express sexual or aggressive impulses that are unacceptable to the conscious mind." Dr. McGuire's ideas reflect
   a. an attribution theory approach to dreaming.
   b. Freud's approach to dream analysis.
   c. the dissociation approach to dreaming.
   d. Hall's research findings on the content of dreams.

7. Bill, age thirty-seven, has the embarrassing problem of going from fully awake to REM sleep in a matter of seconds. This often occurs when he is laughing hard, but it leaves him collapsed on the ground. A reasonable diagnosis for Bill's problem is
   a. sleep apnea.
   b. subliminal perception.
   c. narcolepsy.
   d. SIDS.

8. Norma wants to stop smoking and sees a hypnotist for help. After treatment, whenever she sees a pack of cigarettes she has the uncontrollable urge to tear up the pack and throw it in the trash. Norma's behavior best illustrates
   a. the social role theory of hypnosis.
   b. the hidden observer.
   c. a posthypnotic suggestion.
   d. mesmerism.

9. Your friend is thinking of spending $450 for training in meditation so he can reduce his heart rate and blood pressure. Based on research, you should tell your friend:
   a. "It's worth the money: only meditation can reduce heart rate and blood pressure."
   b. "It's much better to use barbiturates—they're cheaper and you cannot develop a tolerance to them."
   c. "Meditation cannot reduce heart rate or blood pressure, so save your money."
   d. "Relaxation gives the same results as meditation and it's cheaper."

10. Mr. Ford, supposedly an expert on psychoactive drugs, says, "Barbiturates and alcohol are both depressants; cocaine and caffeine are both stimulants. But the only drugs that cause hallucinations are opiates." What statement here is inaccurate?
    a. Opiates do not cause hallucinations.
    b. Caffeine is not a stimulant.
    c. Alcohol is not a depressant.
    d. All psychoactive drugs can cause hallucinations.

Fact and Concept Answers

1. * d. Consciousness changes throughout the day; the changes are in focus (what you are conscious of), degree (the level of awareness), and quality (kind of consciousness you experience). (pp. 119–120)

   a. Consciousness concerns subjective states of awareness.

   b. The three dimensions of consciousness are focus, degree, and quality.

   c. There are many states of consciousness that exist on a spectrum but included are drugged states, hypnosis, and meditation in addition to wakefulness and sleep.

2. * a. We attend to one thing at a time, so attention is selective. We can respond emotionally, however, to stimuli we do not consciously detect in a phenomenon called subliminal perception. (pp. 120, 123–124)

   b. Attention is not objective, though we can observe the results of it; subjective reasoning is irrelevant.

   c. Daydreaming involves conscious awareness of stimuli.

   d. Attention is usually a conscious process; if perception were conscious, we would be responding to stimuli above threshold.

3. * a. Selective attention acts as a filter to screen out distractions so we can focus on important stimuli. (p. 120)

   b. REM is related to sleep and is irrelevant to attention.

   c. Selective attention is also explained in terms of limitations on brain resources and energy.

   d. Because *b* and *c* are incorrect, this cannot be the best answer.

4. * c. Most people's biological clocks are set for 25 hours and must be reset to the solar clock each day. (p. 125)

   a. Without environmental cues, human biological clocks tend to be longer than 24 hours.

   b. It is more difficult to cope with west-to-east travel because our biological clock must be advanced in that direction.

   c. The maximum we seem to be able to rest our clocks is an hour or two in a single day; more than that produces jet lag.

5. * d. Beta waves occur when we are awake and active; alpha waves are associated with relaxation prior to going to sleep. (p. 126)

   a. Delta waves occur when we are deeply asleep.

   b. Beta waves occur when we are awake and active.

   c. Alpha waves occur when we are relaxed; REM waves look much like beta waves.

6. * b. REM sleep is characterized by irregular breathing and heart rate, rapid eye movements, and sexual arousal. (p. 128)

   a. REM sleep does not occur until a full cycle of sleep from Stage 1 to Stage 4 has been completed.

   c. Brain waves are very active during REM sleep; they have the appearance of beta waves.

   d. REM sleep is also called active sleep.

7. * c. After nights of REM deprivation, research subjects dream more intensely and for longer periods. (p. 131)

   a. The opposite of this is true.

   b. These forms of damage have been found only in experimental animals, not people.

   d. Because they would have lost sleep, the opposite would be true.

8. * b. Freud said that sexual and aggressive impulses that are forbidden when awake are symbolically expressed in dreams, when our defenses are weakest. (p. 132)

   a. Attribution theory suggests that random neural activity is "made sense of" by the cortex.

   c. Information processing theories of dreams argue this.

   d. Because *a* and *b* are incorrect, this cannot be the best answer.

9. * d. The latent content is the dream's real meaning, usually involving sexual or aggressive themes. (p. 132)

    a. Freud was unaware of and unconcerned about the chemistry of the brain.

    b. Manifest content is the part of the dream we recognize, how it appears on the surface.

    c. Freud's theory does not deal with how dreams organize or process information.

10. * c. Insomnia is when sleep comes with difficulty or the person wakes up early and cannot get back to sleep. (p. 134)

    a. Insomnia involves difficulty with all sleep and especially with Stage 1 and Stage 2 sleep.

    b. Severe snoring and breathing problems are related to sleep apnea.

    d. Insomnia is not related to REM or non-REM sleep.

11. * a. Narcoleptic attacks of sudden sleep are triggered by emotional incidents, sometimes even by laughter. (p. 135)

    b. The opposite is true: narcolepsy involves sudden attacks of sleep, often involving REM.

    c. Narcolepsy is treated with stimulants.

    d. Snoring and breathing problems in elderly men are symptoms of sleep apnea.

12. * d. Because *a, b,* and *c* are all types of non-REM sleep disorders, this is the best answer. (pp. 135–136)

    a. Sleepwalking is a problem associated with non-REM sleep, but this is not the only correct answer listed.

    b. Bedwetting is a problem associated with non-REM sleep, but this is not the only correct answer listed.

    c. Sleep apnea is a breathing disorder associated with non-REM sleep, but this is not the only correct answer listed.

13. * a. The key factor in hypnosis is suggestion: the hypnotist can suggest actions or thoughts that affect the hypnotized person immediately or on a delayed basis. (p. 137)

    b. Hypnosis does not involve the loss of control over impulses.

    c. The quantity of memory does increase during hypnosis, but this includes many incorrect "memories."

    d. Need for approval is unrelated to hypnosis.

14. * d. Dissociation means that consciousness is split. (p. 138)

    a. These divisions of the nervous system are unrelated to dissociation theory.

b. Role playing is related to social role theories: the opposite side of the hypnosis debate.

c. Drugs are unrelated to the hidden observer issue.

15. * c. Social role theories stress the situational effects of expectation, interpersonal relations, and audience influence. (p. 138)

a. The medulla oblongata is unrelated to hypnosis and social roles.

b. Dreams are unrelated to hypnotized behavior.

d. Experiments supporting social role theories include subjects who are not hypnotized but act as if they were. Therefore, the skill of the hypnotist is considered unimportant.

16. * d. When a person is hypnotized, one hand plunged into ice water can experience no pain from the cold while the rest of the person can report that there is considerable pain. Hilgard calls this the "hidden observer" and uses it to support his dissociation theory of hypnosis. (p. 140)

a. Hypnosis for recall of events experienced when younger is called age regression.

b. The "hidden observer" is within the mind of the hypnotized person.

c. People who are easily hypnotized are called fantasy prone.

17. * a. Imagination seems to be a good explanation for why hypnotized people remember many memories, including ones they make up. (p. 141)

b. Memory under hypnosis is *not* more accurate than memory in the waking state. Therefore, it is not admissible evidence in some courts.

c. The greater the experimenter influence, the more distorted memory would be.

d. Age regression tends to include many made-up memories based on how adults think children ought to act.

18. * d. Physical dependence on drugs is characterized by tolerance, need for the drug to maintain physical functioning, and withdrawal symptoms when the drug is absent. (pp. 144–145)

a. Psychological dependence involves the need for a drug to maintain emotional and behavioral equilibrium.

b. Withdrawal occurs when a person stops taking a drug; tolerance occurs when the drug is still being used.

c. Placebo effects involve behavior changes caused by expectations about the drug's effects rather than the drug itself.

19. * c. Expecting to drink alcohol produces more erotic fantasies regardless of whether one actually drinks alcohol or soft drinks. (p. 145)

a. The drug itself did not produce more fantasies.

b. Expectations of the drug produced more, not fewer, fantasies.

d. Expectations had very significant effects.

20. * a. Amphetamines are manufactured stimulants that have very powerful effects on consciousness. (p. 146)

   b. Opiates are considered depressants, not hallucinogens.

   c. LSD is manufactured, but it is an hallucinogen, not a stimulant.

   d. Barbiturates are manufactured depressants.

Application Answers

1. * b. Selective attention is the filter that focuses consciousness on one thing at a time. (p. 120)

   a. Subliminal perception is the emotional response to stimuli that are below absolute threshold.

   c. The hidden observer is relevant only to hypnosis.

   d. Daydreaming occurs when attention wanders, not when it is focused.

2. * d. Fantasy-prone individuals daydream a good deal and seem to be creative, easily hypnotized, and capable of visualizing things clearly. (p. 123)

   a. Narcolepsy is a sleep disorder unrelated to hypnosis or creativity.

   b. Daydreaming is associated with wandering attention.

   c. Dreaming is unrelated to fantasy-proneness.

3. * a. Most people's biological clocks are set at 25 hours when there are no environmental cues; the subject of one long-term experiment had a 28-hour clock. (p. 125)

   b. Our biological clock is different from the solar clock of 24 hours.

   c. Usually our biological clock is an hour or more longer than 24 hours.

   d. Our biological clocks are quite regular.

4. * d. Alpha waves are associated with relaxation and occur just before we fall asleep. (p. 126)

   a. Stimulant drugs produce active, beta waves.

   b. The deepest stages of sleep are characterized by delta waves.

   c. Beta waves occur when we are fully awake and active.

5. * c. REM sleep (active sleep) involves irregular breathing and heart rate, sexual arousal, brain wave activity that mimics beta waves, and rapid eye movements (REM) under the eyelids. (p. 128)

   a. Stage 1 sleep is a non-REM stage.

   b. Stage 4 sleep is a non-REM stage.

   d. Dreaming and irregular breathing are associated with REM sleep.

6. * b. Freudian dream analysis argues that all dreams are symbolic expressions of sexual and aggressive impulses. (p. 132)

    a. The theory of dreams that says random neural firings while we sleep are constructed into dreams is an attribution theory.

    c. Dissociation is a theory of hypnosis.

    d. Hall's research found little support for the idea that all or most dreams involve sexual or aggressive imagery.

7. * c. Narcolepsy is the rare sleep disorder in which people who are awake rapidly go into an unconscious, REM state. This most often occurs following laughter. (p. 135)

    a. Sleep apnea is a breathing disorder that causes frequent awakening.

    b. Subliminal perception occurs in the waking state and is not a disorder.

    d. SIDS stands for "sudden infant death syndrome" and is related to sleep apnea; Bill is too old for this.

8. * c. A posthypnotic suggestion occurs when a person acts out suggestions after returning to the waking state from hypnosis. (p. 137)

    a. Social role theories of hypnosis discuss the hypnotized person's desire to meet expectations during the hypnotized state.

    b. The hidden observer is a phenomenon of divided consciousness during hypnosis; it is not seen after the hypnotic state ends.

    d. Mesmerism was the term used for hypnosis over a century ago.

9. * d. Holmes et al. found that meditation and relaxation produced the same physiological changes. (p. 143)

    a. Meditation and relaxation appear to produce equivalent changes.

    b. Barbiturates are drugs that do produce tolerance.

    c. Meditation can reduce blood pressure and heart rate.

10. * b. Opiates are depressants, not hallucinogens such as LSD or PCP. (p. 147)

    b. Caffeine is the most widely used psychoactive drug; it is consumed in the morning because it is a stimulant.

    c. Alcohol is a central nervous system depressant.

    d. Many psychoactive drugs such as caffeine, nicotine, and opiates cannot cause hallucinations.

CHAPTER 6

LEARNING

Learning Objectives

1. Define learning and discuss its relationship to acquisition and performance. List the types of learning that do not rely on language. (pp. 151–152)

2. Define classical conditioning. Describe and discuss the components of classical conditioning in Pavlov's experiments with salivating dogs. (pp. 152–153)

3. Describe the acquisition process in classical conditioning. Discuss ways in which classical conditioning occurs in humans, including drug tolerance. (pp. 154–155)

4. Describe and discuss the processes of extinction, spontaneous recovery, and higher-order classical conditioning. Be able to give examples of each in everyday life. (p. 156)

5. Describe generalization and discrimination, and give examples of each. (p. 157)

6. Explain why classical conditioning occurs when there is a contingent relationship between two stimuli and not just a contiguous relationship. (pp. 157–158)

7. Describe the process of aversive conditioning and discuss how it is related to preparedness theory and whether it explains the development of phobias. (pp. 158–159)

8. Describe the development of instrumental conditioning from Thorndike to Skinner. Explain how operant conditioning is different from classical conditioning. Define and give an example of shaping. (pp. 161–163)

9. Describe the acquisition process in operant conditioning. Discuss how continuous reinforcement and partial reinforcement (on fixed-ratio, fixed-interval, variable-ratio, and variable-interval schedules) affect responding. Explain how reinforcement affects choices in responding. (pp. 163–167)

10. Discuss how a token economy is an example of secondary reinforcement. Define and give an example of a discriminated operant. (p. 168)

11. Describe and discuss the cognitive behaviorists' concepts of latent learning and the cognitive map. (pp. 169–170)

12. Define, differentiate between, and give examples of negative reinforcement and punishment. Explain how escape conditioning differs from avoidance conditioning. Discuss the conditions under which punishment is effective. (pp. 170–175)

13. Discuss the evidence that observational learning explains the relationship between watching televised violence and engaging in violence. (pp. 175–177)

Chapter Outline

1. **Learning: a definition** (pp. 151–152)

   Learning is an enduring change in behavior that is the result of experience. *Acquisition* of learning is the process by which our behavioral tendencies change; *performance* takes place when those changes are expressed behaviorally. There are three forms of learning that are not based on language: classical and instrumental conditioning and observational learning.

2. **Classical conditioning: acquisition, human behavior and drug tolerance** (pp. 152–153)

   Classical conditioning is the process of learning to associate a certain response with a certain stimulus. Ivan Pavlov's research with dogs revealed that their first response to a new, neutral stimulus was an *orienting reflex*. He also showed that an *unconditioned stimulus* automatically elicits an *unconditioned response*, but when a neutral stimulus (*conditioned stimulus*) is paired with the unconditioned stimulus, the animal learns a *conditioned response*. Once learning has occurred, the conditioned stimulus alone can elicit the conditioned response. These principles can explain many human emotional experiences as well as the development of tolerance to drugs.

3. **Classical conditioning: phenomena, behaviorism, and aversive stimuli** (pp. 156–161)

   When the connection between a conditioned stimulus and a conditioned response gradually disappears, *extinction* is said to take place. After extinction, the conditioned stimulus may again elicit the original response in a process called *spontaneous recovery*. In a procedure called *higher-order conditioning,* an established conditioned stimulus can be used as an unconditioned stimulus when it is paired with a new neutral stimulus.

   Generalization occurs when learning transfers from one situation to a similar situation. *Discrimination* is the ability to distinguish between similar stimuli by responding in different ways.

For a long time it was believed that classical conditioning occurred because stimuli were paired closely in time (they were contiguous). More recent research shows that conditioning occurs when one stimulus is contingent on another, that is, when one event can predict another.

A stimulus that a subject tries to avoid is called an *aversive stimulus*. Aversive conditioning can be learned very rapidly to stimuli that have survival value to the organism; this supports *preparedness theory*. Aversive stimuli are sometimes responsible for the development of unreasonable fears in people (*phobias*), but preparedness theory does not seem to explain adequately why some phobias are much more common than others.

4. **Instrumental conditioning: development and the acquisition process** (pp. 161–164)

Instrumental conditioning is learning based on the association between our behavior and its consequences. Edward Thorndike began experiments on instrumental conditioning and discovered that responses that are rewarded tend to be repeated, whereas those that are not rewarded are not. He called this the *law of effect*. The process of giving rewards (reinforcers) came to be called *reinforcement*. B. F. Skinner elaborated on Thorndike's work and focused on *operants*—responses emitted by the animal. He called the learning process *operant conditioning*. He also found that learning can be helped by *shaping*, a procedure in which approximations to a wanted response are successively reinforced.

The acquisition process in operant conditioning involves a change in the priority of the organism's responses, where those responses that are reinforced become stronger. The speed of learning can be shown on a learning curve.

5. **Instrumental conditioning: reinforcement schedules, choice, secondary reinforcement, and discriminated operants** (pp. 165–168)

A *reinforcement schedule* describes the frequency with which a wanted response is reinforced. If the subject is rewarded whenever the response is given, there is *continuous reinforcement*. *Partial reinforcement*, when some responses are reinforced, is more common and makes learning and extinction more difficult. Under a *fixed-ratio schedule* of reinforcement, reinforcement is available only after a given number of responses are emitted. With a *fixed-interval schedule* of reinforcement, a given time period must elapse before a response will be reinforced. Fixed-ratio schedules promote higher rates of responding, whereas fixed-interval schedules foster rhythmical bursts of responses corresponding to times when reinforcement is available. *Variable-ratio* and *variable-interval schedules* are irregular patterns of reinforcement that promote faster and steadier responses than fixed schedules.

When people and animals are provided with choices in their responses, they tend to choose those with the highest likelihood of reinforcement. When choices are equal in reinforcement, they tend to alternate.

A primary reinforcer satisfies a biological need. Secondary reinforcement occurs when the response itself is reinforcing. A *token economy* is an example of secondary reinforcement: poker chips, given for appropriate behaviors, can be exchanged for special privileges (primary reinforcers).

Instrumentally conditioned learning includes knowledge that reinforcement is available if a certain response is made. Behaviors that are performed only in the presence of these stimulus signals are called *discriminated operants*.

6. **Instrumental conditioning and behaviorism** (pp. 168–170)

Thorndike and Skinner said that instrumental conditioning was a process of contiguity: the pairing of response and reinforcer. Cognitive behaviorists such as Tolman disagree. They note that learning can occur in the absence of reinforcement, in a process called *latent learning,* and that animals in mazes can learn *cognitive maps* that contradict predictions based on contiguity theory.

7. **Reinforcement versus punishment** (pp. 170–175)

Response strength can be increased through giving the subject something it likes (*positive reinforcement*) or taking away something it dislikes (*negative reinforcement*). *Punishment,* on the other hand, reduces a response's likelihood by either taking away something that is liked or giving something that is disliked.

Negative reinforcement can take two forms. In *escape conditioning,* the subject can make a response that stops an aversive stimulus. *Avoidance conditioning,* a response to a stimulus signaling an aversive stimulus, provides a way of avoiding the negative experience.

Punishment is effective only when very restrictive conditions are met: it must be consistently applied, there must be little delay between response and punishment, and it must be harsh in the first instance given. Punishment has the undesirable side effect of suppressing wanted responses and giving the impression that violence is acceptable.

8. **Learning by observation** (pp. 175–177)

We often learn by watching the behavior of others and the consequences they receive. This is called *observational learning.* Research on watching televised violence shows a strong correlation between exposure to violence and tendencies to act violently. Although this research tends to support observational learning, it cannot be said with certainty that observing violence *causes* violent behavior.

Fill-in-the-Blank Quiz

1. A schedule of reinforcement that does not reinforce every response is called _____ .

2. The process of eliminating a conditioned response by presenting the conditioned stimulus without the unconditioned stimulus is called _____ .

3. A response that acts on the environment is called a(n) _____ .

4. The process of learning to associate a certain response with a certain stimulus is called _____ .

5. The procedure of weakening a response by either taking away something that is liked or giving something that is disliked is called _____ .

6. The idea that organisms are biologically predisposed to acquire and maintain conditioned responses to certain hazards in the environment is called _____ .

7. The partial reinforcement schedule in which a subject must make a certain number of responses before being reinforced is called a(n) _____ .

8. A formerly neutral stimulus that elicits a response by being paired with an unconditioned stimulus is called a(n) _____ .

9. The process of systematically following a response with a reward in order to increase the frequency of that response is called _____ .

10. An enduring change in behavior resulting from experience is called _____ .

11. Learning from watching the behaviors of others and the consequences of those behaviors is called _____ .

12. Thorndike's idea that responses that are rewarded are more likely to be repeated than those that are not is called the _____ .

13. An irregular pattern of reinforcement that rewards the subject after a certain period of time has elapsed is called _____ .

14. The reappearance, with no additional training, of a conditioned response that had been extinguished is called _____ .

15. The frequency with which reinforcement is provided is called _____ .

16. A response to an unanticipated or new stimulus is called a(n) _____ .

17. A form of instrumental conditioning that allows the subject to set the pace of learning is called _____ .

18. The process by which experience changes behavioral tendencies is called _____ .

19. The instrumental learning procedure that strengthens responding by giving the subject something it likes is called _____ .

20. Learning that is not demonstrated immediately is called _____ .

21. The ability to distinguish between similar stimuli by responding to them in different ways is called _____ .

22. A pattern of rewarding the subject whenever it responds correctly is called _____ .

23. A stimulus that automatically elicits a certain response is called a(n) _____ .

24. The successive reinforcement of approximations to a wanted response is called _____ .

25. The demonstration of learning in behavior is called _____ .

26. The form of instrumental aversive conditioning in which the subject learns to avoid the aversive stimulus by responding to a stimulus that signals the onset of the aversive stimulus is called _____ .

27. Learning based on reinforcing consequences is called _____ .

28. A procedure that strengthens learning by taking away from the subject something it dislikes is called _____ .

29. A stimulus that a subject wants to avoid is called a(n) _____ .

30. A mental image of a space learned without direct reinforcement is called a(n) _____ .

31. A behavior that the subject performs only in the presence of a particular stimulus is called a(n) _____ .

32. The tendency to transfer learning from one situation to a similar situation is called _____ .

33. A pattern of reinforcement in which the subject is reinforced for responses made a certain number of seconds or minutes after its last reinforced response is called _____ .

34. The process of eliminating the conditioned response by presenting the conditioned stimulus without the unconditioned stimulus is called _____ .

35. A system of secondary reinforcement that rewards behavior with tokens that later can be exchanged for something the individual wants is called a(n) _____ .

36. Training a subject to respond to a conditioned stimulus by pairing it with the conditioned stimulus from a previous conditioning procedure is called _____ .

37. A form of instrumental aversive conditioning in which the response of the subject terminates aversive stimulation is called _____ .

38. An unreasonable fear that interferes with day-to-day activities is called a(n) _____ .

39. An irregular pattern of reinforcement that rewards the subject after a number of unreinforced responses have been made is called a(n) _____ .

40. A behavior that is automatically emitted after an unconditioned stimulus is called a(n) _____ .

Fill-in-the-Blank Answers

1. partial reinforcement
2. extinction
3. operant
4. classical conditioning
5. punishment
6. preparedness theory
7. fixed-ratio schedule
8. conditioned stimulus
9. reinforcement
10. learning
11. observational learning
12. law of effect
13. variable-interval schedule
14. spontaneous recovery
15. reinforcement schedule
16. orienting reflex
17. operant conditioning
18. acquisition
19. positive reinforcement
20. contingent
21. latent learning
22. discrimination
23. continuous reinforcement
24. unconditioned stimulus
25. shaping
26. performance
27. avoidance conditioning
28. instrumental conditioning
29. negative reinforcement
30. aversive stimulus
31. cognitive map
32. contiguous
33. discriminated operant
34. generalization
35. fixed-interval schedule
36. conditioned response
37. token economy
38. higher-order conditioning
39. escape conditioning
40. phobia
41. variable-ratio schedule
42. unconditioned response

Fact and Concept Questions

1. Which statement about learning is true?
   a. Learning is a change in behavior that is not necessarily the result of experience.
   b. Learning always involves language.
   c. In learning there is no difference between acquisition and performance.
   d. Learning is an enduring change in behavior.

2. _____ is a form of learning in which associations are made between a certain response and a certain stimulus.
   a. Latent learning
   b. Observational learning
   c. Classical conditioning
   d. Operant conditioning

3. In Pavlov's experiments, the clicking of the metronome at first produced _____ but then elicited salivation, so it became a _____ .
   a. an orienting reflex; conditioned stimulus.
   b. an unconditioned response; unconditioned stimulus
   c. anxiety in the animal; unconditioned stimulus
   d. an unconditioned response; conditioned response

4. Classical conditioning and opponent processes combine to provide a good explanation for
   a. the development of fears.
   b. aggressive behavior seen in children.
   c. why some phobias are much more common than others.
   d. the development of drug tolerance.

5. If a conditioned stimulus is no longer paired with an unconditioned stimulus, the conditioned response will _____ in strength because of _____ .
   a. increase; generalization
   b. decrease; extinction
   c. decrease; spontaneous recovery
   d. increase; negative reinforcement

6. Which two terms are opposites?
   a. generalization; spontaneous recovery
   b. generalization; discrimination
   c. positive reinforcement; shaping
   d. extinction; discrimination

7. If the only reason organisms became conditioned is because stimuli and responses occurred at nearly the same time, learning would be caused by
   a. the law of effect.
   b. contingency.
   c. contiguity.
   d. factors other than the environment.

8. Garcia's research on taste aversion and classical conditioning led to the concept of _____ , which stresses the evolutionary importance of learning certain associations.
   a. aversion therapy
   b. spontaneous recovery
   c. cognitive behaviorism
   d. preparedness theory

9. How does instrumental conditioning differ from classical conditioning?
   a. It emphasizes the consequences of our behavior.
   b. It emphasizes the association of stimulus with response.
   c. It emphasizes the memory of the learning organism.
   d. It emphasizes the biological limitations of the organism.

10. Thorndike is to _____ as Skinner is to _____ .
    a. the law of effect; operant conditioning
    b. punishment; positive reinforcement
    c. positive reinforcement; negative reinforcement
    d. classical conditioning; operant conditioning

11. A subject can learn a complicated response if given positive reinforcement for making a crude approximation of the response and then reinforced for responses more and more like the desired one. This process is called
    a. observational learning.
    b. shaping.
    c. higher-order conditioning.
    d. None of the above.

12. Which of the following is an example of a continuous reinforcement schedule?
    a. Every tenth time a person says "Thank you" he/she hears "You're welcome."
    b. Getting paid the same amount whether you make a mistake or not.
    c. Never knowing when you will be paid.
    d. Being complimented on your appearance every time you wear a suit.

13. The difference between a fixed-ratio and a fixed-interval schedule is that in a fixed ratio
    a. the amount of time between reinforcements is always the same.
    b. the importance of the reinforcement remains constant.
    c. Both *a* and *b*.
    d. Neither *a* nor *b*.

14. A token economy is a good example of
    a. secondary reinforcement applied to treatment.
    b. classical conditioning of a phobia.
    c. a fixed-variable schedule of reinforcement.
    d. the fact that partial reinforcement makes learning easier.

15. Discriminated operants are terms in operant conditioning that reflect a similar process in classical conditioning. What is that similar process?
    a. extinction
    b. partial reinforcement
    c. discrimination
    d. higher-order conditioning

16. Experiments with rats in mazes have illustrated the principle of latent learning. The main lesson of latent learning is that
    a. animals can learn without the use of language.
    b. operant conditioning is better than classical conditioning.
    c. learning can occur without being demonstrated immediately.
    d. animals can learn only if they are reinforced for each movement they make.

17. Which statement about negative reinforcement is true?
    a. Like punishment, it reduces the strength of a behavior.
    b. Like positive reinforcement, it increases the strength of a behavior.
    c. It involves giving a subject an undesirable consequence.
    d. It involves rewarding undesirable behaviors.

18. It is a form of negative reinforcement in which the subject learns to respond to a stimulus signaling the onset of an aversive stimulus. It teaches the subject to stay out of aversive situations. "It" is
    a. avoidance conditioning.
    b. punishment.
    c. secondary reinforcement.
    d. escape conditioning.

19. Punishment can be effective as long as
    a. it is delivered immediately after the undesirable response is made.
    b. it is very mild.
    c. Both *a* and *b*.
    d. Neither *a* nor *b*.

20. Long-term studies show a relationship between the amount of time children spend watching violent television shows and their tendency to behave violently later in life. These results
    a. prove that watching violence causes aggression.
    b. support the importance of observational learning.
    c. disprove preparedness theory.
    d. prove that latent learning for aggression occurs in childhood.

Application Questions

1. Little Janie knows that when Mommy calls her by her full name, Jane Margaret Kilpatrick, she is in big trouble. Even as an adult, Jane feels anxious if anyone calls her by her full name. This illustrates
   a. fear based on classical conditioning.
   b. preparedness theory.
   c. escape conditioning.
   d. the shaping of a biological response.

2. Mr. Tobin went to a therapist because he habitually became sexually aroused at the sight of shoes. His therapist repeatedly showed him shoes but in a situation that prevented him from becoming aroused. After a while, shoes were no longer a problem for him. The therapy used the learning process called
   a. a token economy.
   b. higher-order conditioning.
   c. the orienting reflex.
   d. extinction.

3. George was in a car accident on a rainy night. Now he is terrified of driving on either rainy or dry nights. Even when he is not driving, he becomes anxious on rainy nights. The "spread" of George's fears illustrates
   a. the power of spontaneous recovery.
   b. the role of shaping.
   c. the generalization of learning.
   d. preparedness theory's value in explaining phobias.

4. Imagine an experiment in which one group of animals is administered a shock when they see a light. A second group is shocked like the first, but also at times when no light is shone. The second group will not learn a conditioned response to the light because
   a. they were on a partial reinforcement schedule.
   b. although the stimuli were contiguous, they were not contingent.
   c. excessive punishment leads to the suppression of all behavior.
   d. the light became an aversive stimulus for the second group.

5. Dr. Jones has been a therapist for thirty years. He has treated more than one hundred people for fear of snakes, but not a single one for fear of television sets. _____ attempts to explain why so few people are fearful of television sets even though they have much more exposure to them than to snakes.
   a. The law of effect
   b. Contiguity theory
   c. Preparedness theory
   d. Observational learning

6. Circus animals are gradually taught to climb on tall ladders and jump through fiery hoops. Their trainers use positive reinforcement through a process called _____ to get them to learn these complicated movements.
   a. escape conditioning
   b. shaping
   c. discrimination
   d. a token economy

7. Maryanne was in the habit of asking her roommate for lecture notes from Introductory Psychology. Every time she asked for the notes, she got them. Then the roommate suddenly and consistently stopped providing notes. Maryanne stopped asking for them. In operant conditioning terms, what happened?
   a. Maryanne was put on a partial reinforcement schedule.
   b. The roommate began using negative reinforcement.
   c. The request response became an aversive stimulus to Maryanne.
   d. Without continuous reinforcement, the request response was extinguished.

8. Gambling machines in Las Vegas produce strong, steady responses (putting coins in the slots) because, according to operant conditioning, the gamblers are
   a. on a variable ratio reinforcement schedule.
   b. on a continuous reinforcement schedule.
   c. seeking to meet unconscious needs for power.
   d. generalizing a conditioned response to an unconditioned stimulus.

9. Fran is a person with moderate mental retardation. In his treatment, he receives poker chips for engaging in appropriate behaviors such as making his bed and putting his dishes in the sink. The chips can be exchanged for privileges like watching television. The treatment program illustrates
   a. a token economy.
   b. the power of extinction.
   c. shaping.
   d. latent learning.

10. Employees of a company know that when the boss's eyebrows start to twitch, he is going to fly into a rage. They have all learned that when they see twitching eyebrows, it is wise to excuse themselves from the room. In operant conditioning terms, what kind of learning occurred?
    a. punishment
    b. higher-order conditioning
    c. shaping
    d. avoidance conditioning

Fact and Concept Answers

1. * d. Learning is defined as an enduring change in behavior that is a product of experience. (p. 151)

   a. Part of the definition of learning is that it is a product of experience, not simply biological maturation.

   b. All the forms of learning described in Chapter 6 occur without language.

   c. Acquisition (the experience by which behavior change occurs) is distinguished from performance (the expression of changed behavioral tendencies).

2. * c. Classical conditioning emphasizes associations between stimuli and responses. (p. 152)

   a. Latent learning refers to acquisition of new behaviors that are not immediately performed.

   b. Observational learning is behavior change caused by watching others' behavior and the consequences of those behaviors.

   d. Operant conditioning emphasizes associations between responses and their consequences.

3. * a. At first, the clicking sounds got the dogs' ears to prick up—the orienting reflex is an automatic reaction to new stimuli. After being paired with food, the clicks elicited salivation, so they became conditioned stimuli. (pp. 152–153)

   b. The unconditioned response for Pavlov's dogs was salivating; an unconditioned stimulus automatically elicits a biological response—clicking sounds do not do this.

   c. The click produced ear movement, not anxiety.

   d. Clicks are environmental events—stimuli—not responses from the organism.

4. * d. Drug tolerance can be explained as a classically conditioned response to opponent processes: the user learns the drug high is a signal that the opponent process low will soon occur. (p. 155)

   a. Classical conditioning explains the development of fears, but opponent processes are not involved here.

   b. Aggression is much more related to operant and observational learning.

   c. Preparedness theory seeks to explain the frequency of certain phobias.

5. * b. When the unconditioned stimulus is no longer paired with the conditioned stimulus, extinction (the weakening of the conditioned response) occurs. (p. 156)

   a. Without occasional presentation of the unconditioned stimulus, response strength decreases.

   c. Spontaneous recovery is seen when a response reappears after extinction.

   d. Negative reinforcement pertains to operant conditioning.

6. * b. Generalization is learning to make the same response to similar situations; discrimination is learning *not* to make the same response to different situations. (p. 157)

   a. Spontaneous recovery is seen when a response reappears after extinction.

   c. Positive reinforcement is used in shaping.

   d. Extinction involves a decrease in responding; discrimination means learning to respond when reinforcement will occur.

7. * c. Contiguity refers to two events occurring closely in time. (p. 157)

   a. The law of effect was Thorndike's principle that behaviors receiving rewards are repeated more often than those that are not.

   b. Contingency refers to one event's being a good predictor of another event's occurring. This principle explains classical conditioning better than it does contiguity.

   d. Learning almost always requires factors in the environment (stimuli).

8. * d. Preparedness theory came from Garcia's observation that conditioning of nausea to certain tastes occurs very rapidly (as in cases of food poisoning in humans). (p. 159)

   a. Aversion therapy does not deal with evolutionary factors.

   b. Spontaneous recovery is seen when a response reappears after extinction.

   c. Cognitive behaviorism stresses latent learning and such unreinforced mental phenomena as cognitive maps.

9. * a. Instrumental conditioning is the development of associations between responses and their consequences. (p. 161)

   b. The association of a stimulus and response is characteristic of classical conditioning.

   c. Memory and other mental phenomena are aspects of cognitive behaviorism.

   d. The biological limitations of the organism are important in preparedness theory.

10. * a. Thorndike developed the law of effect; Skinner coined the term *operant conditioning* to emphasize the organism's active response to the environment. (pp. 161–162)

    b. Both Thorndike and Skinner were interested in positive reinforcement.

    c. Both Thorndike and Skinner were interested in positive reinforcement.

    d. Thorndike's work set the stage for operant conditioning, not classical conditioning.

11. * b. Shaping is the successive reinforcement of approximations to a desired response. (p. 163)

    a. Observational learning is learning by watching the behavior and consequences of others.

c. Higher-order conditioning is a classical conditioning term referring to the use of an established conditioned stimulus as an unconditioned stimulus in further learning.

d. Because *b* is correct, this cannot be the best answer.

12. * d. Continuous reinforcement occurs when there is reinforcement each time a correct response is made. (p. 165)

a. Getting complimented every tenth time a response is made illustrates a fixed-ratio schedule, or FR 10.

b. Continuous reinforcement pertains to rewards contingent on correct responses.

c. Random reinforcement is the opposite of reinforcement always presented for a correct response.

13. * d. When the amount of time between reinforcements is the same, a fixed-interval schedule of reinforcement is being used; the importance of reinforcement is unrelated to schedules of reinforcement. Therefore, neither *a* nor *b* is correct. (p. 166)

a. Time is relevant in a fixed-interval schedule.

b. Importance is irrelevant to reinforcement schedules.

c. Because both *a* and *b* are incorrect, this cannot be the best answer.

14. * a. Tokens act as secondary reinforcers (they cannot be enjoyed directly as can primary reinforcers) and the token system is a treatment method for improving behavior. (p. 168)

b. Token economies use operant conditioning principles.

c. Tokens can be given on a variety of schedules.

d. Partial reinforcement makes learning more difficult.

15. * c. In discrimination, classically conditioned responses are elicited only by certain stimuli, just as discriminated operants are performed only in the presence of certain stimuli. (p. 168)

a. Extinction occurs when response strength decreases.

b. Partial reinforcement is an operant conditioning term.

d. Higher-order conditioning involves the use of an established conditioned stimulus as an unconditioned stimulus in further learning.

16. * c. Learning where performance indicating behavior change is not immediately evident is a definition of latent learning. (p. 169)

a. Animals learn without language in classical and operant conditioning, and even observational learning.

b. No system of learning is "better" than any other.

d. Latent learning experiments show the opposite: cognitive maps are learned even though specific turns in the maze are not reinforced.

17. * b. Both positive and negative reinforcement increase the probability of a response. (p. 170)

   a. Negative reinforcement increases response strength.

   c. Punishment alone involves giving a subject something it does not like.

   d. Negative reinforcement refers to responses that avoid or escape from negative situations; any kind of response can be reinforced.

18. * a. Avoidance conditioning is a form of negative reinforcement where the response is made to a signal that aversive stimuli are about to happen. (p. 171)

   b. Punishment reduces response strength by giving the subject something that it does not like or taking away something it likes.

   c. Secondary reinforcement refers to consequences that can be converted into primary reinforcers.

   d. Escape conditioning occurs when the response stops aversive consequences but does not prevent them from occurring.

19. * a. Punishment is effective if it is delivered immediately after (within seconds of) the offending response. (p. 174)

   b. Punishment is more effective if it is harsh.

   c. Because *b* is incorrect, this cannot be the best answer.

   d. Because *a* is correct, this cannot be the best answer.

20. * b. A change in behavior related to observing someone else's actions supports the idea of observational learning. (p. 175)

   a. Although it is plausible, there is not sufficient evidence to say that television watching is the cause of aggressive behavior.

   c. Preparedness theory pertains to phobias.

   d. Latent learning is more related to maze running than to television watching.

Application Answers

1. * a. The sound of her name is a conditioned stimulus for a fear response; that anyone making this sound produces fear indicates generalization. (p. 153)

   b. Preparedness theory focuses on the ease with which some phobias develop.

   c. Jane is not escaping from a negative situation.

   d. No successive approximations are being described.

2. * d. Extinction occurs when a conditioned stimulus (shoes) is no longer paired with an unconditioned stimulus (arousal). (p. 156)

   a. Token economies use symbols such as poker chips.

    b. Higher-order conditioning uses an established conditioned stimulus as an unconditioned stimulus in further learning.

    c. The orienting reflex is an automatic response, such as turning one's head, to a new stimulus.

3. * c. The fear response generalized to situations other than the original conditioned stimulus. (p. 157)

    a. Spontaneous recovery would be illustrated if George showed fear long after he no longer responded to rainy nights or driving.

    b. The reinforcement of successive approximations is not seen in this example.

    d. Preparedness would discuss why fear of driving or rain is more likely than some other stimulus.

4. * b. This describes the results of actual research showing that unless stimuli are presented in a contingent manner, conditioning is unlikely. (p. 158)

    a. The experiment describes classical, not operant, conditioning.

    c. Punishment is an operant conditioning concept.

    d. If the light had become an aversive stimulus, conditioning would have occurred.

5. * c. Preparedness theory argues that snake phobias are common because avoiding them has evolutionary significance, but televisions (recent phenomena) have no such biological importance. (p. 159)

    a. The law of effect concerns the probability of making a response after rewarding consequences.

    b. Contiguity refers to events occurring closely in time.

    d. Observational learning would apply if phobias were learned by watching others.

6. * b. The animals' behavior is shaped by using positive reinforcement for each action that approximates climbing and jumping. (p. 163)

    a. Escape conditioning occurs when a response leads to the removal of an undesirable situation.

    c. Discrimination refers to conditioned responses that occur in the presence of certain stimuli but not of others.

    d. A token economy would use poker chips, things animals find uninteresting.

7. * d. Maryanne's roommate had continuously reinforced her requests (she gave up her notes); continuously reinforced behaviors quickly drop out when extinction begins (as when the roommate stopped giving her notes). (p. 165)

    a. If it were partial, she would get notes every so often.

    b. If negative reinforcement were involved, a response would increase.

    c. Perhaps the requests were aversive to the roommate, but not to Maryanne.

8. * a. Never knowing when you will be paid off for behavior is a definition of a variable-interval reinforcement schedule. (p. 167)

   b. If it were continuous, the slot machine would pay off after each coin—there would be nothing to win but your own money!

   c. Behaviorists do not consider unconscious needs.

   d. Unconditioned stimulus is not in the vocabulary of operant conditioning.

9. * a. A token economy uses chips or points as reinforcers for desirable behaviors; they are traded in later for food, privileges, or other desired activities. (p. 168)

   b. Extinction would be used to decrease the strength of undesirable responses.

   c. Shaping would involve reinforcements for successively better attempts at making the bed, for example.

   d. Latent learning refers to learning where immediate performance is not shown.

10. * d. The employees are avoiding the boss's temper by using his eyebrows as a signal of impending aversive stimuli. (p. 171)

    a. If they felt the boss's wrath, that would be punishment.

    b. Higher-order conditioning is a classical conditioning phenomenon.

    c. Shaping would involve positive reinforcement of successive approximations to some desired behavior.

CHAPTER 7

MEMORY

Learning Objectives

1. Define memory and describe the three tasks necessary to any information-retaining system. (p. 179)

2. Describe sensory, working, and long-term memory. Describe what sensory registers do and how George Sperling developed a way to study them. Discuss iconic and echoic memory. (pp. 180–182)

3. Define and discuss eidetic memory. Describe and discuss the duration and capacity of working memory. (pp. 183–185)

4. Discuss the process of moving information from short-term to long-term memory through maintenance rehearsal and chunking. Explain the errors that the chunking of information can cause. (pp. 185–187)

5. Describe elaborative rehearsal and how depth of processing is related to the meaningfulness of what we try to remember. (pp. 187–188)

6. Define semantic network and discuss how this concept explains how words and ideas are stored in terms of meaning. Define and discuss the concept of schema. (pp. 189–192)

7. Define and differentiate between declarative memory and procedural memory. Define and differentiate between semantic memory and episodic memory. (pp. 192–193)

8. Discuss the physiological processes at work during short-term and long-term memory. Discuss the process of consolidation and the physical location of memories in the brain. (pp. 193–195)

9. Describe the semantic and contextual cues that are used in the retrieval process. Discuss what is meant by the tip-of-the-tongue phenomenon, priming, and state-dependent cues. (pp. 196–197)

10. Discuss the concepts of mood-congruent memory, repression, and repressors. Describe research findings about the accuracy of eyewitness testimony and reasons for inaccuracy during retrieval. (pp. 198–200)

11. Describe how forgetting occurs, including proactive and retroactive interference. (pp. 200–202)

12. Describe and discuss such memory mnemonics as the pegword method and the method of loci as well as the role of imagery in assisting memory. (p. 203)

Chapter Outline

1. **The storage and processing of information** (pp. 179–180)

    Memory is a system that allows us to retain what we have learned. Any such system must perform three tasks: *encoding* (choosing relevant information and transforming it into a savable form), *storage* (preserving information until it is needed), and *retrieval* (finding and transforming information back into usable form at a later date).

2. **Encoding** (pp. 180–189)

    It is impossible for the brain to record and store every event we sense. *Sensory memory* briefly stores perceptual information in *sensory registers* until a selection is made to retain what is needed. George Sperling first demonstrated the existence of sensory registers by flashing a picture of many letters for less than half a second. By giving subjects cues for which letters to read back, he discovered that a great deal of visual information is retained for less than 1 second (*iconic memory*). A similar register for sound exists (*echoic memory*), which lasts somewhat longer. Some people, especially young children, can remember scenes very accurately over time. This is called *eidetic memory* and it seems to be a special talent.

    Working memory (short-term memory) is a memory system of limited capacity and duration that holds information for further processing. Without rehearsal, information in short-term memory is lost after about 20 seconds; only about seven (plus or minus two) independent pieces of information can be stored in short-term memory at any one time.

    Long-term memory preserves unlimited amounts of information for very long periods of time. Information can get from short- to long-term memory if it is repeated over and over, a process called *maintenance rehearsal*. Another method is *chunking*, where random elements are grouped by some kind of categorization scheme. Chunking increases the capacity and durability of memory, but it can introduce distortions of information that is remembered.

Transforming information into meaningful units involves *elaborative rehearsal*. The deeper the processing—the more meaning that is required to encode information—the better our memory for it.

3. Storage (pp. 189–196)

A *semantic network*, a network of ideas on a certain subject, helps us store information. Just as in encoding, the greater the meaningfulness of new information and the linkage to semantic networks, the better our ability to remember. Since our memory is stored by meaning rather than discrete events, we can reconstruct details we do not actually remember. *Schemas*, organizing structures, also help us connect new knowledge to old information.

In long-term memory we store facts (*declarative memory*) and ways of performing skills (*procedural memory*). Declarative memory includes both general fact memory (*semantic memory*) and personal experience memory (*episodic memory*).

The storage of information in long-term memory appears to need a process called *consolidation*, when neural circuits have an opportunity to change. Where memories are stored in the brain is not clear, although the temporal lobes, cerebellum, and structures under the temporal lobe are thought to be important.

4. Retrieval (pp. 196–200)

Retrieval is the process of finding information and transforming it back into usable form. In the *tip-of-the-tongue phenomenon* we know we will be able to remember something, although at the time we cannot. The sounds and meanings of words, semantic cues, are helpful in this form of retrieval. Using cues to improve memory is called *priming*.

We tend to remember better when the conditions under which we remember are similar to those under which the learning occurred. These environmental cues are called *state-dependent cues* when memory is impaired during drugged states. Retrieval also improves under conditions of *mood-congruent memory*.

Repression, motivated forgetting, is a real phenomenon; whether it is related to the retrieval process is not clear. As eyewitness testimony research demonstrates, the way a question is worded can alter how incidents are remembered.

5. Forgetting (pp. 200–203)

Forgetting can be a failure at any stage in the process of remembering. A large percentage of what we store is lost rapidly, but some memories are maintained for fifty years or more without rehearsal. Forgetting can also be the result of *interference*, when memory of one thing disrupts memory of another. In *retroactive interference*, early memories are disrupted by later ones; in *proactive interference*, recent memories are disrupted by earlier ones.

6. Improving your memory (pp. 203–205)

To aid in remembering unrelated bits of information we can use *mnemonics*, memory aids. One such mnemonic is the *pegword method*, where new information is linked to a rhyme scheme such as "one is a bun, two is a shoe," etc. Images of the new words linked to the old words (bun, shoes, etc.) help in the retrieval process. The *method of loci* also uses imagery. This time new information is pictured in one location after another as one takes a mental walk. *Imagery*, representation of thought in visual scenes, may improve memory by getting us to use both a verbal code and a visual code for storing and retrieving information.

Fill-in-the-Blank Quiz

1. Memory of personal experiences is called _____ .

2. The ability to remember over time the exact image of a visual experience is called _____ .

3. The memory aid that associates a list of unrelated items with images and mentally places those images in familiar locations is called the _____ .

4. A network of ideas about a particular subject is called a(n) _____ .

5. Another term for motivated forgetting is _____ .

6. The sensory register for visual images is called _____ .

7. The experience of correctly believing you will recall a fact or word although, at the moment, you cannot is called the _____ .

8. The memory system that has limited duration and capacity and that preserves information for processing is called _____ .

9. Memory of facts and words is called _____ .

10. The means of preserving information until it is needed is called _____ .

11. The subtype of memory for performing specific tasks and skills is called _____ .

12. The process of choosing information to be retained and transforming it into a form that can be saved is called _____ .

13. A memory aid can also be called a(n) _____ .

14. The organization of random pieces of information into meaningful wholes is called _____ .

15. The disruption of some memories by other memories is called _____ .

16. The sensory register for auditory information is called _____ .

17. The hypothetical process by which short-term memories are transformed into long-term memories is called _____ .

18. The sensory memory that briefly preserves perceptual information is called _____ .

19. The use of cues to improve memory is called _____ .

20. The memory system that preserves unlimited amounts of information for long periods of time is called _____ .

21. The phenomenon of improved retrieval when the mood at the time of retrieval matches the content of the memory is called _____ .

22. A specific memory system that briefly holds sensory information is called a(n) _____ .

23. The representation of thought in visual scenes is called _____ .

24. An organizing structure for knowledge is also called a(n) _____ .

25. A memory aid that associates a list of unrelated words to a previously memorized set of words is called the _____ .

26. The process of encoding new information into meaningful units by connecting it to existing memories is called _____ .

27. The disruption of an earlier memory by a more recent one is called _____ .

28. The process of retaining information by repeating it over and over again is called _____ .

29. The disruption of a recent memory by an earlier memory is called _____ .

30. Memory of things that can be expressed in words is called _____ .

31. The process of finding stored information and transforming it into usable form is called _____ .

Fill-in-the-Blank Answers

1. episodic memory
2. eidetic memory
3. method of loci
4. semantic network
5. repression
6. iconic memory
7. tip-of-the-tongue phenomenon
8. working memory
9. semantic memory
10. storage
11. procedural memory
12. encoding
13. mnemonic
14. chunking

15. interference
16. echoic memory
17. consolidation
18. sensory memory
19. priming
20. long-term memory
21. mood-congruent memory
22. sensory register
23. imagery
24. schema
25. pegword method
26. elaborative rehearsal
27. retroactive interference
28. maintenance rehearsal
29. proactive interference
30. declarative memory
31. retrieval

Fact and Concept Questions

1. Any memory system must have a process of storing information. What *other* task must a memory system perform?
   a. generate hypotheses and test them
   b. choose information to retain and transform it
   c. disrupt the existence of information
   d. transform external physical stimulation into nerve impulses

2. The memory system that retains all the information our senses gather—but only for several seconds at the most—is called _____ memory.
   a. procedural
   b. short-term
   c. semantic
   d. sensory

3. George Sperling's series of ingenious experiments revealed that our _____ memory can preserve visual images for no longer than _____ .
   a. iconic; 1 second
   b. iconic; 20 seconds
   c. echoic; 3 seconds
   d. echoic; one-quarter of a second

4. Which statement about sensory memory is true?
   a. There is a sensory register for each major sense.
   b. Visual memory lasts much longer than auditory memory.
   c. Everyone has eidetic memory in a sensory register.
   d. Sensory memory does not exist for some individuals.

5. It is also called short-term memory and lasts no more than 20 seconds unless information is repeated. Information in this system undergoes consolidation if it is to be successfully stored for a long time. "It" is
   a. procedural memory.
   b. a schema.
   c. working memory.
   d. long-term memory.

6. In what way are maintenance rehearsal and chunking different?
   a. Chunking helps encode information; maintenance rehearsal doesn't.
   b. Maintenance rehearsal helps encode information; chunking doesn't.
   c. Chunking involves organization into meaningful wholes; maintenance rehearsal doesn't.
   d. Maintenance rehearsal involves organization into meaningful wholes; chunking doesn't.

7. Craik and his colleagues did research on deep processing and found that
   a. the deeper the elaborative rehearsal, the more is remembered.
   b. if elaborative rehearsal is used, consolidation is not necessary.
   c. deep processing is the same encoding method as maintenance rehearsal.
   d. All of the above.

8. If we see an armored truck parked outside a bank, we guess it is carrying more than $15 in cash. We know this because of the things we already know about banks, money, and its transportation. The interconnection of these ideas is called a(n)
   a. sensory memory.
   b. eidetic image.
   c. procedural memory.
   d. semantic network.

9. When we remember, can we reconstruct details we cannot remember independently?
   a. No, memory systems work like computers and cannot reconstruct details.
   b. No, memory systems operate using maintenance rehearsal only.
   c. Yes, short-term memory operates solely on the basis of chunking.
   d. Yes, we can store memories using semantic networks and schemas.

10. Memory for actions is to _____ memory as memory for things expressed in words is to _____ memory.
    a. semantic; episodic
    b. episodic; procedural
    c. procedural; declarative
    d. declarative; semantic

11. Suppose a group of brain-damaged individuals could recall many facts from their earlier lives, such as who their seventh grade English teacher was, but could not remember specific facts about the world such as where Paris is. This would illustrate the difference between
    a. short-term and long-term memory.
    b. episodic and semantic memory.
    c. retroactive and proactive interference.
    d. psychological and physiological cues for retrieval.

12. If consolidation exists, we should be able to prevent information from short-term memory from getting to _____ by giving subjects _____ right after learning new material.
    a. long-term memory; electric shocks
    b. long-term memory; rest and relaxation
    c. sensory memory; rest and relaxation
    d. None of the above.

13. Research suggests that memory is stored in
    a. the cortex.
    b. hippocampus and amygdala.
    c. Both *a* and *b*.
    d. Neither *a* nor *b*.

14. The fact that we can recall childhood memories best when we return to our childhood home is an example of
    a. priming in semantic memory.
    b. environmental cues in retrieval.
    c. repression.
    d. the mnemonic called the method of loci.

15. Guilt, shame, and anxiety can push memories out of our minds through the process psychoanalysts call
    a. interference.
    b. retrieval failure.
    c. retroactive consolidation.
    d. repression.

16. Elizabeth Loftus's research indicates that eyewitness testimony
    a. is much improved when people are hypnotized.
    b. is rarely affected by the manner in which questions are asked.
    c. is far more accurate than most people assume.
    d. is readily distorted by the wording of questions.

17. Which statement about long-term memory is true?
    a. Because long-term memories are permanent, mood and repression have no effect on them.
    b. Long-term memories for Spanish vocabulary words can last 50 years.
    c. Both *a* and *b*.
    d. Neither *a* nor *b*.

18. When learning new information disrupts your ability to remember something you learned a while ago, this is called
    a. consolidation.
    b. mnemonic disruption.
    c. retroactive interference.
    d. repression.

19. Linking a list of unrelated items to a set of already-memorized words (frequently in the form of a rhyme) is a _____ called _____ .
    a. form of interference; the proactive method
    b. mnemonic; the method of loci
    c. mnemonic; the pegword method
    d. form of interference; the method of loci

20. One explanation for the effect that both the pegword method and the method of loci have on memory is that they
    a. make use of a dual code—one verbal, the other visual.
    b. increase the capacity of short-term memory.
    c. reduce the need for a consolidation period in learning new information.
    d. reduce the number of verbal and visual cues to a minimum.

Application Questions

1. Imagine a psychologist flashes for one-half of a second a slide showing ten letters. Immediately afterward, the subject is told to read the letter at either the top or bottom of the picture. The subject will accurately do this because
   a. of echoic memory.
   b. short-term memory is being used.
   c. consolidation was allowed to occur.
   d. of iconic memory.

2. Little Jimmy can study a complicated picture and then remember specific details such as how many whiskers there are on a cat's face when asked much later. This illustrates
   a. eidetic memory.
   b. sensory registers at work.
   c. the method of loci.
   d. maintenance rehearsal in long-term memory.

3. You get lost while driving. You stop for directions and a person tells you that you need to make a right, then a left, then go three blocks, then left, then over a bridge, and right at a Y in the road. Unless you rehearse this information you want to remember, you will forget it in how long?
   a. about 2 or 3 seconds
   b. about one-half of a second
   c. about 20 seconds
   d. several months, depending on retrieval cues

4. Based on what we know about short-term memory, which string of numbers is at the upper limit of the short-term memory capacity?
   a. 792543
   b. 42849026534
   c. 498772435
   d. 3456988438235

5. It is easier to remember TWA-IBM-ATT-GM-NCR than TWAIBMATTGMNCR because of the process called
   a. maintenance rehearsal.
   b. chunking.
   c. procedural memory.
   d. consolidation.

6. If, while studying your psychology text, you write in the margin next to information about sleep disorders "Sounds just like Aunt Edna," you are likely to remember this information better than if you had made no connection. The reason for this is
   a. elaborative rehearsal.
   b. mood-congruent memory.
   c. repression.
   d. semantic memory.

7. Irene says, "I went to this expensive restaurant where they have three forks with each place setting. The waiters were very attentive." Asked if the waiters wore tuxedos, Irene says, "Yes," even though she had not remembered that specific detail. Her recollection of tuxedos illustrates
   a. the reconstruction of memory caused by chunking.
   b. the reconstruction of memory caused by schemas.
   c. the role of consolidation in retrieval.
   d. the role of environmental cues in retrieval.

8. Even though she hasn't played croquet in twenty years, Pauline picks up a mallet and whacks balls through the wickets like a pro. This illustrates _____ memory.
   a. semantic
   b. declarative
   c. episodic
   d. procedural

9. Suppose you are asked the name of Richard Nixon's vice president. You cannot recall the name but know you will. You think, "He resigned, too . . . it starts with an "A" . . . Albert? Aglew? Agnew! yes, Agnew." This illustrates
   a. the tip-of-the-tongue phenomenon.
   b. the ability to retain episodic memory while losing semantic memory.
   c. the value of chunking.
   d. the mnemonic device called the pegword method.

10. Stanley got drunk on Saturday and met Janet, Jessica, and Wendy. He fails to remember their names when sober but recalls them when he is drunk again the next weekend. This illustrates
   a. mood-congruent memory.
   b. repression.
   c. state-dependent cues.
   d. the method of loci.

Fact and Concept Answers

1. * b. In addition to storage, an information-retaining system like memory must encode (choose and transform) information and find stored material and transform it back into usable form, a process called retrieval. (p. 179)
   a. Hypothesis testing is a feature of the scientific method.
   c. Information-retaining systems work against the disruption of information.
   d. Transformation of physical stimulation is a definition of sensation.

2. * d. Sensory memory retains for several seconds virtually all of the information we gather with our senses. (p. 180)
   a. Procedural memory is memory for doing things.
   b. Short-term memory lasts for up to 20 seconds.
   c. Semantic memory is memory for general facts.

3. * a. Sperling flashed pictures of letters (visual information that was recorded in iconic memory); they decayed in less than 1 second. (p. 181)
   b. Short-term memory lasts 20 seconds.
   c. Echoic memory records auditory information.
   d. Echoic memory lasts between 2 and 3 seconds; recent studies have shown iconic memory to be as short as one-quarter of a second.

4. * a. There are sensory registers for vision, hearing, touch, smell, and taste. (p. 181)
   b. Visual (iconic) memory lasts for perhaps one quarter of a second; echoic memory lasts about ten times longer.
   c. Eidetic memory appears to be a special talent found mostly in young children.

d. Since sensory memory is the first stage for all later encoding, anyone with any memory must have this component.

5. * c. Working memory is also called short-term memory because it is our current awareness and holds information for less than 20 seconds before either losing it or transferring it to long-term storage. (p. 184)

a. Procedural memory is memory for doing things.

b. A schema is an organizing structure for knowledge.

d. Long-term memory has no limits on durability: some memories last a lifetime without rehearsal.

6. * c. When unrelated information is formed into meaningful wholes it is said to be chunked; when it is merely repeated, it undergoes maintenance rehearsal. (p. 185)

a. Both chunking and maintenance rehearsal are encoding mechanisms.

b. The reverse of this is true.

d. The reverse of this is true.

7. * a. Material that is processed at a deep level of meaning undergoes elaborative rehearsal; Craik and his colleagues found that the deeper the level, the better the remembering. (p. 187)

b. Consolidation appears to be necessary in all transfer of information from short-term to long-term memory.

c. Maintenance rehearsal involves repetition, not deep processing; maintenance is the shallowest type of processing.

d. Because *b* and *c* are incorrect, this cannot be the best answer.

8. * d. Semantic networks are linkages of information about a topic; we know that banks have large sums of money transported to them and we also know that $15 is not a large sum of money. (p. 189)

a. Sensory memory pertains only to information from the senses and does not link existing knowledge.

b. An eidetic image is a near-photographic memory of a scene.

c. Procedural memory is memory for doing things.

9. * d. When we remember, we reconstruct detailed information on the basis of organizing structures (schemas) and links of previously acquired knowledge (semantic networks). (pp. 190–191)

a. Human memory is more constructive than computer memory.

b. Memory systems use elaborative rehearsal, schemas, and other processes, too.

c. We reconstruct details using long-term memory.

10. * c. Procedural memory is memory for actions and skills; declarative memory is anything you can express in words. Remembering how to swim is procedural; remembering when you learn to swim is declarative. (p. 192)

   a. Semantic memory involves the recollection of general facts.

   b. Episodic memory deals with personal recollections.

   d. Declarative memory pertains to words, not actions.

11. * b. Recalling events in one's personal life illustrates episodic memory; remembering general facts about the world (as one might learn in school) reveals semantic memory. (pp. 192–193)

   a. Short-term and long-term memory differ in capacity (short-term holds seven plus or minus two pieces and long-term is infinite) and duration (short-term lasts 20 seconds and long-term is infinite).

   c. These forms of interference pertain to the order in which material is learned.

   d. Cues are irrelevant to this question.

12. * a. Long-term memories are established after a consolidation process that can be impaired or destroyed with electric shocks. (p. 194)

   b. Rest and relaxation promote consolidation.

   c. Sensory memory occurs prior to short-term memory.

   d. Since a is correct, this cannot be the best answer.

13. * c. Memories for faces are disrupted if the visual cortex is damaged, sounds are forgotten if the auditory cortex is damaged, and the memory deficits of Korsakoff's syndrome are related to impairments in the hippocampus and amygdala. (pp. 194–195)

   a. This is correct, but it is not the only correct answer.

   b. This is correct, but it is not the only correct answer.

   d. Because a and b are correct, this cannot be the best answer.

14. * b. Environmental cues such as the sights and sounds that accompanied original learning improve retrieval. (p. 197)

   a. Priming involves cues that include the sounds of words, not cues from furniture, trees, or the like.

   c. Repression is motivated forgetting.

   d. The method of loci involves remembering unrelated lists of items, not episodic memory.

15. * d. Repression seems to occur when memories are associated with the emotions of shame, guilt, and anxiety. (p. 198)

   a. Interference disrupts memory because of the order in which material is learned.

    b. Retrieval failure occurs when the cues for finding information stored in long-term memory are inadequate.

    c. Retroactive consolidation is a made-up term.

16. * d. Loftus and her colleagues have found that wording distorts memory and can produce faulty eyewitness testimony that witnesses feel as confident about as their accurate memories. (p. 199)

    a. Loftus's work does not involve hypnosis, but research on this topic shows that many incorrect memories are produced under hypnosis (see Chapter 5).

    b. The opposite of this is true.

    c. Eyewitness testimony is alarmingly inaccurate.

17. * b. Harry Bahrick and his colleagues have shown that material learned in school can be retained for fifty years; long-term memory can be virtually permanent. (p. 201)

    a. Mood, repression, and self-schemas can impair long-term memories.

    c. Because *a* is incorrect, this cannot be the best answer.

    d. Because *b* is correct, this cannot be the best answer.

18. * c. Retroactive interference occurs when recent learning disrupts our ability to remember past information (the new "reaches back" to interfere with the old). (p. 202)

    a. Consolidation helps in the formation of long-term memories.

    b. Mnemonics aid in memory, they do not disrupt.

    d. Repression is motivated forgetting.

19. * c. Mnemonics aid in remembering by linking new material with old; in the pegword method, the old material is frequently a rhyme such as "one is a bun, two is a shoe. . . ." (p. 203)

    a. Proactive method is a made-up term.

    b. The method of loci uses a series of visualized places to remember unrelated items.

    d. Linkage is a memory aid, not a form of interference.

20. * b. Paivio (1971) suggests that using both verbal and visual cues (a dual code) makes these two mnemonic devices so effective. (p. 203)

    b. Mnemonics assist long-term memory; only rehearsal can maintain information in short-term memory.

    c. There is no evidence that mnemonics reduce the need for consolidation.

    d. The reverse of this is true.

Application Answers

1. * d. Iconic memory is the sensory register for visual information that lasts less than a second but records everything we see. (p. 182)

   a. Echoic memory is the sensory register for hearing.

   b. Short-term memory lasts more than a fraction of a second.

   c. Consolidation is the process that transfers short-term memories into long-term memory.

2. * a. When visual scenes are recalled in exact detail, a person shows eidetic memory. It is most common in young children. (p. 183)

   b. Sensory registers can hold information for only several seconds or less.

   c. The method of loci is a mnemonic that links unrelated items to visualized locations.

   d. Maintenance rehearsal is the repeating of information to keep it "alive" in short-term memory.

3. * c. The duration in short-term memory of items we feel are important is about 20 seconds unless we rehearse them; unimportant items last only a few seconds. (p. 184)

   a. This is the approximate duration of echoic memory and might have been the right answer for short-term memory if the information had not been important.

   b. Iconic memory lasts about one-half second or so.

   d. Only long-term memory lasts several months, and this is impossible unless there is rehearsal.

4. * c. A string of nine numbers is at the upper limit of short-term memory: seven plus or minus two pieces of information. (p. 185)

   a. Six numbers is just below the average capacity of short-term memory.

   b. Eleven numbers is beyond the limit of nine pieces of information.

   d. Thirteen numbers is beyond the limit of nine pieces of information.

5. * b. The letters are chunked into meaningful units: the acronyms for major corporations in the United States. Fourteen independent pieces of information—the letters—are converted to five names. (p. 185)

   a. Maintenance rehearsal involves the repetition of information without meaning.

   c. Procedural memory is memory for doing things.

   d. Consolidation is the process of transferring information from short-term to long-term memory.

6. * a. In elaborative rehearsal, new information is linked to old information, encoding by meaning. The more one does this, the better one's memory for the new information becomes. (p. 187)

b. Mood-congruent memory occurs when associations are made between information and the mood it creates.

c. Repression is motivated forgetting.

d. Semantic memory is memory of general facts.

7. * b. Schemas about expensive restaurants tell us that waiters wear tuxedos (and that the napkins were made of linen, too). This reconstructive process allows us to remember more than specific details. (p. 191)

a. Chunking alone means forming unrelated elements into meaningful units; it does not relate to the reconstruction of what "should" be there.

c. Consolidation is a storage process.

d. Environmental cues would be relevant if Irene had returned to the restaurant and were reminded of the tuxedos by some cue in the room.

8. * d. Procedural memory involves knowing how to do things, such as play croquet. (p. 192)

a. Semantic memory is memory for general facts.

b. Declarative memory is memory for how to express ideas.

c. Episodic memory is memory for personal experiences.

9. * a. The phenomenon of knowing that a memory will be correctly recalled but not being able to do so presently is called the tip-of-the-tongue phenomenon. Here priming cues are used to get to the right answer. (p. 196)

b. Episodic memory would be the time you shook hands with Spiro Agnew, not remembering a general fact about him (semantic memory).

c. Chunking means forming unrelated elements into meaningful units; that is irrelevant here.

d. The pegword method links unrelated items to words already known, frequently a rhyme.

10. * c. State-dependent cues are those associated with altered states of consciousness (such as intoxication) that make the retrieval of information learned in those states easier. (p. 197)

a. Mood-congruent memory is the fact that retrieval improves when the mood at the time of retrieval matches the content of the memory.

b. Repression is when memories are unavailable because of anxiety, guilt, or other strong emotions.

d. The method of loci is a mnemonic linking unrelated items to visualized places.

CHAPTER 8

THOUGHT AND LANGUAGE

Learning Objectives

1. Briefly define the terms *cognition*, *thinking*, and *language*. (pp. 207–208)

2. Describe and discuss how attributes contribute to the definition of concepts. Explain how prototypes, defining attributes, and characteristic attributes are involved in defining concepts. (pp. 208–210)

3. Discuss how concepts are arranged in hierarchies and linked by propositions. Define and differentiate between inductive and deductive inferences. Give examples of syllogisms. (pp. 210–213)

4. Describe the results of research on imagery and thought; discuss how mental maps organize information. (pp. 213–216)

5. Discuss how structuring problems is the first step in solving them. (pp. 217–218)

6. Define and differentiate between algorithms and heuristics. Describe and give an example of a means-end analysis. (pp. 218–220)

7. Describe and discuss the problems of rigidity and functional fixedness in problem-solving. Discuss the role of incubation, insight, and confirmation bias in problem solving and solution testing. (pp. 220–224)

8. Differentiate between decision making and problem solving. Describe the rational decision-making model. (pp. 224–225)

9. Describe and discuss the representativeness heuristic and the availability heuristic. Explain why studying heuristics that fail reveals more about thought than studying heuristics that succeed. (pp. 226–228)

10. Describe the key characteristics of creativity and the two major tests for creativity. Discuss the factors that interfere with and foster creativity. (pp. 228–230)

11. Define phonemes and discuss how differences in phonemes account for the sound of different languages. Define and discuss morphemes; explain how morphemes combine to produce sentences. (pp. 231–232)

12. Define and discuss syntax and transformational grammar. Discuss the difference between deep and surface structures. (pp. 232–233)

13. Describe and discuss the one-word and two-word stages of language development. Know the age when basic language development is complete. (pp. 233–234)

14. Describe research on animal communications and efforts to teach chimpanzees verbal language. Describe the results of efforts to teach nonverbal language to chimpanzees. (pp. 234–237)

15. Discuss how language may affect what we can and do perceive. (pp. 237–239)

Chapter Outline

1. **Cognition and the tools of thought** (pp. 207–217)

   Cognition is the general term psychologists use to describe all the activities of gathering and using information. *Thinking* is the day-to-day mental activity of integrating cognitive experiences. One way of acquiring, organizing, and expressing our knowledge is through *language*.

   The tools of thought include *concepts*, categories of objects, persons, or ideas. These concepts are defined according to *attributes*, the characteristics of objects that make them similar. We use the best example of a concept—a *prototype*—to define concepts. In particular, we look for attributes that all members of a concept group share (*defining attributes*) as well as characteristics shared by most members (*characteristic attributes*).

   Concepts are linked in hierarchies and by *propositions*, relationships among concepts. The manipulation of these propositions is important in *reasoning* and *logic*. For instance, we can draw conclusions based on specific observations (*inductive inferences*) or move from general principles to specific cases (*deductive inferences*). *Syllogisms* identify a series of premises and the conclusion that follows from them. People use *pragmatic inferential rules* to translate formal logic into concrete language that can help us make inferences in everyday life.

   In addition to words, we use mental pictures or *images* in our thinking. Research indicates that we scan images in much the same way we view physical drawings; we also use mental maps to organize space.

2. **Problem solving** (pp. 217–224)

Problems are questions that appear to have a single answer. The first stage of problem solving is formulating the problem, a process that may require a restructuring of the elements of the problem. Generating solutions is the second stage. *Algorithms* are systematic procedures that always produce a solution to a problem, but they are frequently laborious. *Heuristics* are shortcut rules of thumb that simplify the generation of solutions. Another strategy for determining the way to arrive at a solution and the form it should take is called a *means-end analysis*. The solution of problems is often impaired by *rigidity* of thinking and by *functional fixedness*.

When we take a break from trying to solve problems, a technique called *incubation*, we can return with fresh thinking and often solve them. Only when we test the solution, however, do we decide if the proper answer has been found. The process of *insight* involves instant recognition that the solution is correct. We can, however, engage in *confirmation bias* and believe that the solution is correct when it really isn't.

3. **Decision making** (pp. 224–228)

Though problems have clear-cut answers, *decisions* do not; they require us to choose a course of action. In weighing alternative solutions, every outcome's subjective value and likelihood of occurrence can be evaluated in a process called the rational decision-making model.

We often estimate the probabilities of outcomes with two heuristics. One, the *representativeness heuristic*, uses generalizations about a concept to make judgments. Here decision making is based on stereotypes. The *availability heuristic* is the second way we can simplify decisions. In this case, our estimate of an event's frequency is based on the ease with which we remember its occurrence. Heuristics often assist decision making, but it is through failures that we learn most about the heuristics we actually use.

4. **Creativity** (pp. 228–230)

Psychologists define *creativity* in terms of the ability to come up with new and useful ideas or to combine existing information in new and useful ways. Although creative people are highly intelligent, independent, and self-accepting, many noncreative people are, too. Tests for creativity look at the number of ways familiar objects can be used or ask how one word can fit with groups of others. Rather than thinking of people as creative, however, it is better to think of actions as creative and of situations that foster creativity.

5. **Language** (pp. 231–237)

Language exists at three levels. First, there are the sounds or *phonemes* that make up words. Languages differ in the phonemes they use. The smallest units of meaning, *morphemes*, comprise the second level. Some morphemes are words and others are prefixes and suffixes that modify words. When combinations of words are used to express a relationship, there are phrases and sentences, the third level of language.

Syntax governs the order in which we arrange words. By using *transformational grammar*, we have rules for translating the core meaning of a message (the deep structure) into a wide range of individual sentences (the surface structure).

In infancy, all children babble the same phonemes. Later they select and use the phonemes they hear around them. When they reach the *one-word stage* of language development, they use a single word to convey a variety of thoughts. By two years of age, most children have about fifty words which they can put together in two-word utterances. This *two-word stage* shows a primitive knowledge of syntax and the use of *telegraphic speech*, a condensed form of expression where unnecessary words are omitted. By age six, children have mastered the basic components of language.

Attempts to teach chimpanzees vocal human language have failed. Apes, however, have learned to use American Sign Language and an invented language using plastic symbols. Animals can use language to communicate with humans and each other. Their capacity to learn language quickly and comprehensively is markedly lower than that of humans.

6. **The effect of language on thought** (pp. 237–239)

Benjamin Whorf proposed that language limited what people could perceive. Research has not supported this position but has indicated that language affects what we choose to perceive. One important implication is that supposedly generic terms for people such as "mankind" actually exclude females from consideration.

Fill-in-the-Blank Quiz

1. The sounds that make up words are called _____ .

2. A generalization based on specific observations is called a(n) _____ .

3. The tendency to pay more attention to information that may confirm a hypothesis than information that might disprove it is called the _____ .

4. A mental category of things is also called a(n) _____ .

5. The rules that allow the deep structure of a message to be translated into many different sentences are collectively called _____ .

6. The best example of a concept is called a(n) _____ .

7. A mental representation in thought is a(n) _____ .

8. The period in language development when children use single words is called the _____ .

9. A systematic procedure that always produces the solution to a problem is called a(n) _____ .

10. The clipped form of speech that is characteristic of the two-word stage of language development is called _____ .

11. A procedure for determining the way to arrive at a solution and form that the solution should take is called a(n) _____ .

12. The inability to think of a new use for a familiar object is called _____ .

13. All of the activities involved in gathering and using information is called _____ .

14. The technique of breaking away from a problem for a while so that it can be solved later is called _____ .

15. The mental manipulation of knowledge is also called _____ .

16. An attribute shared by all members of a concept category is called a(n) _____ attribute.

17. The tendency to estimate the frequency of an event by the ease with which we remember it is called the _____ .

18. An idea that links two or more concepts by describing the relationship among them is called a(n) _____ .

19. A series of propositions that leads to a conclusion is called a(n) _____ .

20. The rules of grammar that govern the organization of language are collectively called _____ .

21. A question that appears to have an answer can also be called a(n) _____ .

22. The sudden recognition of the right solution to a problem is called _____ .

23. A medium through which knowledge is acquired, organized, and expressed is called a(n) _____ .

24. The answer to a question that involves choosing a course of action is called a(n) _____ .

25. A characteristic of an object is also called a(n) _____ .

26. The tendency to assume that a person or object must be a member of a category if it represents that category especially well is called the _____ .

27. An attribute shared by many but not all members of a concept category is called a(n) _____ attribute.

28. The ability to come up with new and useful ideas or to combine information in new and useful ways is called _____ .

29. The process of generating new information by manipulating and evaluating old information is called _____ .

30. The period of language development in which children make two-word utterances is called the _____ .

31. A shortcut rule of thumb that simplifies the process of generating solutions is called a(n) _____ .

32. The smallest units of meaning in a language are called _____ .

33. A conclusion about a specific case based on a general principle is called a(n) _____ .

34. The unwillingness to give up a problem-solving strategy that no longer works is called _____ .

35. The rules for manipulating propositions to generate valid inferences are collectively called _____ .

36. The principles that perform the same function as formal logic but in concrete language useful for everyday knowledge are called _____ .

Fill-in-the-Blank Answers

1. phonemes
2. inductive inference
3. confirmation bias
4. concept
5. transformational grammar
6. prototype
7. image
8. one-word stage
9. algorithm
10. telegraphic speech
11. means-end analysis
12. functional fixedness
13. cognition
14. incubation
15. thinking
16. defining
17. availability heuristic
18. proposition
19. syllogism
20. syntax
21. problem
22. insight
23. language
24. decision
25. attribute
26. representativeness heuristic
27. characteristic
28. creativity
29. reasoning
30. two-word stage
31. heuristic
32. morphemes
33. deductive inference
34. rigidity
35. logic
36. pragmatic inferential rules

Fact and Concept Questions

1. _____ are tools that help us organize our experiences. They are categories of things, events, or people that are similar in some way.
   a. Heuristics
   b. Concepts
   c. Prototypes
   d. Syllogisms

2. When deciding that a new object should be included in a certain concept group, we compare it with a prototype. What is a prototype?
   a. An object with attributes that are the opposite of the concept.
   b. An object with one attribute of objects in the concept category.
   c. The relationship between one concept and another concept.
   d. None of the above.

3. Spruces are trees. Trees are plants. Plants are living things. The relationships among these concepts illustrate
   a. inductive inference.
   b. the prototype matching method.
   c. the hierarchical nature of concepts.
   d. the differences between defining and characteristic attributes.

4. The rules of reasoning are called _____ ; the rules used to translate deep structure into different individual sentences are called _____ .
   a. logic; transformational grammar
   b. logic; propositions
   c. propositions; syntax
   d. propositions; morphemes

5. Deductive inference occurs when
   a. a conclusion about a specific case is drawn from a general principle.
   b. syllogisms are not used in the reasoning process.
   c. many individual observations are used to develop a general principle.
   d. the relationship between concepts is presented in specific propositions.

6. Which statement about images is true?
   a. They are always based on words.
   b. They are based solely on actual visual experience.
   c. They cannot be studied scientifically because they cannot be seen.
   d. We scan them the same way we do drawings.

7. Your textbook authors conclude that compared to language, imagery is
   a. not really a form of cognition.
   b. not as important a tool of thought.
   c. unable to help us organize experience.
   d. All of the above.

8. Archimedes jumped out of his bathtub and cried "Eureka!" because, in his effort to solve a problem, he
   a. discovered that he needed to use deductive inference.
   b. used a successful algorithm.
   c. reformulated the problem.
   d. used a means-end analysis.

9. A systematic procedure for finding the best solution is a good definition of _____ ; a shortcut method to simplify problem solving is a good definition of _____ .
   a. a heuristic; deductive inference
   b. an algorithm; insight
   c. rigidity; creativity
   d. an algorithm; a heuristic

10. Both functional fixedness and rigidity have the same effect. They
    a. increase creativity.
    b. make us disregard outcomes that disprove our hypothesis.
    c. help us evaluate syllogisms for the validity of their reasoning.
    d. stop us from thinking in new ways.

11. Albert Einstein used to say that when he was stumped by a difficult problem in physics, the best thing he could do was leave the room and play his violin. When he came back to the problem he was usually closer to solving it. Einstein described what psychologists call
    a. incubation.
    b. insight.
    c. confirmation bias.
    d. means-end analysis.

12. The rational model of decision making involves
    a. using the heuristic called a means-end analysis.
    b. looking at every possible outcome's value and frequency of occurrence.
    c. the development of a general principle based on many individual observations.
    d. the use of insight in order to increase creativity.

13. Which procedure in decision making is most likely to use stereotypes?
    a. the representativeness heuristic
    b. means-end analysis
    c. insight
    d. the availability heuristic

14. Decisions made on the basis of the availability heuristic rely on
    a. a complete evaluation of each alternative's frequency.
    b. our own personal experience.
    c. our capacity to pay whatever the choice costs.
    d. None of the above.

15. Creativity is characterized by
    a. the use of syllogisms and rational decision making.
    b. new ideas that may not be helpful in solving problems.
    c. consistent innovation in all spheres of the creative person's life.
    d. ideas or ways of combining information that are both new and useful.

16. The likelihood of creativity is increased when
    a. people expect their creations will be evaluated by experts.
    b. people focus on the inner rewards of creating something.
    c. the creation is rewarded by money and praise.
    d. None of the above.

17. Phonemes are to _____ as morphemes are to _____ .
    a. ideas; actions
    b. sounds; grammatical rules
    c. sounds; meaning
    d. meaning; sounds

18. Which statement about language is true?
    a. Every language on earth has the same number of phonemes.
    b. Children learn morphemes before they can learn phonemes.
    c. Morphemes can be words or fragments of words such as prefixes.
    d. Languages need phonemes and morphemes but do not require grammar.

19. Telegraphic speech is most likely to occur
    a. during the two-word stage of language development.
    b. when communication uses so-called "deep structure."
    c. in the one-word stage of language development.
    d. at age six, when the basics of language are mastered.

20. Research efforts to teach language to apes indicates that
    a. with practice, apes can speak as well as humans.
    b. apes are unable to learn even the basic concepts of language.
    c. apes are limited in their capacity to learn nonvocal language.
    d. some apes are superior to average human children in developing language.

Application Questions

1. To show her children what a kite is, Mrs. Morgan points out a diamond-shaped one with a long tail made of cloth rather than a round or triangular-shaped one. She was using the best example of "kite." This is an illustration of a
   a. prototype.
   b. heuristic.
   c. characteristic attribute.
   d. concept.

2. "The airports that serve American cities are more crowded than European airports." This statement contains a series of _____ that link concepts.
   a. syllogisms
   b. attributes
   c. propositions
   d. conclusions

3. All birds lay eggs. A pheasant is a bird. Therefore, a pheasant lays eggs. This is an example of
   a. inductive inference.
   b. the availability heuristic.
   c. prototype matching.
   d. a syllogism.

4. Dr. Gant wants some information on a new pain medication. If, while consulting a book listing every medication available to physicians, she looks only under the heading "pain medications" rather than looking at every single medication, she is using
   a. an algorithm.
   b. deductive reasoning.
   c. a heuristic.
   d. a means-end analysis.

5. A student is thinking: "I want to get a better grade in psychology. I need to study longer and better. I will go to the library between classes and in the afternoon because I won't be distracted there." This kind of problem solving illustrates
   a. insight.
   b. the use of an algorithm.
   c. the representativeness heuristic.
   d. a means-end analysis.

6. Which of the following best illustrates insight?
   a. Expecting a tornado to occur on a hot and humid day in June.
   b. Knowing instantly that you can remove chewing gum from any article of clothing if you freeze it first.
   c. Developing a general principle from many individual observations.
   d. Taking time off from thinking about a difficult problem.

7. Despite his critics, Christopher Columbus was sure that he could sail west to reach India. When he reached land (that certainly was *not* India), he concluded he was correct. He even called the area the West Indies. This illustrates
   a. incubation.
   b. confirmation bias.
   c. functional fixedness.
   d. rigidity.

8. Suppose you have frequently driven your car on icy highways without ever getting into an accident. Then, during a snowstorm, you hear announcements on television saying that no one should do unnecessary driving because of treacherous roads. You will probably think you can drive safely because of
   a. the availability heuristic.
   b. the means-end analysis you did.
   c. a rational decision-making process.
   d. confirmation bias.

9. "You did go night last where?" is an incorrectly arranged group of words. Why?
   a. Because it breaks the rules of syntax.
   b. Because it breaks the rules of logic.
   c. Because it confuses phonemes with morphemes.
   d. All of the above.

10. Dr. Mitchell says, "Apes can learn sign language faster than younger children learn vocal language. They can learn grammar and create new words that combine two signs. They can also teach sign language to baby chimps." Dr. Mitchell is *wrong* when she says that
    a. chimps have taught sign language to their babies.
    b. apes learn sign language faster than children.
    c. apes have shown no knowledge of grammar.
    d. no chimps have created new combination signs.

Fact and Concept Answers

1. * b. Concepts are mental groupings of similar objects, events, or people. (p. 208)

   a. Heuristics are rules of thumb used to make decisions.

   c. Prototypes are best examples of a concept group; this answer is too specific.

   d. Syllogisms are series of propositions arranged in premises followed by a conclusion.

2. * d. Since none of the answers given is correct, this is the best answer. (p. 209)

   a. Prototypes are best examples of a concept, so the attributes would not be opposite to the concept being illustrated.

   b. There would be several attributes of the concept so that the example would be clear.

   c. Propositions identify the relationship between one concept and another.

3. * c. Concepts are arranged in hierarchies; in this case, the hierarchy is from a type of tree to a type of plant, to a type of living thing. (p. 210)

   a. Inductive inference involves drawing general conclusions from specific observations.

   b. The prototype matching method involves comparing a specific object with the best example of a concept such as watching a movie and deciding whether it is a comedy or a drama.

   d. Defining attributes are those that all members of a concept group share; characteristic attributes are found in only some of the members.

4. * a. The rules that govern the validity of reasoning are collectively called logic; transformational grammar is Chomsky's term for the system of rules used to translate deep structure meaning into individual sentences. (pp. 212, 233)

   b. Propositions are statements indicating the relationship between one concept and another.

   c. Syntax is the set of rules that governs the organization of words and phrases.

   d. Morphemes are the smallest units of meaning in a language.

5. * a. Deductive inferences work from top down—from general principles to specific cases. (p. 212)

   b. Syllogisms, series of propositions reaching a conclusion, always use general principles to conclude something about a specific case.

   c. Inductive inference uses specific cases personally observed to draw general conclusions (working from bottom up).

   d. The presentation of specific propositions is a characteristic of a syllogism.

6. * d. Research indicates that, just as with drawings we look at, we take longer to scan complex images than simple ones and that we take longer to rotate inverted images than ones that are slightly off center. (p. 213)

   a. Images are examples of cognition without words.

   b. Many images are *not* based on actual visual experience; therefore we make such errors as believing that Montreal is north of Seattle.

   c. Images cannot be seen, but they have been studied scientifically nevertheless.

7. * b. The authors estimate that 90 percent of what you learn in the text will be from words. Language is far more important to cognition than imagery. (p. 216)

   a. Imagery is a form of cognition because it helps organize our experience.

   c. Imagery does organize experience as in the example of using mental maps.

   d. Because *a* and *c* are incorrect, this cannot be the best answer.

8. * c. He reformulated the problem into one having to do with the displacement of water. (p. 218)

    a. Rather than going from general principles about the weight of gold and silver, he used his own experience in the bathtub.

    b. He did not go through a systematic search for answers that would illustrate an algorithm.

    d. A means-end analysis involves the identification of a goal and a purposeful, specified means for reaching it; Archimedes' solution came unexpectedly.

9. * d. An algorithm is a systematic search process for a solution usually involving all possible combinations of alternatives. A shortcut rule of thumb for solving problems is a heuristic. (pp. 218–219)

    a. A heuristic is a shortcut method that may not be systematic.

    b. Insight is the sudden recognition that a particular solution is correct.

    c. Rigidity is a form of thinking that impairs problem solving; creativity involves new and useful ideas.

10. * d. Rigidity—the inability to give up an unsuccessful way of thinking—and functional fixedness (a specific case of rigidity having to do with objects) both restrict problem solving (pp. 220–221)

    a. Creativity requires thinking in new and unrestricted ways.

    b. When we disregard outcomes that disprove our hypotheses we engage in confirmation bias.

    c. Neither uses formal logic.

11. * a. Incubation is the technique of taking a break from a problem so that when we return we are better able to see new solutions. (p. 221)

    b. Insight is the sudden recognition that a solution is correct.

    c. Confirmation bias occurs when we disregard outcomes that disprove our hypothesis.

    d. A means-end analysis involves the identification of a goal and specific steps taken to reach the goal.

12. * b. The rational model is very thorough: every outcome's value and probability of occurrence is evaluated before the best is identified. (pp. 224–225)

    a. The rational model uses an algorithm rather than a heuristic.

    c. General principles based on individual observations are inductive inferences.

    d. The rational model is unrelated to insight or creativity.

13. * a. In the representativeness heuristic, we estimate the probability of an event based on stereotypes about people or objects. (p. 226)

    b. A means-end analysis identifies a goal and the method by which the goal will be achieved.

    c. Insight is the sudden recognition that a solution is correct; it is not a decision-making procedure at all.

    d. The availability heuristic makes use of memories that are most available to us.

14. * b. The availability heuristic uses memories of our personal experience to judge the probability of future events. (pp. 226–227)

    a. The rational decision-making model examines every alternative's frequency of occurrence.

    c. Availability has to do with access in memory, not economic availability.

    d. Because *b* is an accurate answer, this cannot be the best choice.

15. * d. Creativity involves not only new ideas or combination of ideas, but ones that are useful. (p. 228)

    a. Creativity often does *not* involve an exhaustive search for an answer, as we would see in the rational decision-making model.

    b. Besides being new, creative ideas must be useful, too.

    c. People are usually creative in a limited way: in one or two spheres of their lives.

16. * b. The greater the pressure to be creative and the greater the focus on external rewards, the lower the level of creativity. (p. 230)

    a. Research shows diminished creativity when subjects expect their creations will be evaluated by experts.

    c. External rewards seem to reduce creative solutions.

    d. Because *b* is a fine answer, this cannot be the best answer.

17. * c. Phonemes are the smallest units of sound in a language, such as *b* and *ch* in English. Morphemes are the smallest units of meaning and include words such as *ball* and prefixes and suffixes such as *un* (p. 231)

    a. Ideas and actions are irrelevant to phonemes and morphemes.

    b. Morphemes have to do with meaning rather than grammar.

    d. The right answer is reversed here.

18. * c. Morphemes are the smallest units of meaning, whether these are words, suffixes, or prefixes. (p. 232)

    a. Languages differ, in part, because they use different phonemes; English, for example, does not have the trilled *r* of Spanish.

    b. Children first make sounds (phonemes) before they can express meaning (morphemes).

    d. Languages need all three.

19. * a. Telegraphic speech, streamlined language that omits unnecessary words such as prepositions, occurs during the two-word stage. (p. 233)

b. Deep structure is the meaning of an arrangement of words in a sentence; even when the surface structure changes, the deep structure can be maintained.

c. Telegraphic speech involves arrangements of words, which are impossible when only one word is spoken.

d. By age six, children speak according to most of the rules of grammar, which require the use of modifiers, prepositions, and the other niceties that are omitted in telegraphic speech.

20. * c. The speed of language learning, the size of vocabulary, and the completeness of understanding grammar are much lower in apes than in average humans. (pp. 73–74)

a. Even after years of training, apes are only able to make a few utterances.

b. Apes have learned hundreds of words and the rules for grammatically putting them together.

d. The average child learns 2,000 words by age two; no ape has ever learned 1,000.

Application Answers

1. * a. A prototype is a best example or most typical case of a concept, such as a diamond-shaped kite. (p. 209)

b. Heuristics are shortcut rules of thumb used in problem solving.

c. A characteristic attribute is one that some members of a concept group share.

d. A concept is a mental grouping of similar objects, events, or people.

2. * c. Propositions show relationships between concepts. In this case, there are the propositions that airports serve cities, that American cities and European cities both have airports, and that American airports are more crowded. (p. 212)

a. A syllogism is a series of premises that reach a conclusion.

b. Attributes are characteristics of a concept.

d. Conclusions are drawn at the end of a syllogism.

3. * d. This illustrates a series of propositions that lead to a conclusion. This is a definition of a syllogism. (p. 212)

a. Syllogisms always rely on general principles; inductive inference does not.

b. The availability heuristic deals with event probability estimates.

c. Prototype matching occurs when a new object is compared with the standard for a concept group.

4. * c. By looking in one section of the book, the doctor is taking a shortcut to finding a solution—that is, she is using a heuristic. (p. 219)

    a. An algorithm is a thorough, systematic search process that examines all possible combinations. Had the doctor looked at every listing, she would have used an algorithm.

    b. Deductive reasoning uses a general principle to arrive at a conclusion about a specific case.

    d. A means-end analysis identifies a goal and specific steps for reaching it.

5. * d. This illustrates a procedure for determining the way to arrive at a solution: it is a means-end analysis. (p. 219)

    a. Insight is the sudden recognition of a correct solution.

    b. An algorithm is a thorough, systematic search for a solution.

    c. The representativeness heuristic is a probability estimating method.

6. * b. When you suddenly know that the solution you have arrived at is correct, you experience insight. (p. 222)

    a. Past experience may lead one to expect tornados under these circumstances, thus illustrating the availability heuristic.

    c. Inductive inference occurs when general principles are concluded on the basis of individual observations.

    d. Incubation occurs when we take time off from a problem.

7. * b. The tendency to disregard outcomes that disprove our hypotheses is called the confirmation bias. (p. 223)

    a. Incubation is when we take time away from a problem before returning to it.

    c. Functional fixedness is the inability to see new ways of using objects.

    d. Rigidity means the unwillingness to give up a problem-solving strategy that does not work; it is unrelated to inflexibility in looking at results.

8. * a. The availability heuristic is used when available memories (often from personal experience) are employed to estimate the probability of events. (pp. 226–227)

    b. There is no evidence here of having determined a way of solving a problem or identifying the form the solution should take.

    c. Rational decision making involves an evaluation of every alternative's value and probability.

    d. Confirmation bias occurs when people look for support of their initial belief rather than proof that it is wrong.

9. * a. The rules of syntax govern the arrangement of words in a sentence. (p. 232)

    b. Logic is concerned with propositions that lead to appropriate conclusions; it is unrelated to rules for word organization.

    c. Phonemes are units of sound, whereas morphemes are units of meaning. There is no confusion here.

    d. Because *b* and *c* are incorrect, this cannot be the best answer.

10. * b. Dr. Mitchell is in error thinking that apes are faster than children. Though the average infant learns 2,000 words in two years, no chimp has ever learned 1,000 words in a lifetime. (p. 236)

    a. Chimps are reported to use sign language with each other and to teach it to their young.

    c. Apes can learn rules of grammar.

    d. Chimps have coined new combination words, such as "finger bracelet" for a ring.

CHAPTER 9

MOTIVATION

Learning Objectives

1. Define and differentiate among the concepts motivation, drives, and incentives. Contrast intrinsic and extrinsic motivation. Discuss the role of homeostatic mechanisms in motivation. (pp. 241–243)

2. Discuss the instinct theory of motivation and the problem of the naming fallacy. Discuss and differentiate between the psychoanalytic, drive reduction, and optimal arousal theories of motivation. (pp. 244–247)

3. Discuss and differentiate between the opponent-process and cognitive theories of motivation. Explain the overjustification effect. Describe Maslow's hierarchy of needs theory of motivation and the concept of self-actualization. (pp. 248–249)

4. Describe the physiological components of hunger and explain the checking account and savings account analogies. Discuss the physiological cues for hunger, including taste, stomach cues, liver cues, and hypothalamus involvement. (pp. 250–253)

5. Describe how energy outgo is controlled through exercise and brown fat. Describe the symptoms and causes of anorexia and bulimia nervosa. (pp. 254–255)

6. Discuss the set point and social cue theories of obesity. (pp. 255–257)

7. Discuss the scientific study of physical sexuality. Describe research findings on the factors involved in sexual attraction. (pp. 258–260)

8. Discuss what is known about the development of sexual orientation. Describe the forms of sexual dysfunction. (pp. 260–261)

9. Describe the need for achievement and discuss its relationship to parenting and task choice. (pp. 261–263)

10. Discuss the relationship between gender and the need for achievement. (pp. 264–265)

Chapter Outline

1. **What is motivation?** (pp. 241–243)

A reason for a particular behavior is called a motive. All the factors that energize behavior and direct it are called *motivation*. An internal stimulus that pushes behavior is called a *drive;* an external stimulus that pulls behavior is an *incentive*. Some behaviors are *intrinsically motivated,* that is, the behavior is pleasurable in and of itself. When behavior is motivated by the consequences of that behavior, it is said to be *extrinsically motivated*.

Much of our behavior is motivated by biological needs. *Homeostatic mechanisms* are responsible for monitoring the level of internal variables and triggering corrective action to bring them into normal levels. Some motives are clearly social, some clearly biological, and others are combinations.

2. **Explaining motivation: the theories** (pp. 244–250)

Instinct theories of motivation argue that innate tendencies to respond to certain stimuli explain behavior. These theories have gradually disappeared because, in part, they fall victim to naming a phenomenon rather than explaining it. *Sociobiological theory* is a modern version of instinct theory. It claims that all behavior, including altruism, stems from genetic selfishness. Freud's psychoanalytic motivation theory suggests that the basic drives of sex and aggression are frustrated and redirected into social motives through a process called *sublimation*.

Drive reduction theory is a behavioral motivation theory that claims that behavior is a response to *drive stimuli*—the unpleasant experience of unmet biological needs. After a behavior reduces a biological drive state, it is associated with the conditioning situation and, through secondary reinforcement, becomes an incentive itself.

Motivation based on the body's desire for a moderate level of nervous system excitement is called *optimal arousal theory*. Sensory deprivation research supports this belief. Opponent process theory explains why some people have higher needs for stimulation than others.

Cognitive theories of motivation emphasize how people think about and justify their behavior. In the *overjustification effect*, intrinsically motivated behaviors are weakened when rewards are supplied for those behaviors.

Abraham Maslow's motivation theory proposes that humans must meet basic biological needs before moving on to social needs and finally *self-actualization*, the need to develop fully our capacity to feel and understand the world. His classification of motives is called a *hierarchy of needs*.

3. **Hunger and eating: the energy account and controlling energy intake** (pp. 250–253)

Hunger is a biological motive related to glucose, the energy source for the body. Like a checking account, food represents deposits of energy and activity represents withdrawals. The balance in the account must remain in a narrow range. Energy can be saved in the body in the form of liver starch and body fat. The amount of energy savings the body tries to maintain is called the set point.

How much we eat is influenced by the taste of food and, to some extent, the cues we detect from the stomach. Biochemical cues from the liver and activity in the hypothalamus region of the brain play major roles, too. In addition to biological cues, hunger and satiety are affected by social cues such as others' expectations and social stress.

4. **Hunger and eating: controlling energy outgo and eating disorders** (pp. 254–257)

Energy can be used up through exercise, which directly burns energy and indirectly increases the rate of metabolism. Brown fat, a heat-releasing structure in the body, also regulates energy expenditure.

In the eating disorder called *anorexia nervosa*, people starve themselves. When people maintain weight levels by alternately binging on food and then purging, the disorder is called *bulimia nervosa*. These are disorders most often found in young women, a fact that may point either to hormonal changes as the cause or to socially determined body images, self-esteem, and issues of personal control.

Obesity, being 25 percent or more above normal body weight, occurs in more than one-quarter of all people in the United States. One explanation for obesity is an inappropriately high set point, which may be due to genetics or overfeeding in infancy. A different view of obesity stresses oversensitivity to social cues rather than biological ones.

5. **Sexual motivation** (pp. 257–261)

Sexual motivation is a biological motive that involves an interaction of stimuli and responses between males and females called *courtship*. Masters and Johnson's scientific studies of physical sexuality showed that as sexual motivation increases, pleasurable sensations from *erogenous zones* become more and more important. After *orgasm*, sexual motivation declines for a time.

Cultural factors strongly influence the physical characteristics we see as sexually attractive. Sexual behavior is also affected by how we think of ourselves.

Survey research shows that 13 percent of males and 8 percent of females have had homosexual contacts; even more report a desire for such relationships. Though no clear cause for homosexuality exists, childhood gender nonconformity is reported by many adult homosexuals.

Sexual dysfunction is a problem that limits sexual satisfaction for one or both partners in a relationship. Masters and Johnson claim they can successfully treat most of these dysfunctions.

6. **Achievement motivation** (pp. 261–265)

One of the social motives Henry Murray identified was a *need for achievement*, the desire to meet challenges and accomplish one's goals. Measured with the Thematic Apperception Test (TAT), this motive is associated with high performance in school and business. When parents set high standards for independence and excellence for their children, the children tend to grow up with high needs for achievement. Those with high needs for achievement choose tasks of moderate difficulty. This may be explained in terms of the payoffs available, personal control over success or failure, or the *diagnosticity* of the action—the information the behavior provides about one's ability.

Most studies of the need for achievement focused on men. Matina Horner's research showed what she termed a fear of success in women. Other explanations have been offered including an accurate reflection of social sanctions against successful women.

Fill-in-the-Blank Quiz

1. The condition in which people maintain body weight over 25 percent above average weight is called _____ .

2. A circumstance or environmental stimulus that pulls the organism to behave in certain ways is called a(n) _____ .

3. The eating disorder in which a person starves himself or herself is called _____ .

4. A mechanism that regulates the level of a physiological variable is called a(n) _____ .

5. The exchange of stimuli and responses between males and females that leads to intercourse is called _____ .

6. The theory that claims that a genetic selfishness is the motive for all human behaviors, including such social behaviors as altruism, is called _____ .

7. When the intrinsic motivation for a behavior is weakened by supplying an extrinsic motive, this is called the _____ .

8. The idea that behaviors become incentives when they relieve a biological drive is called _____ .

9. The social motive to meet challenges and accomplish one's goals is called _____ .

10. Motivation derived from the consequences of behavior is called _____ .

11. The eating disorder in which people regulate their weight by alternately binging and purging is called _____ .

12. Motivation derived from the pleasure in behaving in a particular way is called _____ .

13. In Maslow's theory, the need to develop fully our capacity to feel and understand the world is called _____ .

14. An internal stimulus that pushes an organism to act in a particular way is called a(n) _____ .

15. In Maslow's theory, the classification of motives from physiological ones to self-actualization is called the _____ .

16. The psychological factors that energize behavior and determine its direction are collectively called _____ .

17. The strong rush of sexual pleasure that occurs at the climax of sexual interaction is called _____ .

18. According to Freud, the process by which the energy of a biological drive is redirected to a social motive is called _____ .

19. A sensitive part of the body whose stimulation increases sexual motivation is called a(n) _____ .

20. An innate tendency to respond to certain stimuli in certain ways is called a(n) _____ .

21. The capacity of a task to give information about the skills of the person who performs it is called _____ .

22. The idea that certain behaviors are motivated by the need to maintain a moderate level of excitement in the nervous system is called _____ .

23. A problem that limits the sexual satisfaction of either or both partners in a relationship is called a(n) _____ .

24. The discomfort caused by a biological need that increases the biological drive is called a(n) _____ .

Fill-in-the-Blank Answers

1. obesity
2. incentive
3. anorexia nervosa
4. homeostatic mechanism
5. courtship
6. sociobiological theory
7. overjustification effect
8. drive reduction theory
9. need for achievement
10. extrinsic motivation
11. bulimia nervosa
12. intrinsic motivation
13. self-actualization
14. drive
15. hierarchy of needs
16. motivation
17. orgasm
18. sublimation
19. erogenous zone
20. instinct

21. diagnosticity
22. optimal arousal theory

23. sexual dysfunction
24. drive stimulus

Fact and Concept Questions

1. External stimuli that pull behavior are called _____; internal stimuli that push behavior are called _____ .
   a. instincts; incentives
   b. incentives; drives
   c. drives; intrinsics
   d. motives; drives

2. When we are motivated by behaviors we find pleasurable in themselves, we are said to be
   a. high in need for achievement.
   b. low in need for achievement.
   c. extrinsically motivated.
   d. intrinsically motivated.

3. Homeostatic mechanisms are most crucial to which kind of motivation?
   a. biological
   b. cognitive
   c. achievement
   d. social

4. Sublimation is to _____ motivation theory as innate tendencies to respond to certain stimuli are to _____ theories.
   a. cognitive; drive reduction
   b. psychoanalytic; instinct
   c. instinct; drive reduction
   d. psychoanalytic; cognitive

5. It explains motivation in terms of a desire for not too much nor too little neural activity. It is supported by research on sensory deprivation. It fails to explain, however, why some people are motivated to take extraordinary risks. What is "it"?
   a. psychoanalytic theory
   b. Maslow's hierarchy of needs
   c. optimal arousal theory
   d. drive reduction theory

6. What does the overjustification effect explain?
   a. Why people with high needs for achievement choose nearly impossible tasks.
   b. Why we are sexually attracted to certain people.
   c. Why associating certain behaviors with the reduction of a drive makes that behavior an incentive in itself.
   d. Why supplying rewards for intrinsically interesting activities weakens our interest in them.

7. Self-actualization is a part of which motivational theory?
   a. Maslow's hierarchy of needs
   b. Freud's psychoanalytic theory
   c. opponent process theory
   d. None of the above.

8. Can glucose energy be stored in the body?
   a. No, it must be used as quickly as it is "deposited" when we eat.
   b. No, the set point makes this impossible.
   c. Yes, it is converted into glucagon in the brown fat.
   d. Yes, it is converted into body fat and liver starch.

9. Which of the following are cues involved in controlling eating?
   a. the taste of food
   b. glucose receptors in the liver
   c. Both *a* and *b*.
   d. Neither *a* nor *b*.

10. Brown fat is involved in the regulation of energy because
    a. it stores unused glucose.
    b. it upsets the body's natural set point.
    c. it releases heat when energy is oversupplied.
    d. it reduces the metabolic rate.

11. Self-starvation is to _____ as binging and purging are to _____ .
    a. anorexia nervosa; obesity
    b. anorexia nervosa; bulimia nervosa
    c. bulimia nervosa; anorexia nervosa
    d. bulimia nervosa; obesity

12. Which of the following statements about obesity is true?
    a. It occurs in less than 10 percent of people in the United States.
    b. It is unrelated to genetics.
    c. It rarely presents any serious health risks.
    d. It may be explained by a too-high set point.

13. How are obese people supposed to be different from people of normal weight in their response to social cues?
    a. They are less influenced by social stress.
    b. They are more responsive to external cues about when to eat rather than biological cues to eat.
    c. They are less responsive to external cues about when to eat rather than biological cues to eat.
    d. They are more responsive to signals sent from the liver that it is time to eat.

14. In what way is sexual motivation different from hunger motivation?
    a. It is not related to a physiological deficit.
    b. It is not a biological motivation.
    c. It is not influenced by cultural factors.
    d. It does not involve an interaction with others.

15. Erogenous zones are important in _____ motivation.
    a. sexual
    b. hunger
    c. achievement
    d. cognitive

16. Which statement about sexual attraction is true?
    a. The same physical features are considered sexually attractive in women all over the world.
    b. Sexual attraction is affected only by sexual motives.
    c. Adolescents' choice of partner may be a reaction to parental attitudes.
    d. In our culture today, there are no specific physical characteristics preferred in sexual partners.

17. Childhood gender nonconformity is most related to
    a. adult homosexuality.
    b. sexual dysfunction in women.
    c. eating disorders in adolescent women.
    d. sex differences in need for achievement.

18. Henry Murray and David McClelland both used the Thematic Apperception Test (TAT) to study
    a. physical changes that occur during the phases of physical sexuality.
    b. the causes of eating disorders such as anorexia and bulimia nervosa.
    c. why some children grow up with a homosexual sexual orientation.
    d. the need to meet challenges and accomplish one's goals.

19. Children with high needs for achievement probably have parents who
    a. allow them to set whatever goals they wish.
    b. protect them from life's difficulties.
    c. expect them to be independent and successful.
    d. are harsh and cool with their children.

20. Matina Horner's research on women and achievement led her to believe that some women are fearful of success. An alternative explanation is that women
    a. are given too few experiences with failure.
    b. are too interested in the diagnosticity of tasks.
    c. tend to choose moderately difficult tasks.
    d. accurately describe society's reaction to successful women.

Application Questions

1. Murray goes to work at a fast-food restaurant because he wants to earn enough money for a new car and because his father will yell at him if he doesn't. Murray is
    a. intrinsically motivated.
    b. motivated by drive reduction.
    c. motivated by instincts.
    d. extrinsically motivated.

2. Eileen says, "Obese people have an instinct to eat too much when they see food; shy people have an instinct to be silent when they are around strangers." The problem with Eileen's thinking is that it
    a. falls victim to the naming fallacy.
    b. is based on the overjustification effect.
    c. mixes psychoanalytic theory with instinct theory.
    d. assumes that biological motives can be influenced by social cues.

3. Dr. Portini says, "The reason people continue to do pain-inducing things like lifting weights is because while they engage in those activities endorphins that reduce pain are released; when they stop there is a rush of pleasure." Dr. Portini's ideas reflect the _____ theory of motivation.
    a. psychoanalytic
    b. opponent process
    c. optimal arousal
    d. hierarchy of needs

4. According to the overjustification of effect, intrinsic motivation for playing baseball should be
    a. highest in professionals who are well paid.
    b. lowest in professionals who are well paid.
    c. lowest in adolescents who play for the fun of it.
    d. highest in adolescents who are unsuccessful.

5. Dr. Minor believes that the cause of obesity and anorexia can be found in a particular structure in the body because research has shown that damage to this structure can turn off or turn on eating. Dr. Minor's research is probably focused on
   a. the erogenous zones.
   b. the stomach.
   c. the hypothalamus.
   d. brown fat.

6. Jill eats tremendous quantities of high-calorie food and then gets rid of it by vomiting or taking laxatives. Jill's behavior is characteristic of
   a. obesity.
   b. anorexia nervosa.
   c. an inappropriate set point.
   d. bulimia nervosa.

7. Webster is a quite obese adult: his weight is 70 percent higher than normal weight. Research suggests that he was
   a. raised in a family with at least one obese parent.
   b. overweight as a child.
   c. Both *a* and *b*.
   d. Neither *a* nor *b*.

8. Brent says that he has an immediate decline in sexual interest right after orgasm. It is not troubling to him or his partner. He goes to a psychologist and asks, "Do I have a form of sexual dysfunction?" What should the psychologist say?
   a. "Yes, men usually have no loss of interest after orgasm."
   b. "Yes, any limitation in sexual performance is a sexual dysfunction."
   c. "Yes, the decline in interest should occur before orgasm, not after it."
   d. "No, the decline in interest is normal and if it is not troubling to either person it isn't a dysfunction."

9. A high school basketball player with a high need for achievement is shooting baskets by himself. Where is he likely to stand on the court?
   a. Between 15 and 20 feet from the basket—where making shots is difficult but not impossible.
   b. Between 2 and 5 feet from the basket—where making shots is almost a certainty.
   c. Between 25 and 30 feet from the basket—where making shots happens once in a hundred times.
   d. Need for achievement makes no prediction about the tasks individuals choose.

10. Lana, a student with a high need for achievement, enrolls in an intermediate French course because, she says, "it will tell me if I really have the ability to speak a foreign language." Lana's reasons reflect the _____ theory of need for achievement.
    a. psychoanalytic
    b. decision
    c. fear of success
    d. diagnosticity

Fact and Concept Answers

1. * b. Incentives pull behavior from external stimuli such as monetary payment; drives are internal stimuli that push behavior, such as a dry mouth motivating drinking water. (p. 241)

   a. Internal stimuli are called drives.

   c. Intrinsics is not a psychological term; intrinsic motivation refers to behavior stemming from pleasurable behaviors.

   d. Both incentives and drives are motives.

2. * d. Intrinsic motivation occurs when behaviors happen because of the pleasure they bring, not the external rewards they promote. (p. 241)

   a. High need for achievement involves a desire to accept challenges and accomplish personal goals.

   b. Low need for achievement involves a lack of interest in challenges and goals.

   c. Extrinsic motivation occurs when behavior is explained in terms of the rewards the behavior produces or the punishments it helps avoid.

3. * a. Homeostatic mechanisms keep biological variables inside the body within a certain range, as for example, the maintenance of body temperature near 98.6 degrees Fahrenheit. (p. 242)

   b. Cognitive theories stress the need to understand our actions and the world around us.

   c. Achievement motivation is a social motive and is unrelated to maintaining internal equilibrium.

   d. Social motives are unrelated to maintaining internal equilibrium.

4. * b. Psychoanalytic theory argues that sexual and aggressive impulses are transformed into social motives through sublimation; instinct theories explain behavior in terms of innate tendencies. (pp. 244, 246)

   a. Sublimation is an unconscious phenomenon, not a cognitive effort at understanding personal behavior.

   c. Drive reduction theorists reject the notion of instincts.

   d. Cognitive theories stress how we think about actions, not automatic instinctive tendencies.

5. * c. Optimal arousal theory proposes that we are motivated to maintain a middle range of nervous system arousal and that we take action to reduce excessive arousal or to increase inadequate arousal. (p. 247)

   a. Psychoanalytic theory stresses unconscious motives.

   b. Maslow's theory includes biological, social, and self-actualization motives.

   d. Drive reduction theory emphasizes the elimination of biologically produced drive states.

6. * d. When an intrinsically motivated behavior (like playing video games) is rewarded, our interest in the activity is weakened because we can explain our behavior as extrinsically motivated. (p. 248)

   a. Those with high needs for achievement choose moderately difficult tasks.

   b. Overjustification is unrelated to sexual attraction.

   c. This answer is relevant to drive reduction theory, a noncognitive theory of motivation.

7. * a. In Maslow's hierarchy of needs, self-actualization needs are the last to be met. (p. 249)

   b. Freud's motives are biological and unconscious: aggression and sexuality.

   c. Opponent-process theory focuses on the effects of pleasure and pain.

   d. Because *a* is a correct answer, this cannot be the best answer.

8. * d. When energy is not immediately needed, glucose is stored (through a process involving insulin) as fat or starch so it can be used later. (p. 250)

   a. Our body has a savings account for energy.

   b. The value at which a person's weight stabilizes is the set point; it is possible only because fat storage occurs.

   c. Brown fat expends energy; glucagon reconverts fat and starch into glucose.

9. * c. Food loses its taste as we eat, and this effect is related to the time when we stop eating. Glucose receptors in the liver can detect when the body needs more energy (food) and when sufficient replacement has occurred. Therefore, *c* is the best answer. (pp. 250–251)

   a. Food tastes are important, but this is not the only correct answer.

   b. Glucose receptors are important, but this is not the only correct answer.

   d. Because both *a* and *b* are correct, this cannot be the best answer.

10. * c. Brown fat, found in the armpits, around the kidneys, and in the back, is a tissue that releases a great deal of heat in order to regulate weight. (p. 254)

    a. Regular fat stores unused glucose; brown fat is very different.

    b. Brown fat does not upset the set point.

    d. Brown fat does not reduce the body's metabolism.

11. * b. Anorexia nervosa is an eating disorder involving self-starvation; bulimia nervosa is an eating disorder in which weight is maintained by alternately eating large quantities of high-caloric foods (binging) and then vomiting or taking laxatives (purging). (p. 254)

    a. Binging and purging are featured in bulimia.

    c. Bulimics usually have average or above-average weight.

    d. Bulimics usually have average or above-average weight.

12. * d. If the set point is too high, the body stores too much fat and keeps the person at an obese level. (p. 255)

    a. Obesity occurs in roughly one-quarter (25 percent) of people in the United States.

    b. Genetics are strongly implicated in the cause of obesity.

    c. Obesity can lead to heart disease, stroke, diabetes, gall bladder ailments, and other serious medical conditions.

13. * b. According to Schachter's work, obese people are more responsive than people of normal weight to external cues for eating such as clocks showing the time 6 o'clock. (p. 256)

    a. Social stress has a significant effect on eating for a range of individuals.

    c. The reverse of this seems to be true.

    d. This is the kind of internal cue to which obese people have been found to be deficient in responding.

14. * a. If we do not eat, there is an obvious physiological deficit; if we do not have sex, there is no analogous deficit. (p. 258)

    b. Both are biological motivations.

    c. Sexual behavior and sexual attraction are both influenced by cultural expectations.

    d. Sexual motivation involves courtship, an involved set of interactions.

15. * a. Sexual motivation involves the stimulation of erogenous zones—areas of the body that increase the likelihood of orgasm. (p. 258)

    b. Hunger motivation is unrelated to erogenous zones.

    c. Achievement motivation is unrelated to erogenous zones.

    d. Cognitive theories of motivation are unrelated to erogenous zones.

16. * c. Cohen and Friedman (1975) suggest that adolescents may choose sexual partners who help them become independent of their parents' influence. (p. 260)

    a. Cultures vary tremendously in what they consider sexually attractive.

    b. Nonsexual motives such as needs for power affect sexual attraction.

    d. Men prefer slender women with large eyes and small chins.

17. * a. Surveys with adult homosexuals show that many report having done fewer of the things children of their sex are "supposed" to do (such boys who refuse to play sports or girls who are uninterested in dolls) and that they did not identify strongly with members of their own sex. (p. 260)

    b. Sexual dysfunction is unrelated to gender nonconformity.

    c. Eating disorders are unrelated to gender nonconformity.

    d. Sex differences in achievement motivation are unrelated to gender nonconformity.

18. * d. Need for achievement is the need to meet challenges and accomplish personal goals. Henry Murray and his student David McClelland have been two of the earliest researchers in the area. (p. 261)

    a. Masters and Johnson studied physical sexuality.

    b. Neither Murray nor McClelland studied eating disorders.

    c. Gender nonconformity was studied with questionnaires, not with the TAT.

19. * c. Parents who push their children to be independent and excellent but who are also warm and encouraging tend to rear children with high needs for achievement. (p. 262)

    a. Parents who provide no standards and do not push for excellence rarely have children with high achievement needs.

    b. Overly protective parents do not rear children with high achievement needs.

    d. Parents with high-achievement children are warm and encouraging.

20. * d. If women describe the fate of successful women in negative terms, they may be accurate reporters of sanctions such women must face in a society that still engages in sex discrimination. (pp. 264–265)

    a. If anything, these responses may indicate too many experiences with failure (especially in male-dominated situations).

    b. Interest in the diagnosticity of tasks is related to high achievement motivation, not low motivation.

    c. Selecting moderately difficult tasks is a sign of high achievement motivation, the opposite of what Horner said she found.

Application Answers

1. * d. Extrinsically motivated behavior is influenced by the consequences of our actions—the rewards for doing it or the punishments we avoid by not stopping. (p. 241)

    a. Intrinsically motivated behavior occurs when the activity is pleasurable in and of itself.

    b. Drive reduction involves the elimination of a biological need.

    c. Only if Murray said he had an inborn tendency to flip burgers would an instinct theory apply.

2. * a. A significant problem with instinct theory is that it names phenomena rather than explaining them; saying shy people have a shyness instinct does not advance our knowledge. (p. 244)

    b. Overjustification is part of the cognitive theory explaining changes in intrinsically motivating behavior after reward.

c. No psychoanalytic concepts are mentioned here.

d. All biological motives can be influenced by social cues.

3. * b. Opponent process theory suggests that since pleasure and pain are opposites, we are motivated to continue pain- or risk-inducing actions because of a rebound effect after the activity ends. (p. 248)

a. Psychoanalytic theory focuses on sex and aggression.

c. Optimal arousal theory emphasizes moderation.

d. Maslow's hierarchy of needs theory is unrelated to pain.

4. * b. The more ball players are rewarded, the better they can justify their actions as the result of money, not the joy of playing the game. (pp. 248–249)

a. Overjustification suggests that intrinsic motivation will sink as payment rises.

c. Playing for the fun of it is a definition of intrinsic motivation.

d. It is doubtful that unsuccessful athletes feel their efforts are pleasurable.

5. * c. Certain areas of the hypothalamus seem to control or partially control hunger and satiety. When such areas of the rat's brain are stimulated, rats can go for long periods without eating or eat so much they become obese. (p. 253)

a. Erogenous zones are related to sexual motivation.

b. Stomach cues play only a minor role in hunger.

d. Brown fat gives off heat; it is not involved in anorexia.

6. * d. Bulimia nervosa is an eating disorder characterized by binging on high-caloric food and purging it through vomiting or laxatives. (p. 254)

a. Obesity may involve eating high-caloric foods (although often it does not) but not purging.

b. Anorexia is characterized by self-starvation; purging occurs only on rare occasions.

c. Inappropriate set point is involved in obesity; bulimics often do not show weight much above normal.

7. * c. Obese people are usually raised by at least one obese parent; they tend to have a lifelong problem with being overweight. Because both statements are true, c is the best answer. (p. 256)

a. Obese people are usually raised by at least one obese parent, but this is not the only correct answer.

b. Obese people tend to have lifelong problems with weight, but this is not the only correct answer.

d. Because there are two correct answers, this cannot be true.

8. * d. Sexual dysfunction occurs when limitations on sexual satisfaction affect either person or both. Since this is not true in Brent's case, there is no dysfunction. The reduction in sexual motivation after orgasm is common anyway. (pp. 260–261)

   a. Loss of sexual motivation after orgasm is common.

   b. Only limitations that are problems for the couple are dysfunctions.

   c. Sexual motivation increases until orgasm.

9. * a. High need for achievement is illustrated by choosing difficult, not impossible, challenges. (p. 261)

   b. These would represent no challenge: something those with high needs for achievement avoid.

   c. These would represent low-probability chances for success: something those with high needs for achievement avoid.

   d. Need for achievement predicts the choice of moderately difficult challenges.

10. * d. Individuals with high needs for achievement may choose tasks that provide information on their abilities. These are tasks with high diagnosticity, according to Trope. (p. 262)

    a. Psychoanalysis has little to say about achievement needs.

    b. Decision theory argues that Lana would choose in order to get better payoffs (better grades).

    c. Fear of success is associated with low needs for achievement.

CHAPTER 10

EMOTION AND STRESS

Learning Objectives

1. Define and differentiate between emotion and stress. Discuss the emotional actions involved in the emotional response. (pp. 268–269)

2. Describe and discuss the autonomic responses in emotions. Describe what polygraph machines record and discuss why they may be ineffective in detecting lying. (pp. 269–271)

3. Describe the function of human emotional expressive behaviors. Discuss whether expressive behaviors are innate or socially learned. Explain how emotional behaviors are integrated. (pp. 271–273)

4. Discuss how the conscious experience of emotion fits into the James-Lange theory of emotion. Describe research that supports this theory. (pp. 273–274)

5. Describe the Cannon-Bard theory of emotion. Discuss how it is the same as and different from the two-factor theory. Explain the roles of attribution and misattribution in two-factor theory. (pp. 275–276)

6. Discuss the ethics of deception in research such as Schachter and Singer's. Explain how feelings distinguish human emotional responses from animal responses. (pp. 275–279)

7. Discuss the need for cognition in emotional responses. Discuss how social constructions shape our emotional responses. (pp. 280–281)

8. Describe the areas of the nervous system involved in emotional responses. (pp. 282–283)

9. Define and discuss the basic emotions. Discuss primary and secondary emotions, positive and negative emotions. (pp. 283–285)

10. Describe the three stages of the general adaptation syndrome. Discuss research on challenges that are correlated with stress. Define "life change units" and "hassles." (pp. 286–288)

11. Describe the Type A personality and the characteristics most associated with heart disease. Give explanations why this relationship exists. (pp. 289–290)

12. Describe and discuss how resistance to stress can stem from humor, the hardy personality, self-efficacy, and optimism. (p. 291)

13. Discuss research on responses to extreme challenges, including posttraumatic stress disorder. (pp. 291–292)

14. Describe and discuss problem- and emotion-focused coping styles. Describe the relaxation techniques of biofeedback, meditation, and progressive muscle relaxation. Discuss the role of exercise in coping with stress. (pp. 291–294)

Chapter Outline

1. **Introduction** (p. 268)

   An *emotion* is a complex automatic response to a situation comprising an action, autonomic responses within the body, facial expressions, and feelings. *Stress* is an emotional response that disrupts our equilibrium.

2. **The emotional response** (pp. 268–273)

   One component of an emotional response is our physical behavior in the situation. Plutchik has argued that emotional actions are a product of evolution; we engage in some emotional actions, however, because of cultural learning.

   The autonomic nervous system responds during emotions with the *fight or flight response*. Lie detector machines (polygraphs) do not detect lies as much as they measure autonomic changes in heart rate, respiration, and skin resistance to electrical current (GSR).

   Expressive behaviors are the facial and gestural behaviors we show when we exerience a feeling. People in very different cultures appear to express emotions the same way. Cultures, however, also have *display rules*, norms that govern the expression of emotions. The three behavioral components of emotion interact: changing one component changes the others.

   Feelings are the conscious experience of emotions, the names we give to our responses.

3. **The James-Lange, Cannon-Bard, and two-factor theories of emotion** (pp. 273–280)

   The *James-Lange theory* runs counter to common sense by saying that the conscious experience of emotions follows the behavioral components of emotional reactions. This idea is supported by research in which people's feelings change when, for instance, they alter their facial expressions.

The *Cannon-Bard theory* of emotion argues that the thalamus interprets situations and simultaneously signals changes in the autonomic nervous system (internal arousal) and cortex (feelings). Cannon suggested that all emotional responses have a nearly identical autonomic response.

Stanley Schachter and his colleagues developed the *two-factor theory* of emotion, which draws on both James-Lange and Cannon-Bard. It states that the level of arousal one experiences governs the intensity of an emotional experience, but how a person understands the situation in which the emotion occurs determines the emotion he or she experiences. The labeling of emotions depends on *attribution* and *misattribution*, the processes of interpreting and misinterpreting situations.

Schachter's research into the attribution of emotions involved deceiving subjects. Recent concerns about ethics have required researchers to obtain the informed consent of subjects.

Human awareness of our emotional responses is probably what most distinguishes our emotions from those of animals.

4. The emotional situation and the role of the brain in emotion (pp. 280–283)

Psychologists disagree on whether we must think about and evaluate situations before we experience emotions. Some of the controversy comes from definitions of cognition and whether there must be a conscious interpretation. Clearly, social factors shape our interpretations of situations and the emotions we experience in them.

Emotional responses are coordinated by the cortex and limbic system of the brain. Although both sides of the brain are involved in emotion, the right hemisphere plays a major role in the recognition and experience of emotion; the left hemisphere is active when we are angry.

5. The range of emotion (pp. 283–285)

People disagree on which experiences warrant the term "emotion." Plutchik lists certain primary emotions from which secondary emotions are created. Positive emotions are more prevalent in most people; negative emotions help us deal with emergencies.

6. Vulnerability and resistance to stress responses (pp. 285–291)

According to Hans Selye, we automatically respond to challenges with a three-phase response he called the *general adaptation syndrome (GAS)*. The syndrome includes alarm, resistance, and exhaustion stages. Exhaustion is characterized by immune system changes that may hasten disease.

Stress is a response to challenges that, according to Holmes and Rahe, may include both positive and negative major changes in life measured as life change units. Daily hassles, however, are better predictors of future illness than major events.

People with the *Type A personality* are chronically aroused because they are impatient, competitive, and hostile. Compared with Type B personalities, Type As (especially hostile ones) are more prone to heart disease. Type As are relatively unaware of their bodies' limitations and tend to create stressful circumstances.

Humor has proven to be useful in resisting stress. So, too, is the *hardy personality*, a set of traits including a sense of commitment to activities, control over events, and acceptance that change is part of life. A related concept is *self-efficacy*, the belief that one is competent and can achieve what one wants. Optimism is also related to health as pessimism is related to illness.

7. Coping with stress (pp. 292–294)

Extreme challenges such as tornados and violent crimes tend to cause stress responses regardless of a person's resistance mechanisms. However, research has failed to support Kübler-Ross's idea that there are set stages in coping with such crises. In posttraumatic stress disorder there are long-range psychological and physical consequences to experiencing crises.

There are two major ways of coping with stress: problem-focused coping (which changes the challenging circumstances) and emotion-focused coping (which may involve accepting circumstances or changing our feelings). Problem-focused coping is more effective and is used when we think we can manage the situation.

One emotion-focused strategy is to relax. *Biofeedback* achieves relaxation by using machines to control autonomic responses. *Meditation* and progressive muscle relaxation are other means. Exercise has also proven to be useful in managing stress.

Fill-in-the-Blank Questions

1. The personality traits involving control, commitment, and acceptance of change that seem to protect the individual from illness are collectively called the _____ .

2. We call the conscious experience of emotion our _____ .

3. The three-stage stress response, including alarm, resistance, and exhaustion, is called the _____ .

4. The emotional reaction to elements that threaten to or actually disrupt our equilibrium is called _____ .

5. The techniques that focus attention and produce a calming effect on feelings and autonomic activities is collectively called _____ .

6. The theory of emotion that proposes that arousal level determines emotional intensity, but that our understanding of emotional situations determines the quality of the emotion we have, is called the _____ .

7. The sense of competence that we can achieve what we want to is called _____ .

8. The theory of emotion that proposes that feelings are the result of emotional behaviors is called the _____ .

10. Cultural norms that govern the expression of emotions are called _____ .

11. The misinterpretation of events is called _____ .

12. We call the complex automatic responses (including actions, internal changes, facial expressions, and feelings) to situations _____ .

13. The heart disease–prone personality that experiences chronic arousal is called the _____ .

14. The facial expressions, postures, and gestures that convey information about our emotional states are called _____ .

15. Cannon called the pattern of autonomic responses that prepare the organism for intense action the _____ .

16. The interpretation of events is called _____ .

17. A relaxation technique that allows us to control the body's autonomic responses by using machines that monitor internal changes is called _____ .

18. The theory of emotion that proposes that the thalamus interprets emotional situations and simultaneously signals a conscious experience of feelings and an autonomic response is called the _____ .

Fill-in-the-Blank Answers

1. hardy personality
2. feelings
3. general adaptation syndrome (GAS)
4. stress
5. meditation
6. two-factor theory
7. self-efficacy
8. James-Lange theory
9. display rules
10. misattribution
11. emotion
12. Type A personality
13. expressive behavior
14. fight-or-flight response
15. attribution
16. biofeedback
17. Cannon-Bard theory

Fact and Concept Questions

1. An emotion is a complex response that includes all but one of the following. Which is not included in an emotion?
    a. expressive behavior such as smiling or scowling
    b. autonomic responses such as a pounding heart
    c. environmental settings such as crowding or excessive heat
    d. feelings such as sorrow or anxiety

2. Which statement about evolution and emotional actions is most accurate?
    a. Although many action tendencies are products of evolution, many others are culturally influenced.
    b. Emotional actions are the product of our evolutionary biology and are not influenced by culture.
    c. Cultural influences are so strong in emotional actions that evolutionary history plays no role.
    d. Neither evolution nor cultural influence helps explain why people have the emotional action tendencies they do.

3. _____ triggers the autonomic responses that Walter Cannon called the _____ .
    a. Reductions in heart rate and respiration; fight or flight response
    b. Release of adrenalin; general adaptation syndrome
    c. Increases in heart rate and respiration; relaxation response
    d. Release of adrenalin; fight or flight response

4. Why can't polygraphs always detect lies?
    a. They measure only one autonomic response: heart rate.
    b. Potential subjects rarely believe that they work.
    c. They can measure only autonomic responses, not truthfulness.
    d. They make distinctions between big lies and small "white" ones.

5. Research on facial expressions indicates that
    a. like autonomic responses, they are not influenced by culture.
    b. like emotional actions, they are innate but influenced by culture.
    c. people from non-Western cultures are unable to recognize emotions expressed by Westerners.
    d. display rules for every culture determine how each emotion is expressed.

6. In the James-Lange theory of emotion, our conscious experience of emotions occurs
    a. before we ever experience an autonomic response.
    b. at the same time we experience an autonomic response.
    c. after we experience an autonomic response.
    d. when we attribute an emotional experience to a specific environmental cause.

7. How is the Cannon-Bard theory different from the James-Lange theory?
   a. Cannon-Bard says that feelings and autonomic responses occur at the same time.
   b. Cannon-Bard says that every emotion has its own pattern of autonomic responses.
   c. Cannon-Bard does not consider the importance of the brain.
   d. Cannon-Bard does not examine the role of adrenalin in emotional responses.

8. Attribution and misattribution are concepts that are most important in the
   a. general adaptation syndrome (GAS).
   b. two-factor theory of emotion.
   c. Cannon-Bard theory of emotion.
   d. evolutionary theory of emotion presented by Darwin.

9. Which aspect of the human emotional response most differentiates our emotions from those of animals?
   a. the intensity of the human autonomic response
   b. our inability to be aware of our feelings
   c. the low number of emotional expressions we can produce
   d. our awareness of our emotional patterns

10. Which statement about cognition in emotion is most accurate?
    a. Emotional responses can occur only after we consciously process information.
    b. Almost all of our emotional responses occur without cognition.
    c. Cognition tends to reduce the intensity of our emotional responses.
    d. Cognition can be so automatic that we can feel emotions without being aware of the cognitions involved.

11. In animal research, damage to the brain structures called the _____ and _____ can produce such emotional behaviors as snarling, hissing, and extraordinary docility.
    a. thalamus and pituitary
    b. amygdala and hippocampus
    c. cerebellum and medulla
    d. thalamus and medulla

12. There is wide agreement that anger, sadness, happiness, disgust, and fear
    a. are not controlled by any evolutionary or hereditary factors.
    b. are the product of other emotions.
    c. are the basic emotions.
    d. cannot be "mixed" to produce other emotions.

13. When it comes to the balance of negative versus positive emotional states, we tend to
    a. list many more negative ones than positive ones.
    b. overestimate the occurrence of positive ones.
    c. use the positive ones to cope with emergencies.
    d. None of the above.

14. The second stage of the general adaptation syndrome is called the _____ stage.
    a. exhaustion
    b. resistance
    c. alarm
    d. hardiness

15. The _____ stage of the general adaptation syndrome is marked by impairment of the immune system that can leave us open to disease.
    a. alarm
    b. resistance
    c. hardiness
    d. exhaustion

16. Which of the following tends to be the best predictor of physical and psychological illness?
    a. hassles
    b. major positive life events
    c. major negative life events
    d. Type B personality pattern

17. The Type A personality is
    a. prone to develop heart disease.
    b. chronically overaroused.
    c. unlikely to notice when he or she is experiencing stress.
    d. All of the above.

18. According to Kobasa, the hardy personality is characterized by three Cs. These are:
    a. compassion, calm, and cheerfulness.
    b. cholesterol, chronic overarousal, and conceit.
    c. control, change, and commitment.
    d. carefulness, cautiousness, and concern for others.

19. Which statement about response to extremely stressful situations is most accurate?
    a. Elisabeth Kübler-Ross's stage model has been strongly supported by research.
    b. Although these situations can affect mental health, they do not affect physical health.
    c. In some cases, there can be long-term problems called posttraumatic stress disorder.
    d. Although these situations can affect physical health, they do not affect mental health.

20. This effective coping method emphasizes changing the circumstances that presented problems. What is being described?
    a. problem-focused coping
    b. relaxation and meditation
    c. emotion-focused coping
    d. biofeedback

Application Questions

1. If we found that all people who were angered, no matter what their culture, ran at and physically attacked the source of their anger, we could conclude that
   a. autonomic emotional responses are innate.
   b. emotional actions are innate.
   c. autonomic emotional responses are learned.
   d. feelings are learned.

2. Dr. Harvey says, "Humans have many more facial expressions than animals. That is because they are more social creatures and these expressions evolved as adaptive means of predicting human behavior." Dr. Harvey's ideas are similar to
   a. Selye's views on the general adaptation syndrome.
   b. Schachter's two-factor theory of emotions.
   c. Zajonc's proposal that all emotions are innate.
   d. Darwin's view of emotionally expressive behaviors.

3. Darren and Mollie fell in love during a devastating hurricane. The _____ theory of emotion explains this by suggesting they misattributed their arousal to love when they were actually afraid.
   a. two-factor
   b. Cannon-Bard
   c. James-Lange
   d. general adaptation

4. Psychologist X is replicating Schachter and Singer's famous study in which subjects received injections of adrenalin but is also giving subjects informed consent about the procedures. What can we say about psychologist X's study?
   a. It is unethical because psychologists can no longer inject subjects with any chemical.
   b. It is unethical because psychologists are not allowed to give informed consent.
   c. It will not replicate Schachter and Singer's study because subjects will have information about the injections.
   d. It will not replicate Schachter and Singer's study because it will deceive the subjects.

5. Brenda is hooked up to an EEG machine and is feeling especially happy. Research suggests that in her brain
   a. there is excessive stimulation in the hippocampus.
   b. her amygdala is quite active.
   c. the right hemisphere is extensively damaged.
   d. her front right hemisphere is quite active.

6. Walking down a dark street, you are confronted by a mugger pointing a gun. Your heart pounds and your breathing speeds as adrenalin pumps through your bloodstream. According to Hans Selye, what is happening?
   a. You are experiencing the alarm stage of the general adaptation syndrome.
   b. You are expressing the basic emotion called disgust.
   c. You are experiencing a stress response called posttraumatic stress disorder.
   d. You are using problem-focused coping.

7. Vernon is a subject in a research study. He is asked to fill out the Social Readjustment Rating Scale for events over the past six months. What is the researcher assessing in Vernon?
   a. whether he is a Type A personality
   b. whether he has experienced a large number of hassles
   c. how many life change units he has experienced
   d. how hardy a personality he has

8. When Sharon is in ambiguous situations, she assumes that she is able to control her behavior and is confident that she can achieve the goals she desires. Sharon has the stress-resistant personality trait called
   a. Type B.
   b. self-efficacy.
   c. transcendental meditation.
   d. Type A.

9. Ron is looking at a meter on a machine that shows him if the muscles in his forehead are getting more or less tense. With practice, he can control the muscle tension and relieve his headaches without medication. Ron is using the stress-reduction strategy called
   a. problem-focused coping.
   b. meditation.
   c. psychotherapy.
   d. biofeedback.

10. Julie is depressed and anxious. She is strongly against taking any medications to relieve her stress-related symptoms. Which of the following techniques might help reduce her stress levels and improve her mood?
    a. exercising
    b. meditating
    c. progressive muscle relaxation
    d. All of the above.

Fact and Concept Answers

1. * c. Emotions are responses to environmental circumstances; they do not include the situation itself. (p. 268)

   a. Expressive facial responses are one of the crucial elements of an emotion.

b. Emotions involve internal changes controlled by the autonomic nervous system: accelerated heart rate, respiration, and sweating (among others).

d. We are aware of our emotional state we experience a feeling such as happiness, fear, or sadness.

2. * a. Like animals, we tend to run when afraid and attack when angry: adaptive responses that are innate. We are influenced to express these behaviors in socially approved ways, however. (p. 269)

b. Culture influences the intensity and manner of our emotional actions.

c. Since there is universality in emotional actions, many psychologists consider them innate, the product of evolution.

d. Both evolution and culture have been helpful in explaining human emotional reactions.

3. * d. When adrenalin is released, autonomic responses, including increased heart rate and respiration, are triggered. Cannon called these changes the fight-or-flight response because they prime the organism to attack or run. (p. 269)

a. The fight-or-flight response is characterized by increased heart rate and respiration.

b. The general adaptation syndrome was Selye's work and involves a long-term, generalized response to threat.

c. The relaxation response represents the opposition of the fight-or-flight response since it involves reduced arousal.

4. * c. Polygraphs measure changes in such physiological responses as heart rate, respiration, and galvanic skin response. They cannot measure *why* changes in arousal occur; they cannot assess intentions or truthfulness. (pp. 270–271)

a. They are called polygraphs because they measure several physiological changes simultaneously.

b. Most people believe they work; this is a principal reason for their effectiveness.

d. Polygraphs cannot distinguish between lies, only between intensities of arousal.

5. * b. Ekman and Izard's research with varied cultures shows universality of emotional expression—indicating that it is innate; display rules, however, point up the cultural factors in the setting and manner for showing expression. (p. 272)

a. Display rules are cultural influences.

c. For the basic emotions, recognition is accurate even for cultures having no contact with one another.

d. Display rules are only important for certain emotions in certain situations.

6. * c. According to the James-Lange theory, the feeling occurs after our body has reacted to a stimulus. For example, we feel frightened because we are aware of our hands shaking. (p. 273)

    a. No theory of emotion suggests that we experience feelings before autonomic changes occur.

    b. Cannon-Bard theory argues that autonomic changes and feelings occur simultaneously.

    d. Attribution is a central feature of two-factor theory.

7. * a. The Cannon-Bard theory argues that autonomic changes and feelings are signalled simultaneously by the thalamus; the James-Lange theory says that autonomic changes occur first. (pp. 273–274)

    b. Cannon argued that we usually are *not* able to detect any differences in the autonomic responses for different emotions.

    c. Cannon put special emphasis on a structure of the brain: the thalamus.

    d. Cannon put special emphasis on adrenalin as the trigger for all autonomic responses.

8. * b. In two-factor theory, feelings occur when we attribute (or misattribute) the cause of our autonomic responses to events in the world. (pp. 275–276)

    a. The general adaptation syndrome is Selye's formulation of what occurs during stress.

    c. Cannon-Bard theory deals almost exclusively with physiological factors, not cognitive ones.

    d. Darwin's evolutionary ideas focus on adaptation and inheritance, not thinking.

9. * d. Your textbook authors argue that our awareness of emotional responses—our feelings—make our emotional experiences different from an animal's. (p. 279)

    a. There is no reason to believe that the intensity of human emotional responses are systematically different from those of all animals.

    b. The opposite of this statement is true.

    c. Humans have a larger number of emotional expressions than animals.

10. * d. Zajonc's research shows that we can have feelings about objects without consciously processing information. (p. 281)

    a. Results of Zajonc's work show that we can respond emotionally when we have not consciously processed information.

    b. Typically, we respond emotionally after we have consciously interpreted stimuli.

    c. Cognition can increase our emotional response (consider the worrywarts among us) or decrease our responses (consider the deniers among us).

11. * b. Both are structures in the limbic system. A damaged amygdala produces docility, whereas stimulation of the hippocampus produces snarling and other defensive behaviors. (p. 282)

    a. The thalamus and pituitary are not central to emotional responses.

    c. The cerebellum and medulla are not central to emotional responses.

    d. Because both *a* and *c* are incorrect, this cannot be the best answer.

12. * c. Psychologists agree that these five emotions form the basic five, the primary emotions from which others may be produced. (p. 283)

    a. Expression of these emotions is so universal, it would appear they are innate, hereditary responses.

    b. These are the basic emotions. They combine to produce the other emotions, not the other way around.

    d. Plutchik and others believe that these primary emotions are mixed to produce secondary emotions.

13. * a. Perhaps because happiness is considered typical, we tend to list many more negative emotions than positive ones. (p. 285)

    b. We tend to overestimate (or at least pay more attention to) negative emotional states.

    c. Your textbook authors suggest that we cope with emergencies by using negative emotions.

    d. Because *a* is an accurate statement, this cannot be the best answer.

14. * b. According to Selye, during the first stage there is an alarm reaction, after which the body engages in resistance against the threat. (p. 286)

    a. The exhaustion stage is the third phase—after resistance.

    c. Alarm is the first, emergency phase of the general adaptation syndrome.

    d. Hardiness is a personality pattern, not a phase of the general adaptation syndrome.

15. * d. During exhaustion, the body has for so long resisted the threat that immune function is impaired, leaving the body open to infection and disease. (p. 286)

    a. The alarm stage is the first response and is not associated with illness.

    b. Resistance is the prolonged second stage and is not associated with illness.

    c. Hardiness is a personality pattern.

16. * a. Hassles like losing one's keys are better predictors of physical and psychological illness than major life events. (p. 288)

    b. Positive life events are not very good predictors of stress reactions.

    c. Hassles are better predictors than major negative events.

    d. Compared to Type As, who show great hostility, Type Bs have a reduced risk of heart disease.

17. * d. The Type A personality is characterized by competitiveness, hostility, and time pressure, all of which chronically increase arousal. Because of overarousal and the Type A's unawareness of body changes, this personality is particularly prone to heart disease. (pp. 289–290)

a. This is true, but so is *b* and *c*.

b. This is true, but so is *a* and *c*.

c. This is true, but so is *a* and *b*.

18. * c. The hardy personality feels personal control in many situations, sees change as a challenge rather than a threat, and is committed to a personal course of action. (p. 291)

a. The Cs are control, change, and commitment.

b. The Cs are control, change, and commitment.

d. The Cs are control, change, and commitment.

19. * c. In extremely stressful situations, there are long-term effects such as headaches, recurring bouts of anxiety and depression, sleep disturbances, and social and sexual impairments that are globally called posttraumatic stress disorder. (p. 292)

a. Kübler-Ross's stage model, though plausible, has not held up to research scrutiny; in fact, no set pattern for response to crisis seems apparent.

b. Crises affect both mental and physical health.

d. Crises affect both mental and physical health.

20. * a. Problem-focused coping entails attempts to remove the sources of stress. It tends to be more effective than emotion-focused coping. (p. 292)

b. Relaxation and meditation are emotion-focused forms of coping.

c. Emotion-focused coping involves attempts to endure stress by changing how one is emotionally responding to circumstances.

d. Biofeedback is another emotion-focused coping strategy.

Application Answers

1. * b. Emotional actions are believed to be innate to the extent that they serve an adaptive purpose and are universal within the species. (pp. 268–269)

a. Running and attacking are emotional actions, not physiological changes such as autonomic responses.

c. If responses are learned, there would be cultural differences.

d. Feelings are our awareness of emotions, not our actions in response to stimuli.

2. * d. Darwin suggested that the wide range of emotional expressions seen in humans was the evolutionary legacy of the fact that we are such social animals. (p. 272)

a. The general adaptation syndrome is a stress response seen in humans and animals and is unrelated to facial expression.

b. Two-factor theory is unrelated to facial expression.

c. Zajonc proposed that emotions could occur in the absence of cognitions; he said nothing about whether emotions are innate.

3. * a. Two-factor theory states that the arousal felt in dangerous situations is readily misattributed and labeled as love; love affairs are facilitated by such arousing situations as hurricanes. (p. 279)

   b. Cannon-Bard theory does not include issues of attribution and misattribution.

   c. James-Lange theory suggests that feelings are the result of experiencing particular autonomic response patterns.

   d. The general adaptation syndrome is a stress response and is unrelated to attribution or falling in love.

4. * c. Schachter and Singer could test their theory only by manipulating information (and deceiving subjects). Recent ethical standards that require informed consent make the replication of their work impossible. (p. 279)

   a. Injections are still ethical as long as subjects willingly participate after being informed of the possible discomfort and side effects.

   b. It is now unethical *not* to provide informed consent.

   d. By providing informed consent, the researcher has eliminated any deceptions (and made replication of the original work impossible).

5. * d. Research indicates that when people are experiencing happiness, there is considerable activity in the right front hemisphere of the cortex. (p. 283)

   a. Stimulation of the hippocampus of animals can produce snarling and other defensive behaviors.

   b. The amygdala is most involved in rage reactions and extreme docility.

   c. People with right hemisphere damage have trouble experiencing emotion or identifying facial expressions that convey emotions.

6. * a. The first stage in responding to threat is the alarm stage of the general adaptation syndrome, when the release of adrenalin increases heart and respiration rates. (p. 286)

   b. The emotion experienced in such situations is probably panic.

   c. Posttraumatic stress disorder is a long-term response to extreme situations and entails attention disturbances, depression, anxiety, and physical problems.

   d. Problem-focused coping occurs when one seeks to solve the source of a stress-related problem.

7. * c. The Social Readjustment Rating Scale lists forty-three stressful life events, such as death of a relative or change in job and rates each in terms of life change units. (p. 287)

   a. The assessment of the Type A personality would ask about feelings of time pressure, hostility, and competitiveness.

   b. Hassles include small "events" such as a car's not starting, losing someone's address, or arriving late for an appointment.

d. Hardiness would be assessed through questionnaire items concerning feelings of personal control in situations and how one views the benefits or costs of change.

8. * b. Self-efficacy is the tendency to feel confident in one's actions and to sense that one has personal control in situations where it is ambiguous whether such control is present. (p. 291)

a. Type B personality is assessed in terms of one's ability to relax and take on tasks one at a time.

c. Transcendental meditation is a relaxation strategy in which one silently repeats a word or phrase to achieve focused attention.

d. The assessment of the Type A personality would ask about feelings of time pressure, hostility, and competitiveness.

9. * d. In biofeedback, machines monitor internal body changes such as heart rate or muscle tension so that individuals can actively change these signs of tension. (p. 292)

a. Problem-focused coping seeks solutions to the source of stress, not a reduction in one's response to it.

b. Meditation uses the silent repetition of words or phrases to focus attention and reduce muscle tension.

c. Psychotherapy makes no use of machinery.

10. * d. Exercise has proven helpful in reducing depressive symptoms, meditating is a proven way to reduce tension, and progressive muscle relaxation also produces a psychological calm. Since all of these statements are true, *d* is the best answer. (p. 294)

a. This is correct, but so are *b* and *c*.

b. This is correct, but so are *a* and *c*.

c. This is correct, but so are *a* and *b*.

CHAPTER 11

THE ORIGINS OF DEVELOPMENT

Learning Objectives

1. Define development and discuss the assumptions relevant to the continuity and discontinuity concepts of development. (pp. 297–298)

2. Describe and discuss nativism and empiricism; trace the historical roots of nativism and empiricism in philosophy. Discuss the stance of early and current psychologists on the nature-nurture controversy. (pp. 298–300)

3. Describe the process of forming the genotype. Explain the role of genes and DNA in the inheritance of traits. (pp. 301–302)

4. Discuss how identical and fraternal twins differ; describe and discuss how twin studies can identify the contribution of heredity to development. (pp. 302–304)

5. Describe and discuss the duration of, and events that take place during, the germinal, embryonic, and fetal phases of the prenatal period. Describe the role of the placenta. Discuss the environmental hazards and teratogens that threaten the embryo. Discuss evidence that learning begins during the fetal period. (pp. 305–306)

6. Discuss the reasons for the neonate's immaturity of behavior. Describe the neonatal reflexes. Describe the direction and rate of physical development in the first year. (pp. 307–308)

7. Describe and discuss the techniques used to study infant perceptions and preferences. Analyze the strengths and weaknesses of these methods. (pp. 309–311)

8. Discuss which neonatal perceptual systems are developed and which are undeveloped at birth. Discuss what is known about the infant's face perception. (pp. 312–313)

9. Describe Piaget's concepts of accommodation and assimilation. Describe the abilities of the infant during the six sensorimotor periods. Explain the process of decentration. Discuss challenges to Piaget's concept of object permanence through experiments with impossible events. (pp. 314–316)

10. Describe the infant's social development and its links to parental behavior and expectations. Discuss motherese and the development of attachment in the second half of the first year. Discuss the continuity of temperament. (pp. 316–319)

11. Describe and discuss Bowlby's ideas on attachment and Lorenz's on imprinting. Discuss the evidence concerning attachment needs based on Harlow's research with infant monkeys. (pp. 320–322)

12. Describe Ainsworth's research on securely attached, insecure-avoidant, and insecure-resistant children. Discuss the long-term impact of early attachment and the evidence concerning any negative effects of early daycare. (pp. 322–324)

Chapter Outline

1. **The process of, and influences on, development: the debate** (pp. 297–301)

   Development is the predictable sequence of physical and psychological changes that we pass through as we age. Some theorists believe that development passes through distinct *stages*, separated by *transitions* that may need to occur at *critical periods*. These theorists subscribe to a discontinuity approach. Continuity theory argues that development occurs in gradual increments. Psychologists also disagree on the importance of *genes* that determine the developmental process of *maturation*. Those who emphasize inheritance endorse nativism; those who stress the role of environment endorse empiricism. Nativism can be traced to the French philosopher Jean-Jacques Rousseau; empiricism stems from the English philosopher John Locke. J. B. Watson was a psychologist who favored the empiricist view of development. G. Stanley Hall, Arnold Gesell, and Sigmund Freud all took a nativist-discontinuity point of view. Today, most psychologists accept that both genes and environment influence development.

2. **Genetic origins of development** (pp. 301–305)

   Development begins at conception, when *chromosomes* from the father's sperm join those from the mother's ovum. Chromosomes are composed of segments of *deoxyribonucleic acid (DNA)* called genes. The genes determine the individual's *genotype*, which is expressed in the form of *traits*, which, collectively, are called the *phenotype*. Most traits are affected by many genes.

   With the exception of *identical twins*, no two people have the same genotype. *Fraternal twins* share no more than half their genes, but are born at the same time. Twin studies clarify the degree to which inheritance contributes to such traits as temperament.

3. **The prenatal period: conception to birth** (pp. 305–307)

The *prenatal period* (between conception and birth) lasts roughly thirty-eight weeks. During the *germinal phase* the fertilized egg (zygote) travels toward the uterus to become implanted on the uteran wall. During the *embryonic phase* (lasting six weeks), the *embryo* is linked to the mother through the *placenta*. More than half of all conceptions end in spontaneous abortions caused by genetic abnormalities or environmental factors. Surviving embryos face threats from such *teratogens* as alcohol and other drugs as well as diseases such as rubella and AIDS. From eight weeks after conception until birth the *fetus* develops. During this *fetal phase,* the unborn child begins to move about and respond to its environment. The fetus is capable of learning.

4. **Neonatal behavior and perception and the research methods used to study them** (pp. 307–313)

The human newborn, or *neonate,* is relatively helpless, but among its special skills are *neonatal reflexes.* The rooting and sucking reflexes help the infant locate food and eat it. The grasping and Moro reflexes help the infant protect itself. In the first year and a half of life, there is dramatic physical growth. By about five months, the infant can remain in a seated position; at eight months most infants crawl; at a year of age, most begin to walk.

Developmental psychologists can study infant behavior by measuring sensory organ responses and measuring habituation to stimuli. Other methods use high-amplitude sucking and head turning to measure preferences and discriminations.

At birth, infants have a good sense of touch, smell, taste, and hearing. Visual acuity and depth perception are weak, however. Infants at two to three months of age prefer to look at human faces.

5. **Cognitive development** (pp. 314–316)

Jean Piaget believed that cognitive development was based on two processes: *accommodation* (adapting schemas to new experiences) and *assimilation* (adapting new experiences to existing schemas). He called the first stage of cognitive development the sensorimotor stage and noted six periods within it. In the first sensorimotor period (birth to one month), responses are reflexive. In the second (one to four months), the infant begins to adapt her relexes to her experience. The third period (four to eight months) shows the first voluntary and repetitive responses to interesting outcomes. *Object permanence* (knowledge that objects out of sight still exist) is believed to be learned in the fourth period (eight to twelve months). At twelve to eighteen months (the fifth sensorimotor period), the child varies the activities that can produce effects in the world. In the sixth period (eighteen months to two years), the child, secure in object permanence, learns that objects can be altered while out of sight. Throughout the sensorimotor stage, there is a process of *decentration*—a distinction of self from other people and objects in the world. Research by Baillarageon and her associates has used the surprising disappearance of objects to challenge Piaget's notion that object permanence develops only at eight months of age or later.

6. **Social development** (pp. 316–319)

Newborns can control those around them. Parents are responsive to infant noises. Parents often communicate with infants in an exaggerated, high-pitched form of speech called motherese. An exclusive attachment to the caregiver develops around eight months. Primitive language appears between twelve and eighteen months. Very young infants can recognize and respond to adult facial expressions.

Temperament, an individual's fundamental disposition, can be seen in early infancy. Infant temperament seems to continue into childhood, although some studies point out discontinuity and others show continuity.

7. **Attachment** (pp. 320–325)

A bond that psychologists call *attachment* forms between the infant and its primary caregiver. John Bowlby's research argues that attachment to one person must occur in the first year or there will be impairment of future relationships. This idea was influenced by Konrad Lorenz's research with baby geese and *imprinting*.

Research by Harry Harlow using infant monkeys separated from their mothers showed that monkeys need something soft to cling to and that they need to interact with their peers to develop normally. One can only cautiously generalize these results to human babies.

Human attachment research by Mary Ainsworth uses the strange situation—in which the infant is briefly separated from the mother, exposed to a stranger, and reunited with her. Ainsworth has categorized children's responses as showing secure attachment, insecure-avoidant, and insecure-resistant attachment. Attachment patterns at age one affect later development.

Daycare experiences in early infancy may increase avoidant responses in the strange situation, but proponents of daycare argue that these findings do not necessarily prove that early daycare is a bad idea.

Fill-in-the-Blank Questions

1. Two individuals who are conceived by the same parents and born at the same time but who do not share the same genotype are called _____ .

2. An individual's fundamental disposition is also called his or her _____ .

3. The expression of an individual's genotype is called the _____ .

4. The process of adapting a new experience to an existing schema is called _____ .

5. A strand of genetic material found in the nucleus of every cell is called a(n) _____ .

6. An infant who is one month old or less is called a(n) _____ .

7. The basic unit of heredity that gives a blueprint for the production of specific proteins is called a(n) _____ .

8. A substance that causes physical defects in an embryo is called a(n) _____ .

9. A period in which behavior and experience change very little is called a(n) _____ .

10. The period of prenatal development following implantation, when the placenta forms and the basic body organs develop, is called the _____ .

11. A period in which behavior and experience change very rapidly is called a(n) _____ .

12. The developing human at two to eight weeks following conception is called a(n) _____ .

13. The large complex molecules that form the chromosomes are called _____ .

14. A behavior pattern that is present at birth and that helps the newborn survive is called a(n) _____ .

15. Individuals who are conceived and born at the same time and who have the same genotype are called _____ .

16. According to Piaget, the infant's recognition that an object exists outside his or her experience with it is called _____ .

17. The period of prenatal development from conception to implantation is called the _____ .

18. The process of learning an attachment during a sensitive period early in life is called _____ .

19. A time of special sensitivity in the development of an organism, during which certain events must occur or others must be avoided for the individual to develop normally, is called a(n) _____ .

20. The structure in the pregnant mother through which nutrients and oxygen are delivered to the embryo and through which wastes are removed is called the _____ .

21. The developmental processes that are determined by the individual's biological inheritance are called _____ .

22. The developing human from about eight weeks after conception until birth is called a(n) _____ .

23. A reliably observed characteristic is called a(n) _____ .

24. The last period of prenatal development, from eight weeks until birth, is called the _____ .

25. An individual's genetic makeup is called the _____ .

26. The process of adapting behavior and thinking to meet the demands of a new situation is called _____ .

27. According to Piaget, the process by which the infant comes to distinguish the self from other people and objects is called _____ .

28. The period of development from conception until birth is called the _____ .

29. The process by which a bond is formed between the infant and his or her primary caregiver is called _____ .

30. The regular sequence of physical and psychological changes that we pass through as we age is called _____ .

Fill-in-the-Blank Answers

1. fraternal twins
2. temperament
3. phenotype
4. assimilation
5. chromosome
6. neonate
7. gene
8. teratogen
9. stage
10. embryonic phase
11. transition
12. embryo
13. deoxyribonucleic acid (DNA)
14. neonatal reflex
15. identical twins
16. object permanence
17. germinal phase
18. imprinting
19. critical period
20. placenta
21. maturation
22. fetus
23. trait
24. fetal phase
25. genotype
26. accommodation
27. decentration
28. prenatal period
29. attachment
30. development

Fact and Concept Questions

1. If a psychologist believes that certain events must occur at a specific time during development or else the individual develops abnormally, the psychologist believes
   a. in continuity theory.
   b. in empiricism.
   c. that stages do not exist.
   d. that critical periods exist.

2. _____ thought that children were born like a blank slate on which parents and teachers write. This idea illustrates the _____ position on development.
   a. John Locke; nativist
   b. Jean-Jacques Rousseau; empiricist
   c. John Locke; empiricist
   d. Jean-Jacques Rousseau; nativist

3. Most psychologists today view development as determined
   a. solely by inheritance.
   b. by both genes and environment.
   c. solely by the environment.
   d. solely by maturation.

4. There are twenty-three pairs of _____ in each cell.
   a. chromosomes
   b. genes
   c. DNA molecules
   d. genotypes

5. Which statement is accurate?
   a. Most psychological traits are caused by a single gene.
   b. Genes are blueprints for proteins that direct the activities of cells.
   c. Fraternal and identical twins have the same genotypes although they may have different phenotypes.
   d. Fraternal and identical twins have the same phenotypes although they may have different genotypes.

6. Research on identical twins reared in different environments
   a. proves that all traits are inherited.
   b. indicates that heredity has almost no influence on intelligence or temperament.
   c. indicates the environment determines temperament.
   d. shows that both inheritance and environment affect psychological traits.

7. Which statement about the prenatal period is true?
   a. It lasts about twenty-three weeks.
   b. It consists of the time from conception until implantation.
   c. It is made up of two phases: the germinal and fetal phases.
   d. It lasts about thirty-eight weeks.

8. During the _____ phase of prenatal development, the _____ begins to develop and the basic body organs are formed.
   a. germinal; uterus
   b. fetal; placenta
   c. embryonic; placenta
   d. germinal; fetus

9. What are teratogens?
   a. Substances like tobacco and prescription drugs that can harm the embryo or fetus.
   b. The stimuli that a fetus can hear and respond to after it is born.
   c. Deformed arrangements of DNA that lead to spontaneous abortions.
   d. The automatic behaviors that newborns display that help them survive a hostile world.

10. The grasping and Moro reflexes are most related to the neonate's ability to
    a. see and imitate others.
    b. protect itself.
    c. feed itself.
    d. None of the above.

11. To measure an infant's ability to discriminate one stimulus from another, researchers use
    a. the high-amplitude sucking (HAS) technique
    b. the head-turning (HT) technique
    c. Both a and b.
    d. Neither a nor b.

12. In the first few days after birth, a neonate
    a. can hear about as well as an adult.
    b. can see about as well as an adult.
    c. cannot taste or smell.
    d. cannot recognize others' voices or its own cry.

13. When it comes to perceiving faces, infants
    a. prefer nonhuman faces to human faces.
    b. show a true preference for human faces within the first ten days of life.
    c. at two or three months prefer complex facelike stimuli.
    d. at two or three months prefer nonfaces to simple, scrambled faces.

14. Accommodation and assimilation are key concepts in _____ theory of child development.
    a. Harry Harlow's
    b. Jean Piaget's
    c. John Bowlby's
    d. Mary Ainsworth's

15. Which of the following is a good definition of object permanence?
    a. the child's tendency to lose interest in objects that are consistently present
    b. the child's psychological bond with a caregiver who provides consistent nurturance
    c. the child's tendency to distinguish itself from other people and objects
    d. None of the above.

16. The infant's changing ability to communicate and respond to the caregiver is an example of
    a. physical development.
    b. social development.
    c. cognitive development.
    d. temperament development.

17. Which statement about temperament is true?
    a. Temperament continues from infancy to childhood.
    b. All infants have pretty much the same temperament.
    c. Temperament determines whether a child learns object permanence.
    d. Adult temperament and infant temperament are usually the same.

18. The process of bonding between an infant and primary caregiver is called
    a. sensorimotor development.
    b. decentration.
    c. attachment.
    d. temperament development.

19. Ainsworth's research identified "insecure-avoidant children" who are
    a. abnormally clingy: they do not seem to trust the bond with their mothers.
    b. almost always the result of having attended daycare.
    c. uninterested in interacting with their mothers.
    d. too fearful to explore a new room environment.

20. There is little debate that, compared to children cared for at home, children who have attended daycare are _____ .
    a. less assertive and independent.
    b. slower to develop intellectually.
    c. more maladjusted.
    d. less obedient to parents and more aggressive with peers.

Application Questions

1. Dr. Thomas considers herself a nativist. We can expect that she emphasizes the importance of _____ and _____ in development.
   a. learning and the environment
   b. genetics and maturation
   c. empiricism and continuity
   d. stages and the environment

2. Two individuals developed when two separate ova were fertilized by two separate sperm. They have the same mother, however, and were born on the same day. What can we say about these individuals?
   a. They are identical twins.
   b. They have the same phenotype.
   c. They are fraternal twins.
   d. They have the same genotype.

3. Mrs. Gilliam is four days pregnant. We can say with certainty that
   a. the embryo inside her is attached to the wall of the uterus.
   b. her fetus has already begun to develop its basic body organs.
   c. the placenta is already nourishing the embryo inside her.
   d. the zygote inside her is in the germinal phase of development.

4. Dr. Platt says this about neonates: "They are born when their brains are fully developed but when they are also immature relative to other animals. This is because the human mother's wide birth canal and pelvis interferes with her walking upright." Which statement Dr. Platt made is incorrect?
   a. The statement that neonate's brains are fully developed.
   b. The statement that humans are born less mature than other animals.
   c. The statement that width of pelvis interferes with walking.
   d. None of the statements is incorrect.

5. Tammy, a six-month-old, looks at a stuffed toy for five minutes and then turns away. This lack of interest in an object that is no longer novel occurs when the preference
   a. undergoes assimilation.
   b. responds to object permanence.
   c. is seen during sensorimotor intelligence.
   d. habituates.

6. Brad is a two-month-old. We can anticipate that, in terms of perceptual development, he
   a. can respond to some depth cues.
   b. can see colors.
   c. Both a and b.
   d. Neither a nor b.

7. A five month-old watches a toy rabbit move along a track, disappear behind a screen, and *not* appear through a cutout in the screen. The child's eyes widen when it fails to see the rabbit through the cutout. This illustrates
   a. a significant challenge to Piaget's assertion that object permanence occurs after eight months of age.
   b. the fact that infants do not begin to show decentration until they are twenty-four months or older.
   c. Piaget's assertion that object permanence is impossible before twelve months.
   d. the fact that social development depends on physical development.

8. Mrs. Johannsen talks to her infant, Lars, with a high-pitched, exaggerated form of speech that her infant seems to love. This form of speech, which psychologists call _____ , is important in the social development of infants.
   a. a teratogen
   b. attachment behavior
   c. accommodation
   d. motherese

9. Valerie works at the zoo with infant monkeys. Last week one infant monkey's mother died suddenly. Based on Harlow's research, this infant monkey will need two things to develop normally:
   a. baby monkeys to interact with and something fuzzy to cling to
   b. food to eat and an artificial "mother" made of wire mesh
   c. enough warmth to keep it comfortable and enough water to drink
   d. baby monkeys to interact with and an artificial "mother" made of wire mesh

10. Stacey, Tracy, and Lacy are all fifteen months old and securely attached. Stacey and Tracy attend a high quality daycare, but Lacy receives at-home parent care. Two years from now we can expect that
   a. Lacy will have stronger attachment to her mother than Stacey and Tracy will to their mothers.
   b. all three will be popular with their peer group and well adjusted.
   c. Stacey and Tracy will have stronger attachment to their mothers than Lacy to hers.
   d. Lacy will be more avoidant in the strange situation than Stacey or Tracy.

Fact and Concept Answers

1. * d. Critical periods are times when events must occur in order for normal development to proceed. They are a key component of discontinuity theory. (p. 298)
   a. Continuity theory suggests that development is gradual and that events need not occur at crucial times.
   b. Empiricism stresses the role of the environment in development; critical periods are more closely associated with nativism, inheritance, and maturation.
   c. Stages are times of relative calm in development separated by transitional periods; critical periods are transitions that must occur at a certain point in development.

2. * c. John Locke was a British philosopher who argued that newborns come into the world with a *tabula rasa* (blank slate) and that all behaviors and thoughts are the result of experience. This philosophy is called empiricism. (p. 299)

    a. John Locke was an empiricist, not a nativist.

    b. Jean-Jacques Rousseau was a French philosopher who believed that children are profoundly different from adults and that differences are caused by biology; this is a nativist philosophy not an empiricist philosophy.

    d. Rousseau was a nativist, but nativists do not maintain the *tabula rasa* view of young children.

3. * b. Most psychologists accept the importance of *both* nature and nurture; they differ only on the degree of importance for each on different behaviors. (p. 300)

    a. Even nativist-oriented psychologists accept that environmental factors influence behavior.

    c. Even empiricist-oriented psychologists accept that inheritance influences behavior.

    d. Maturation, a biologically driven process, is important, but most psychologists accept that environmental factors combine with it to determine behavior.

4. * a. Twenty-three chromosomes from the mother and twenty-three chromosomes from the father combine as pairs to form a zygote; these pairs are copied in every cell of the body of the offspring. (p. 301)

    b. There are thousands of genes on each of the twenty-three pairs of chromosomes.

    c. Billions of DNA molecules wind together to form genes that, in turn, make up the twenty-three pairs of chromosomes.

    d. Genotype is a collective term for all the genetic material in an individual.

5. * b. Genes, portions of DNA strands, form a template that guides the manufacture of proteins, which are influential in cell growth and activity. (p. 302)

    a. Few psychological traits are controlled by a single gene; single genes do influence physical traits such as hairline.

    c. Identical twins have identical genetic material (genotype), but fraternal twins share only about one-half of their genes.

    d. Phenotypes are the observable traits in individuals. Fraternal twins are not identical in appearance, so they cannot have identical phenotypes.

6. * d. Similarities in identical twins reared apart argue that genetics cause this, but since differences do exist, environment must play a role. (p. 303)

    a. Since there are psychological traits on which identical twins do not show identical behavior, this statement is incorrect.

    b. Identical twins reared apart show remarkable similarity in intelligence and temperament. This is evidence that these traits are strongly influenced by genetics.

    c. Because there is a strong similarity in the temperaments of identical twins reared apart, environmental factors cannot completely determine temperament.

7. * d. The prenatal period, incorporating three separate phases, lasts about thirty-eight weeks. (p. 305)

    a. The prenatal period lasts thirty-eight weeks.

    b. The germinal phase lasts from conception to implantation on the wall of the uterus.

    c. There are three phases: germinal, embryonic, and fetal.

8. * c. After implantation on the uterine wall, the placenta develops so that the embryo can receive nutrients and oxygen and have a way for body wastes to be removed. This occurs during the embryonic period (roughly two weeks to six weeks after conception). (p. 305)

    a. In the germinal phase, body organs are not forming; the uterus is present before conception.

    b. The fetal phase occurs after all the basic body organs have begun to develop.

    d. The fetus does not develop until the fetal phase—about six or seven weeks after conception. The germinal phase consists of the first week or so after conception.

9. * a. Teratogens are substances that can harm the physical and psychological development of the developing human. (p. 305)

    b. There is no specific name given to the stimuli, such as a mother's voice that the fetus can hear and later respond to.

    c. There is no specific name given to deformed strands of DNA.

    d. Automatic behaviors shown by newborns are called neonate reflexes.

10. * b. In the Moro reflex the neonate "hugs" with its arms and legs after support for the head is released; the grasping reflex is also an instinctive response to hold onto a supporting object. Both reflexes help the child protect itself from falls and damage. (p. 308)

    a. Seeing clearly and, consequently, imitating are abilities not available to the neonate.

    c. The rooting and sucking reflexes are involved in feeding.

    d. Since *b* is an accurate completion of the sentence, this cannot be the best answer.

11. * c. Psychologists measure infant preference and discrimination by recording how long and how hard the child sucked on a pacifier (HAS) and, in older infants, how quickly and for how long it turns its head toward an object. (pp. 310–311)

    a. This is true, but head turning is also used.

    b. This is true, but high-amplitude sucking is also used.

    d. Since *a* and *b* are correct, this cannot be the best answer.

12. * a. Neonates have a fine sense of hearing at birth. (p. 309)

    b. Visual acuity is quite poor at birth; if they were adults, we would consider neonates to be legally blind.

    c. Taste and smell sensitivity are quite good in neonates.

    d. Newborns can recognize voices and respond to recordings of their own crying.

13. * c. Research shows that ten-to-fifteen week infants prefer to look at facelike stimuli, particularly if they are scrambled and therefore more complex. (p. 313)

    a. Human infants prefer to look at human faces.

    b. Since their poor eyesight prohibits such observations, we cannot assume that such young children prefer human faces.

    d. Infants at two or three months prefer complex faces.

14. * b. Jean Piaget, the Swiss biologist-psychologist, generated a theory of cognitive development in which the basic processes are accommodation and assimilation. (p. 314)

    a. Harry Harlow's work involved attachment and development in infant monkeys.

    c. John Bowlby's theories pertain to attachment in humans.

    d. Mary Ainsworth's research is on secure and insecure attachment in children.

15. * d. Object permanence is the child's understanding that things continue to exist even when the child cannot directly see, feel, hear or otherwise experience them. Because none of the other options states this, "none of the above" is the best answer. (p. 314)

    a. The child (or adult) who loses interest in an object shows habituation.

    b. The child's bonding with a caregiver is called attachment.

    c. The child's tendency to distinguish self from nonself is, in Piaget's terminology, decentration.

16. * b. Social development is the growth in interaction shown through communication. This includes child-to-adult as well as child-to-child interaction. (p. 316)

    a. Physical development pertains to changes in the body such as growth, motor ability improvement, and the like.

    c. Cognitive development is the child's ability to understand the world and mentally manipulate it.

    d. Temperament is the fundamental disposition of the individual; some would argue that it does not develop (change) much over childhood.

17. * a. Temperament, the fundamental disposition of the individual, has been shown to be remarkably consistent throughout childhood. There is less consensus about its continuity into adulthood. (p. 319)

    b. Infants differ in temperament from the first hours or days of life. Some infants are highly irritable, others are placid.

    c. Temperament is unrelated to the learning of object permanence.

    d. It is unclear whether infant temperament continues through to adulthood.

18. * c. Attachment is the process of creating an emotional bond between infant and caregiver. It is also the term for the bond itself. (p. 320)

    a. Sensorimotor development is a term that Piaget employs to describe the infant's changes in cognitive style.

    b. Decentration is Piaget's term for the infant's tendency to distinguish itself from other people and objects.

    d. Some would argue that if temperament remains constant throughout the life span, there is no temperament development.

19. * c. Infants showing insecure-avoidant patterns of attachment do not use their mothers as anchor points in the strange situation; they seem aloof and uninterested in their mothers. (p. 323)

    a. Insecure-resistant children tend to cling to their mothers; they do not explore the strange situation because they seem not to have trust in their mothers.

    b. There is no relationship between daycare and insecure-avoidant patterns of attachment.

    d. Insecure-avoidant children explore the room but do so without using their mothers as a resource.

20. * d. Children younger than five years old who are raised solely in the home environment tend to be more obedient to their parents and less aggressive with their peers than those exposed to daycare. (pp. 323–324)

    a. The reverse of this is true: daycare children are, if anything, more assertive and independent.

    b. There is some evidence that daycare children show faster intellectual development.

    c. There is considerable debate on this: aggressiveness (maladaptive behavior) in some eyes is assertiveness and independence (adaptive behavior) in other eyes.

Application Answers

1. * b. Nativism stresses the role of inheritance and genetics. It also argues that most of the changes in behavior we see are the result of maturation—the unfolding of biologically blueprinted changes. (p. 298)

    a. Empiricism stresses the environment and learning.

    c. Nativists are more likely to emphasize a discontinuity approach; they take the opposite viewpoint from empiricists.

    d. Nativists downplay the role of the environment.

2. * c. Fraternal twins come from different ova (and zygotes), so their genetic similarity is roughly the same as siblings; they do share the same birthday. (p. 302)

    a. Identical twins come from one zygote that separates to produce two individuals with identical genetic material.

    b. Fraternal twins are not identical in appearance or behavior, so they cannot have the same phenotypes.

    d. Fraternal twins do not have the same genetic material, so they cannot have the same genotypes.

3. * d. The germinal phase consists of the first seven or so days after conception. (p. 305)

    a. The embryo does not attach to the uterine wall until day seven after conception.

    b. The fetal phase does not begin until six weeks after conception.

    c. The placenta does not begin to develop until the embryonic phase (roughly a week or two after conception).

4. * a. The neonate is relatively immature because it is born before the brain is fully developed. (p. 307)

    b. Humans are far less mature. For instance, other mammals can walk within hours or days of birth, whereas infants take twelve or more months to do the same thing.

    c. The wider the birth canal, the wider the pelvis and the harder it is to walk upright.

    d. Because *a* is an accurate answer, this cannot be the best response.

5. * d. A child (or adult) habituates when a stimulus is presented for so long that its novelty wears off. (p. 310)

    a. Assimilation is a Piagetian term for the process of adapting a new experience to an existing schema.

    b. Object permanence is the knowledge that objects out of one's experience continue to exist.

    c. Habituation occurs throughout life.

6. * c. At two months, infants can respond to the depth cue of objects getting larger or smaller and they can see colors. Therefore, the best answer is both *a* and *b*. (p. 312)

    a. This is true, but so is *b*.

    b. This is true, but so is *a*.

    d. Because *a* and *b* are both accurate completions of the sentence, this cannot be the best answer.

7. * a. Renée Baillarageon's research is being described. This "impossible event" seems to startle even five-month-olds, a fact at variance with Piaget's timetable for object permanence. (pp. 315–316)

    b. Decentration, the distinction of self and nonself, is a process seen throughout infancy.

c. This five-month-old's response shows some knowledge of object permanence, so Piaget's assertion is challenged, not supported.

d. This experiment is irrelevant to both physical and social development.

8. * d. Motherese is the term psychologists coined for the high-pitched, exaggerated, singsong type of speech infants respond to that fosters social development. (p. 317)

a. A teratogen is a substance such as alcohol or heroin that can damage the developing embryo or fetus.

b. Attachment is the bonding of infant and caregiver; it may be improved with motherese, but they are separate concepts.

c. Accommodation is Piaget's term for the changing of mental schemas in response to new experiences.

9. * a. Harlow's work showed that normal development in orphaned monkeys required interaction with young monkeys and an object that was soft and fuzzy. (pp. 321–322)

b. Food is not enough. The wire mesh substitute mothers did not provide the fuzzy, comforting contact monkeys apparently need.

c. Warmth and water are not enough.

d. Interaction is important, but wire mesh substitutes did not provide the contact comfort monkeys need.

10. * b. Children with strong attachment at fifteen months are more popular and better adjusted two years later than children who are not; being at a high-quality daycare does not diminish this effect. (pp. 323–324)

a. High-quality daycare does not interfere with the attachment process.

c. High-quality daycare does not improve on at-home attachment.

d. Daycare children show more avoidance in the strange situation than children reared at home.

CHAPTER 12

THE STAGES OF DEVELOPMENT: CHILDHOOD THROUGH ADULTHOOD

Learning Objectives

1. Describe the components of a stage theory of development. (pp. 327–328)

2. Describe the basic ideas in Piaget's stage theory of cognitive development, Kohlberg's stages of moral reasoning, and Erikson's psychosocial theory. (pp. 328–332)

3. Describe the changes in the body and the brain that take place in late infancy and early childhood. Discuss the importance of representational thought in the cognitive development of children. (pp. 332–333)

4. Describe the cognitive abilities of the child in Piaget's preoperational stage. Discuss egocentrism, conservation, and how the method for testing conservation challenges Piaget's assumptions. (pp. 333–336)

5. Compare preconventional and conventional stage moral reasoning. Describe and discuss psychosocial development in childhood. Describe how play behavior changes from solitary to cooperative. Discuss and explain sex differences in children's play behavior. (pp. 336–338)

6. Describe research on the effects of family and televised violence on children. (pp. 338–340)

7. Describe and discuss the physical changes that occur in adolescence, including primary and secondary sex characteristics. Describe and discuss the cognitive changes that occur at puberty and the ways these changes are studied. (pp. 341–343)

8. Describe postconventional reasoning and discuss how it comes about. Discuss the limitations of Kohlberg's theory. Describe and discuss the changes in sexuality that affect adolescents. (pp. 344–346)

9. Distinguish the three responses to the adolescent identity crisis. Discuss the forms that adolescent vulnerability can take including responses to suicidal intentions. (pp. 346–347)

10. Explain how cross-sectional and longitudinal research designs can examine cohort effects. Discuss the stages of family development and the role of historical and economic events in development. (pp. 348–350)

11. Describe the physiological aging process after the early twenties. Discuss reproductive aging and the quality of life in late adulthood. (pp. 350–351)

12. Describe cognitive changes in adulthood, including dialectical reasoning, general cognitive abilities, and crystallized and fluid intelligence. (pp. 352–353)

13. Describe changes in social development during adulthood, including generativity, Levinson's life structures, and midlife crisis. (pp. 354–356)

Chapter Outline

1. **Stage theories: Piaget, Kohlberg, and Erikson** (pp. 328–332)

   Stage theories of development assume that stable periods of behavior (stages) are separated by periods of rapid change (transitions) and that *developmental norms* indicate the time in life when these stages occur. Stage theories suggest typical behavior at certain ages, but they cannot define any individual's development.

   Jean Piaget's theory of cognitive development suggests that people respond to disequilibrium through accommodation and assimilation. Thinking capacity changes over four stages from infancy (sensorimotor) to preschool years (preoperational) to grade school years (concrete operational) to adolescence (formal operations). Lawrence Kohlberg devised a three-stage theory of moral reasoning development. Erik Erikson, a psychoanalyst, devised an eight-stage *psychosocial theory* of social development that assumes we resolve critical issues at different ages throughout life.

2. **Ages two to twelve years: physical development and cognitive development** (pp. 332–336)

   From ages two to twelve, physical growth slows down from the explosive growth of infancy. A two year old's brain has a denser network of connections than an adult's does, perhaps to accommodate the learning of skills and information in childhood. Language development allows *representational thought*, the ability to talk about things that are not present. According to Piaget, in the preoperational stage (ages 2–6), children do not have the ability to perform *operations* in which internalized actions are reversed. They show egocentrism, the inability to take another's perspective. *Conservation* concepts for number, volume, and mass develop only in the concrete operational stage. Research using alternative testing methods has challenged Piaget's ideas about developmental norms for conservation tasks.

3. **Ages two to twelve years: moral development and social development** (pp. 336–341)

In Kohlberg's theory, children go from preconventional moral reasoning, which is based on fear of consequences, to conventional moral reasoning, which emphasizes social expectations and conventions.

Socialization, the process of learning social customs and attitudes, influences the social development of children. Children's play behavior changes from solitary to parallel to associative and finally to cooperative play. Sex differences in play behavior are noted throughout childhood and can be explained by both parental expectation and biological differences.

Childhood aggressiveness is partially explained by exposure to aggressive models. Nonexperimental studies of televised violence find associations between exposure and actual aggressive behavior. Experimental evidence suggests that televised violence may cause aggression, but the artificiality of experiments makes this speculation at the current time.

4. **Adolescence: physical, cognitive, and moral development** (pp. 341–344)

Puberty, the period of physical change that prepares the body for reproduction, triggers changes in physical growth as well as in *primary* and *secondary sex characteristics*. The timing of the onset of puberty varies greatly from person to person and has implications for social development.

Piaget argued that adolescence was characterized by formal operational thinking in which formal logic could be used. The pendulum test shows the use of formal operations. The capacity for abstract thought also contributes to *adolescent egocentrism*, the tendency to assume that others are thinking the way one is thinking, at the same time and in the same way.

Moral reasoning also changes in adolescence. Postconventional reasoning considers principles that go beyond the law. Some argue that Kohlberg ignores the importance of culture in moral reasoning: Gilligan finds that women's moral reasoning is based on values different than men's.

5. **Adolescence: social development** (pp. 345–347)

The comparative freedom of adolescence allows for new interactions. Increased sexuality holds the threat of sexually transmitted diseases such as AIDS and teenage pregnancy.

According to Erikson, adolescents go through a period of intense self-examination to resolve questions of identity. Three responses to the identity crisis are identity foreclosure, negative identity formation, and identity diffusion. Adolescence is a time of increased vulnerability to substance abuse, criminal behavior, and suicide. Generally, though, adolescence is not as turbulent a period as we might be led to believe.

6. **Adulthood: research methods and physical development** (pp. 348–351)

Cohort effects (historical influences that affect behavior) confuse the results of *cross-sectional studies*, in which people of different ages are compared at one point in time. *Longitudinal studies*, which examine the same cohort repeatedly, can clarify changes that occur solely because of age. A life span perspective on development can focus on family changes as well as historical and economic events that shape behavior.

The decline in physical functioning that begins in adulthood is gradual. Perception is impaired, fertility declines (in women, this occurs during *menopause*), and sexual activity may decline. For most, however, the quality of life among the elderly is quite satisfactory.

7. **Adulthood: cognitive and social development** (pp. 352–356)

Riegel and Basseches have suggested that *dialectical reasoning* is a stage of cognitive development that follows formal operations. This kind of reasoning recognizes the logic of two arguments and applies abstract thinking to everyday events.

The elderly do less well than younger adults on cognitive tests requiring quick responses, but on other tasks cognitive ability improves with age. *Crystallized intelligence* (that which is memorized and used in familiar situations) and *fluid intelligence* (the ability to learn new information) may have opposite changes in old age: fluid intelligence gets worse, whereas crystallized intelligence improves.

Erik Erikson emphasizes the need to be productive, to show generativity, in middle adulthood. In late adulthood, people reflect on their lives. Roger Gould suggests that at each stage we cast off false assumptions; Daniel Levinson focuses on changes in life structures. Levinson examines career and family choices. Research tends not to find frequent and clear-cut crises in adulthood.

Fill-in-the-Blank Questions

1. The process by which children learn the customs and attitudes of their community is called _____ .

2. Knowledge and skills that have been memorized and can be put to practical use in familiar situations is called _____ .

3. The inability to see the world from another's perspective is called _____ .

4. The cessation of menstruation that normally occurs in middle adulthood is called _____ .

5. Erik Erikson's theory that at different stages of life the individual must resolve a critical issue is called _____ .

6. The human reproductive organs are called the _____ .

7. The average age at which an important behavior is performed is called a(n) _____ .

8. The period of change in early adolescence that prepares the body for reproduction is called _____ .

9. Piaget's term for an action that a child can carry out and reverse entirely in his or her imagination is called a(n) _____ .

10. The tendency of adolescents to assume that everyone else is thinking the same way and about the same things at the same time that they do is called _____ .

11. The developmental period between childhood and adulthood is called _____ .

12. The ability to learn new information and skills is called _____ .

13. The ability to talk about events and people who are not present at the moment is called _____ .

14. The physical traits of the two genders that are not essential for reproduction are called _____ .

15. Piaget's term for the ability to understand that certain properties of an object stay the same despite changes in its shape or position is called _____ .

16. The stage of cognitive development after formal operations, when principles of abstract reasoning can be applied to everyday issues, has been provisionally called _____ .

Fill-in-the-Blank Answers

1. socialization
2. crystallized intelligence
3. egocentrism
4. menopause
5. psychosocial theory
6. primary sex characteristics
7. developmental norm
8. puberty
9. operation
10. adolescent egocentrism
11. adolescence
12. fluid intelligence
13. representational thought
14. secondary sex characteristics
15. conservation
16. dialectical reasoning

Fact and Concept Questions

1. What does a developmental norm tell you?
   a. when, during an individual's life, a specific behavior will occur
   b. the average age at which an important behavior occurs
   c. the number of stages that an individual passes through in order to fully develop a behavior
   d. when, during an individual's life, a stage of development can be skipped

2. Kohlberg's developmental theory emphasizes
   a. how a person's social interactions change across life.
   b. the correctness of moral decisions that individuals make.
   c. the changes in physical characteristics that occur in childhood.
   d. how a person reasons when making moral decisions.

3. Erikson is to _____ development as Piaget is to _____ development.
   a. social; cognitive
   b. cognitive; physical
   c. cognitive; social
   d. social; physical

4. Piaget used the three-mountain test to investigate the point when children can take the perspective of other people. This test is most likely to be used
   a. to see if adolescents can solve conservation problems.
   b. before there is representational thinking.
   c. to see if formal operations are present.
   d. during the preoperational stage to assess egocentrism.

5. According to Piaget, how is the cognitive ability of the concrete operations child different from that of the preoperational child? The concrete operations child can
   a. use abstract and dialectical reasoning.
   b. use representational thinking.
   c. solve conservation problems.
   d. reduce disequilibrium through accommodation and assimilation.

6. Preconventional moral reasoning has the theme:
   a. "Don't do it if you wind up getting hurt by it."
   b. "Everybody has to obey the rules because without them we wouldn't be safe."
   c. "Do the right thing and people will like you."
   d. "The law doesn't make it right; universal principles of morality are what matter."

7. Which statement about sex differences in children's play behavior is most accurate?
   a. There are no differences that any research has been able to confirm.
   b. Any differences have *not* been related to socialization.
   c. One possible explanation may be the higher testosterone levels found in boys.
   d. One possible explanation may be that boys are frustrated by girls' more rough-and-tumble play.

8. Which statement about aggression in children is most accurate?
   a. As children grow older, their verbal aggression decreases.
   b. Nonexperimental studies link aggressive behavior with televised violence but cannot distinguish cause and effect.
   c. Laboratory experiments distinguish cause and effect but do *not* find a relationship between aggressive behavior and televised violence.
   d. Children from violent families are no more aggressive than children from nonviolent families.

9. Between the ages of ten and fifteen, an individual's pituitary gland increases its output of hormones controlling the thyroid and sex glands. This, in turn, triggers
   a. puberty.
   b. the development of secondary sex characteristics.
   c. Both *a* and *b*.
   d. Neither *a* nor *b*.

10. According to Piaget, what cognitive changes occur in adolescence?
    a. the ability to think abstractly and to analyze the correctness of the reasoning process
    b. the elimination of all forms of egocentric thinking
    c. the ability to use representational thinking and language to solve problems
    d. the need to examine oneself and develop a personal sense of identity

11. Because adolescents have increased exposure to different kinds of people and because they can use formal operations, Kohlberg assumes
    a. their moral reasoning emphasizes social conventions and laws.
    b. they are too confused to use principles for making moral decisions.
    c. they will fail the pendulum string length test.
    d. their moral reasoning will go from conventional to postconventional.

12. Which statement about adolescent sexuality is accurate?
    a. Roughly 20 percent of all AIDS cases in the United States involve people between the ages of thirteen and twenty-one.
    b. The great majority of adolescents knows how sexually transmitted diseases can be prevented and takes action to protect themselves.
    c. Both *a* and *b*.
    d. Neither *a* nor *b*.

13. What happens when adolescents resolve their identity crisis with identity foreclosure?
    a. They drift aimlessly, planning one career one day and another the next day.
    b. They fix on an identity closely related to the expectations of their parents.
    c. They fix on an identity their parents strongly disapprove of.
    d. They put aside practical issues and absorb themselves in self-examination.

14. For most adolescents,
    a. conflicts with parents are so intense that parents are seen as enemies.
    b. the changes they go through are seen as gradual rather than sudden crises.
    c. there are no changes in sexual behavior or social stresses.
    d. hormonal changes do not affect physical development.

15. Longitudinal research studies are especially helpful because they can distinguish which changes in behavior occur because of age and which occur because of
    a. family systems changes.
    b. cognitive development.
    c. cohort effects.
    d. the dropout rate of respondents in the study.

16. The family systems approach and stages of family development are most closely associated with
    a. a life span perspective on development.
    b. Reigel and Basseches's ideas on dialectical reasoning.
    c. cross-sectional studies of development.
    d. critics of Erikson's view of social development.

17. Fertility declines with age, but
    a. for males it increases and for females it decreases.
    b. for males it decreases sharply and for females it decreases gradually.
    c. for males it decreases gradually and for females it decreases sharply.
    d. for males it decreases and for females it increases.

18. Survey research on the elderly shows that
    a. most fears that early and middle adults have about being old occur only in a small percentage of the elderly.
    b. physical health declines regardless of the number of social contacts one has.
    c. more than three-quarters of the elderly experience loneliness and poor housing as very serious problems.
    d. not having enough to do and not having enough friends are the two most pressing problems for the elderly.

19. If a person can recognize the logic of two arguments and apply abstract reasoning principles to everyday issues, that person demonstrates
    a. fluid intelligence.
    b. crystallized intelligence.
    c. generativity.
    d. dialectical reasoning.

20. Levinson's stages of adult development focus on changes in
    a. intelligence.
    b. the individual's life structure
    c. beliefs about other people.
    d. physical development.

Application Questions

1. Brad believes that children advance through four stages of cognitive ability. At each point, they must deal with new experiences that challenge already existing mental ways of understanding the environment. Brad's beliefs most closely match those of
    a. Erik Erikson.
    b. B. F. Skinner.
    c. Jean Piaget.
    d. Daniel Levinson.

2. Dr. Jameson says, "Erikson proposed a theory of social development. Some of the key issues in the theory are trust, identity, moral reasoning, and intimacy." Which idea in this statement is inaccurate? The idea that
    a. Erikson's theory is about psychosocial development
    b. trust is important in the theory
    c. identity is important in the theory
    d. moral reasoning is important in the theory

3. Charles is four years old. According to Piaget, Charles
    a. can engage in imaginative play because he has representational thought.
    b. will be able to solve conservation tasks because he shows egocentrism.
    c. will be able to think using formal operations because he shows egocentrism.
    d. will demonstrate he can take another's perspective on the three-mountain test.

4. Pat is a seven-year-old boy. Patti is a two-year-old girl. What assumptions can we make about their play behavior?
    a. Pat is more aggressive and loud than Patti.
    b. Patti engages in more cooperative play than Pat.
    c. Pat engages in more solitary play than Patti.
    d. Neither is able to show parallel or associative play.

5. Martha has just entered adolescence. Which of the following changes can we expect in her?
   a. a new awareness that morality is based on whether the consequences of actions affect her personally
   b. a reduced involvement with peers and increased attachment to her parents
   c. an increase in estrogen levels in the bloodstream and the appearance of secondary sex characteristics
   d. a belief that no one else thinks the way she does or thinks about the same things

6. Suppose a psychologist uses Kohlberg's methods for assessing the moral reasoning of a group of adolescent boys and girls. What are the results likely to be?
   a. They will show the same level of reasoning: postconventional.
   b. Girls will seem to be at a conventional level because their concern for personal relationships will go unconsidered.
   c. Boys will be at a conventional level, whereas girls will be at a postconventional level.
   d. Neither boys nor girls will be at the postconventional level.

7. In 1990, twenty year olds may show less political awareness than forty year olds. This difference may be because of changes that occur with age, but they may also be because, in their youth, the forty year olds lived through the political upheavals of the 1960s. The second explanation
   a. illustrates the importance of accommodation and assimilation.
   b. can be ruled out using a cross-sectional study.
   c. would probably be given by Piaget or Kohlberg rather than Erikson.
   d. illustrates a cohort effect.

8. Tom and Jane are in late adulthood, and they are in average health. Compared to early adulthood, their current
   a. vision and hearing are less acute.
   b. muscles are less powerful and their joints less limber.
   c. taste and smell sensitivity is reduced.
   d. All of the above.

9. Warren says, "I can see both sides of the death penalty issue: society must protect itself from murderous people, but a society that murders is no better than the criminal." This kind of thinking illustrates
   a. the moral reasoning of almost all adults.
   b. dialectical reasoning.
   c. conventional moral reasoning.
   d. what Erikson called "identity foreclosure."

10. Gladys is a sixty year old. According to Horn and other psychologists interested in cognitive changes in later adulthood, Gladys has probably
    a. decreased in both fluid and crystallized intelligence over the past thirty years.
    b. decreased in fluid intelligence over the past thirty years.
    c. increased in fluid intelligence over the past thirty years.
    d. increased in both fluid and crystallized intelligence over the past thirty years.

Fact and Concept Answers

1. * b. Developmental norms indicate the average age for the appearance of important behaviors such as walking or talking. (p. 328)

   a. Norms cannot tell what specific individuals will do; this limitation presents a major criticism of stage theories of development.

   c. The number of stages in a theory is irrelevant to the notion of a developmental norm.

   d. Stage theories argue that stages cannot be skipped; developmental norms simply suggest the age at which important behaviors occur.

2. * d. Kohlberg's theory examines the changes in moral reasoning that occur between young childhood and adolescence. (pp. 329–330)

   a. Social interaction is of more interest to Erikson and other theorists on social development than it is to Kohlberg.

   b. Kohlberg is not concerned with the actual moral decision an individual makes; his theory is about the reasoning behind the decision.

   c. Physical development is irrelevant to Kohlberg's theory of moral development.

3. * a. Erikson proposed his psychosocial theory to explain social development; Piaget's theory concerns changes in mental ability (cognitive development). (pp. 328, 330)

   b. Erikson's theory concerns social development; Piaget did not focus on physical changes.

   c. These are the reverse of the correct answer.

   d. Piaget focused on the mental changes in children, not the physical changes.

4. * d. Egocentrism, the inability to see another's perspective, is tested using the three-mountain test. Piaget discovered that egocentrism is characteristic of preoperational children (roughly ages two to six). (p. 334)

   a. Conservation problems require the changing of an object's shape to see if the person being tested understands that basic properties in the object remain constant. For example, identical volumes of water may fill different-shaped glasses to different levels, but their volume remains the same.

   b. Representational thinking uses language; children normally have language in the preoperational stage.

   c. Formal operations are observed in adolescents and are illustrated by an ability to use abstract thinking.

5. * c. Solving conservation problems—understanding that the properties of objects remain constant even if their shape changes—is possible in the concrete operations stage (roughly ages seven to eleven). (pp. 334–335)

   a. Dialectical reasoning is an idea that came after Piaget.

b. Representational thinking is found in every two- or three-year-old child, long before the concrete operations period.

d. The reduction of disequilibrium through accommodation and assimilation is basic to thinking at all stages of development, according to Piaget.

6. * a. Preconventional moral reasoning focuses on the personal consequences of moral decisions such as potential punishment. (p. 336)

   b. Obedience to the law is characteristic of conventional moral reasoning.

   c. Moral reasoning based on being liked is characteristic of conventional moral reasoning.

   d. Concern for universal moral principles is characteristic of postconventional reasoning.

7. * c. Testosterone levels are higher in male than in female children, and this may cause their more vigorous and physical style of play. (p. 338)

   a. Sex differences are strong, consistent, and appear at an early age.

   b. Socialization, the cultural shaping of behavior, has an important role in play behavior.

   d. Girls tend to be frustrated by boys' rough-and-tumble play.

8. * b. Correlational studies of exposure to televised violence and actual aggressive behavior are not able to clarify which comes first. The association between the two is strong and consistent, however. (pp. 339–340)

   a. Verbal aggression tends to increase with age.

   c. Laboratory studies also find a relationship between televised violence and aggressive behavior but cannot demonstrate such a cause-and-effect relationship in nonexperimental settings.

   d. One of the best predictors of childhood aggressiveness is exposure to aggressive family members.

9. * c. Puberty, the time of physical changes that prepare the body for reproduction, occurs between ages ten and fifteen, when gonadotrophins produce changes in such secondary sex characteristics as facial hair (boys) and breasts (girls). Changes in thyroid function also produce a growth spurt. (pp. 341–342)

   a. This is correct, but so is *b*.

   b. This is correct, but so is *a*.

   d. Because both *a* and *b* are correct, this cannot be the best answer.

10. * a. Abstract reasoning and the ability to see faulty reasoning are characteristics of formal operations, the cognitive capacity of the adolescent. (pp. 342–343)

    b. Adolescents engage in adolescent egocentrism: they think everyone else is thinking about them and thinking the same way that they are.

    c. Representational thinking occurs in every normal two or three year old.

    d. Erikson discusses self-examination as an issue in social development.

11. * d. The ability to grasp universal principles of morality is, Kohlberg believes, a function of the adolescent's exploration of widening circles of people and situations. (p. 344)

    a. Social conventions are important in conventional moral reasoning and are likely when one has had little exposure to alternative ideas.

    b. Exposure to different people and the ability to think abstractly should lead to principled thinking, not to confusion.

    c. Those who have mastered formal operations should "pass" the pendulum string length test: they will examine one factor at a time, in the manner of the scientist.

12. * d. Because none of the alternatives is accurate, this is the best answer. (pp. 345–346)

    a. Only about 1 percent of AIDS cases in the United States are adolescents.

    b. An alarmingly small minority of adolescents understand basic issues in sexually transmitted diseases, including how to protect oneself against them.

    c. This cannot be the best answer because neither *a* nor *b* is true.

13. * b. Identity foreclosure occurs when the resolution of identity issues occurs without experimentation: the expectations of the parents are largely internalized. (p. 346)

    a. This kind of drifting is characteristic of those with identity diffusion.

    c. This kind of rebellion is characteristic of negative identity formation.

    d. All adolescents may put aside practical considerations and examine themselves in a process called moratorium.

14. * b. Longitudinal research on adolescents shows that most see their changes as gradual rather than sudden. (p. 347)

    a. To the contrary, most adolescents name their parents as their personal heroes.

    c. Adolescence, by its nature, involves changes in sexuality and identity that produce social stresses.

    d. Hormonal changes affect thyroid function, which, in turn, leads to a growth spurt.

15. * c. By measuring behavior repeatedly in the same people (something possible only in longitudinal studies), we can learn how much change is due to age alone. Cohort effects are the influences of events that affect whole age groups. (p. 349)

    a. If family system changes occurred as people aged, longitudinal studies would *not* be able to separate these two effects.

    b. If cognitive development is associated with aging, longitudinal studies would *not* be able to separate these two effects.

    d. One of the more serious problems with longitudinal studies is that biased groups of respondents may drop out.

16. * b. The lifespan perspective tends to include information on family development and take a family systems approach. (p. 348)

    b. Dialectical reasoning is associated with cognitive development after adolescence and is unrelated to the lifespan perspective.

    c. Cross-sectional research does not answer most lifespan questions; longitudinal studies are far more suitable.

    d. Erikson includes many concepts that are attractive to the lifespan approach: personality development throughout life and the influence of family interactions.

17. * c. Only in females is there menopause, a sudden loss in fertility. (p. 351)

    a. Fertility declines in both sexes.

    b. The reverse of this is true.

    d. Fertility declines in both sexes.

18. * a. Research shows that whereas 50 percent or more of the public think crime, health, and loneliness will be very serious problems in old age, only 23 percent or less of the elderly actually report this. (p. 351)

    b. The number of social contacts one has in old age is strongly associated with health.

    c. Only 12 percent of the elderly report loneliness as a very serious problem; only 4 percent report poor housing.

    d. Not having enough to do and not having enough friends are ranked seventh and eighth on the list of ten very serious problems.

19. * d. Dialectical reasoning is the term Reigel uses to describe the capacity to see two sides of an argument and use abstract reasoning in everyday life. (p. 352)

    a. Fluid intelligence is the ability to solve new problems.

    b. Crystallized intelligence is the storehouse of memorized information and skills that we can use in familiar situations.

    c. Generativity is Erikson's term for the middle adult's need to be productive.

20. * b. Levinson coined the term "life structure" to convey the underlying design of a person's life that explains social and career development in adulthood. (p. 355)

    a. Levinson's work is unrelated to intelligence.

    c. Beliefs are central to Roger Gould's thoughts on social development.

    d. Physical development is unrelated to Levinson's work.

Application Answers

1. * c. Piaget's theory of cognitive development suggests four stages (sensorimotor, preoperational, concrete operations, and formal operations) that occur when accommodation and assimilation are used to deal with disequilibrium. (pp. 328–329)

    a. Erikson developed psychosocial theory.

b. B. F. Skinner argued that development did not occur in stages at all but was continuous.

d. Levinson examined life structure changes in adulthood.

2. * d. Moral reasoning is important in Kohlberg's theory, not Erikson's. (p. 329)

a. Erikson's theory is a psychosocial one because it examines social change from a psychoanalytic perspective.

b. Trust versus mistrust is the first psychosocial crisis in Erikson's model.

c. Identity is the key question for adolescents, according to Erikson.

3. * a. Imaginative play occurs when children can think about things that are not present—a characteristic of representational thinking and the preoperational child. (p. 333)

b. Conservation tasks are not supposed to be capable of solving by four year olds; concrete operations children (over age 7) begin to understand conservation.

c. Formal operations occurs in adolescence.

d. The three-mountain test is a way to see that four year olds *are* subject to egocentrism.

4. * a. Boys at all ages are more aggressive in their play than girls. (p. 338)

b. Cooperative play occurs late in childhood and is virtually impossible for two year olds.

c. Solitary play is the earliest occurring form of play; Patti probably plays that way.

d. Parallel and associative play are common in preschool children: Pat is probably able to play this way.

5. * c. Estrogen is the female sex hormone and increases in estrogen levels occur in puberty when secondary sex characteristics appear. (p. 342)

a. Moral reasoning based on personal consequences such as punishment is seen in preschoolers and is supposed to disappear in adolescents.

b. Adolescence is marked by increased peer involvement.

d. People of Martha's age show adolescent egocentrism: the belief that others think like she does.

6. * b. Carol Gilligan argues that Kohlberg's scoring method emphasizes the abstract logic involved in moral reasoning and not the values that women place on personal interactions; for that reason, postconventional girls appear to use conventional reasoning. (p. 344)

a. Research shows apparent sex differences in moral reasoning.

c. The reverse of this seems to be true.

d. Boys may be at a postconventional level.

7. * d. A cohort effect is the influence of historical events, such as the political changes that occurred in the 1960s, on an age group's behavior. (p. 349)

   a. Accommodation and assimilation are part of Piaget's theory and are unrelated to historic events.

   b. Cross-sectional studies are unable to distinguish development from cohort effects.

   c. Piaget and Kohlberg would emphasize internal thought processes; Erikson is more likely to look at social changes.

8. * d. Vision, hearing, taste, and smell sensation and perception all decline in middle and late adulthood. Physical fitness also tends to decline. Since all of these occur, this is the best answer. (pp. 350–351)

   a. This is true, but so is *b* and *c*.

   b. This is true, but so is *a* and *c*.

   c. This is true, but so is *a* and *b*.

9. * b. Dialectical reasoning occurs when two sides of an argument can be accepted and abstract reasoning is used in everyday life issues. (p. 352)

   a. Research shows rather little support for the idea that dialectical reasoning is widespread.

   c. Conventional moral reasoning focuses on laws and the need for others to like one's decisions.

   d. Identity foreclosure occurs when adolescents choose, without experimentation, a life path that coincides with their parents' expectations.

10. * b. Fluid intelligence, the ability to solve new problems, tends to decrease with age, although this is difficult to say with certainty since any test of fluid intelligence includes some crystallized intelligence. (p. 353)

    a. There is evidence that crystallized intelligence increases over middle adulthood.

    c. Fluid intelligence is likely to decrease because reaction times decrease.

    d. Cognitive ability remains the same or decreases over middle and later adulthood.

CHAPTER 13

PSYCHOLOGICAL ASSESSMENT

Learning Objectives

1. Describe and explain how theoretical constructs such as self-monitoring are used as the basis for developing psychological tests. (p. 360)

2. Define reliability and the statistical technique called correlation. Discuss how the correlation coefficient assesses test-retest reliability but is confused by stability concerns. Describe alternate-forms reliability, split-half reliability, and internal consistency. Discuss how internally consistent a test should be. (pp. 361–364)

3. Define criterion validity and discuss the types of tests that require it. Compare criterion validity with face validity and construct validity. Describe traits that correlate with high self-monitoring and the way in which construct validity develops. (pp. 364–367)

4. Describe the clinical interview. Define behavioral assessment and discuss methods of self-observation. Discuss the strengths and weaknesses of self-predictions. (pp. 367–369)

5. Define objective tests. Differentiate between aptitude and achievement tests. Describe self-report personality measures and the reasons that indirect measurement is used. Describe and discuss projective techniques. (pp. 370–371)

6. Describe the origins of intelligence testing and what Binet's early test was designed to do. Discuss how the intelligence quotient (IQ) is calculated with the Binet test. Explain why IQ cannot be calculated this way for adults and what a standard score is. (pp. 372–375)

7. Discuss how group means, the distribution of scores on the normal curve, and standard deviations are used to interpret individual scores. Apply this method to IQ scores for adults. (pp. 376–377)

8. Discuss the problems of defining intelligence. Define the concepts *g*, *verbal IQ*, and *performance IQ*. Contrast these approaches with Gardner's and Sternberg's. (pp. 375–379)

9. Describe what the field of behavior genetics seeks to understand. Discuss the relationship between IQ score correlations and genetic similarity. Discuss the evidence that environmental factors influence IQ. (pp. 380–381)

10. Describe and discuss the socioeconomic factors involved in differences in IQ scores between black and white Americans. Discuss the cultural biases that exist in IQ tests and the idea of culture-fair tests. (pp. 381–383)

11. Describe the method and usefulness of the following personality tests: the Minnesota Multiphasic Personality Inventory (MMPI), the Rorschach Inkblot Test, and the Thematic Apperception Test (TAT). Discuss clinical versus statistical prediction. (pp. 385–389)

12. Evaluate the strengths and weaknesses of objective and projective personality tests. Discuss the problems of using personality tests in the employee selection process. Discuss what a battery of tests is and how it is used. (pp. 389–391)

Chapter Outline

1. **Properties of effective measures** (pp. 360–367)

   To illustrate how psychologists develop tests, the text uses a test of *self-monitoring* as an example. The Self-Monitoring Scale is an outgrowth of *theoretical constructs* about how people differ in how much they change their behavior to fit with a given situation. We measure the reliability of a measure by using the statistical technique called *correlation*. The *correlation coefficient*, which ranges from +1.00 to –1.00, indicates the direction of relationship and its strength. In *test-retest reliability*, the correlation coefficient measures consistency over time or *stability*. *Alernate-forms reliability* indicates consistency by using two different forms of the same measure; *split-half reliability* compares scores on one half of the test with scores on the other half. The relationship between each item in a measure and all the other measures is called *internal consistency*.

   A measure is valid if it measures what it was designed to measure. If we correlate test scores with a specific observable outcome, we learn the test's *criterion validity*. If a measure looks as though it is a good measure of relevant factors, it is said to have *face validity*. A more complex form of validity is *construct validity*: when, over many research studies, the measure proves to support its underlying theoretical construct. Theory plays a major role in the definition of reliability and validity for any measure, but the results of research on the measure help to refine the theory, too.

2. **Assessment techniques** (pp. 367–372)

The most common assessment technique is the *interview*. Interviews provide the assessor with great freedom and are easy to do, but the reliability of the information they provide is often low. *Behavioral assessment*, involving direct or indirect observation, is often used by behaviorists, who focus on concrete actions. *Self-predictions* can be quite accurate as long as individuals are not likely to bias their answers.

Objective tests use a question and response format that is the same for everyone taking the test. *Aptitude tests* are objective tests that measure the ability to do some task; *achievement tests* measure what the subject has already done. Objective personality tests (self-report measures) can ask people to describe themselves directly or use indirect methods to get around problems of dishonesty or unawareness.

Projective tests measure motives or emotions indirectly by asking for responses to ambiguous stimuli.

3. **Measures of intelligence** (pp. 372–385)

Measures of intelligence can predict school performance but not much else. The origins of intelligence testing go back to France in 1904, when Alfred Binet and Theodore Simon developed a test to identify those children who needed special schooling. They created subtests based on children being able to answer them at different ages. A *mental age* of 12, for instance, means that a child performs like the average twelve year old. *Intelligence quotient (IQ)* is calculated by dividing mental age by chronological age and multiplying by 100. IQ is now used more generally to refer to the score on an intelligence test. After childhood, chronological age no longer has relevance, so IQ for adults is based on *standard scores:* a score comparing the individual with others who have taken the test.

A group's performance on a test is described in terms of a group mean or average. How the scores are distributed, perhaps conforming to the normal curve, is also identified. The standard deviation (approximately the average differences of all individual scores from the mean) indicates the spread of scores. Using the individual's score and the standard deviation we can calculate the percentage of all people taking the test who did better (or worse) than the individual.

Intelligence is a difficult term to define, but most agree it pertains to the ability to solve problems and cope successfully with one's environment. Some psychologists have argued that there is one general ability, what Spearman called *g*. Wechsler has suggested that there are two: *verbal IQ* and *performance IQ*. Others have listed from several to many dozens of separate abilities. Sternberg, for instance, identifies componential skills (the analytical skills used in school), experiential skills (creative thinking), and contextual skills (practical intelligence for getting things done).

The subdiscipline of *behavioral genetics* examines the relationship between heredity and behavior. As the closeness of a relationship increases, so does the correlation of IQ scores. Only by separating genetic similarity from environmental similarity can we learn how much inheritance contributes to these correlations. Adoption studies and those comparing identical and fraternal twins indicate that IQ is strongly influenced by genetics. When children are raised in unstimulating environments, however, IQ scores go down, indicating that the environment plays a role, too.

African Americans, on the average, score fifteen points lower on IQ tests than white Americans. Asian Americans score higher than white Americans. Some have argued that these differences are due to genetics. Blacks, however, generally have less education and opportunity. Further, when race is determined by blood tests, the degree of white ancestry does not relate to IQ. IQ tests may be unfair to individuals and cultural groups because of the items used. Culture-fair tests avoid language and other cultural influences.

4. **The assessment of personality** (pp. 385–391)

Tests of personality are used for many purposes—research, diagnosis, advising, and making hiring decisions. One of the most widely used tests is the Minnesota Multiphasic Personality Inventory (MMPI), which consists of 556 true-false items. The MMPI has ten clinical scales that correspond to psychological disorders and does predict diagnostic categories moderately well. A controversy exists over whether statistics can predict behavior better than clinical judgment. When measures are valid and there is a specific prediction to make, statistics do seem superior. The most famous projective test is the Rorschach Inkblot Test, which is based on the assumption that things seen in inkblots reveal something about psychological functioning. Neither the reliability nor the validity of the Rorschach is very good, however. The Thematic Apperception Test (TAT) is another projective test that has been used to measure achievement and other needs.

Although the reliability and validity of objective personality measures like the MMPI are good, these measures may be inaccurate in predicting future behavior and cannot measure all aspects of personality.

Psychological tests are used to help make selection decisions because interviews have questionable reliability and validity. Interest tests like the Strong-Campbell Interest Inventory can indicate broad categories of work that are suitable to an individual. Most psychologists perform clinical assessments with a battery of tests and interviews.

Fill-in-the-Blank Questions

1. The capacity to solve problems and cope successfully with one's environment is called _____ .

2. The average age of the people who performed at the same level as the subject on a test that predicts school performance or intelligence is called _____ .

3. An instrument that indirectly measures motives or emotions by asking the subject to respond to an ambiguous stimulus is called a(n) _____ .

4. The degree to which a test appears to measure what it is supposed to measure is called _____ .

5. An estimate of reliability obtained by dividing a test in half and relating the score on one half to the score on the other half is called _____ .

6. An estimate of reliability obtained by administering two different forms of the same test at two different times is called _____ .

7. An estimate of the reliability of a psychological measure obtained by relating each item of a multi-item measure to every other item is called _____ .

8. An assessment technique that uses the individual's predictions about his or her own behavior or performance in some future situation is called a(n) _____ .

9. The tendency to be especially aware of the expectations of others and to adjust one's behavior to fit those expectations is called _____ .

10. A statistical technique used to measure the degree to which two variables are related is called a(n) _____ .

11. A concept or idea that is part of a theory is called a(n) _____ .

12. The degree to which a test that is designed to predict an observable outcome actually does predict that outcome is called _____ .

13. A measure of the degree to which two variables are related is called the _____ .

14. The degree to which a test produces similar scores on two separate occasions and thereby measures an instrument's reliability is called _____ .

15. The score that compares the individual's score with the scores of all the other people who have taken a test is called the _____ .

16. An instrument that measures what the subject already has done is called a(n) _____ .

17. The kind of validity built up over time and much research for a test of a theoretical construct is a(n) _____ .

18. A score on an IQ test that reflect the subject's ability to carry out nonverbal tasks is called _____ .

19. An estimate of reliability obtained by administering the same test twice, separated by a span of time, is called _____ .

20. An instrument that measures the subject's ability to perform a task is called a(n) _____ .

21. An assessment technique that uses verbal questions and answers to collect information about the subject is called a(n) _____ .

22. An assessment technique that uses the direct observation of an individual's behavior as a predictor of future behavior is called _____ .

23. An assessment technique in which the questions and the response format are defined and the same for everyone tested is called a(n) _____ .

24. A score on an intelligence test—originally, mental age divided by chronological age and multiplied by 100—is called a(n) _____ .

25. A score on an IQ test that reflects the subject's ability to carry out tasks involving words is called _____ .

Fill-in-the-Blank Answers

1. intelligence
2. mental age
3. projective test
4. face validity
5. split-half reliability
6. alternate-forms reliability
7. internal consistency
8. self-prediction
9. self-monitoring
10. correlation
11. theoretical construct
12. criterion validity
13. correlation coefficient
14. stability
15. standard score
16. achievement test
17. construct validity
18. performance IQ
19. test-retest reliability
20. aptitude test
21. interview
22. behavioral assessment
23. objective personality test
24. intelligence quotient (IQ)
25. verbal IQ

Fact and Concept Questions

1. The Self-Monitoring Scale was designed to measure
   a. a person's ability to predict his or her future behavior.
   b. a person's tendency to be aware of others' expectations and to adjust his or her behavior to these expectations.
   c. a person's tendency to think about personal motives and feelings and to act on them.
   d. a person's ability to tell interesting stories when presented with ambiguous pictures.

2. A correlation coefficient of −.90 indicates that
   a. there is a very weak negative relationship between two variables.
   b. one variable causes the other variable to happen.
   c. one variable is completely unrelated to the other variable.
   d. there is a very strong negative relationship between two variables.

3. When a psychological test is given to the same people twice, separated by a period of time, the kind of reliability being measured is called
   a. test-retest.
   b. split-half.
   c. construct.
   d. alternate-forms.

4. If a test had perfect _____ , one item would be all you would need because it would correlate perfectly with every other item.
   a. validity
   b. test-retest reliability
   c. internal consistency
   d. stability

5. If the Self-Monitoring Scale has high criterion validity, we can predict that
   a. the scale appears to measure what it was designed to measure.
   b. after much research, it would correlate with other theoretical constructs.
   c. scores on it will predict observable outcomes.
   d. the scale will have low internal consistency and stability.

6. The most common assessment technique is the
   a. interview.
   b. MMPI.
   c. ability test.
   d. intelligence test.

7. Because interviews are flexible and often unstructured they typically have
   a. very high test-retest reliability.
   b. poor reliability.
   c. very high construct validity.
   d. None of the above.

8. It is unwise to use self-predictions to assess
   a. whether people will be successful in such programs as weight loss or smoking cessation treatment.
   b. an individual's future behavior.
   c. fairly concrete behaviors.
   d. abstract personality traits or behaviors about which people are embarrassed.

9. When a test has the same questions and format for everyone taking it and the answers are marked as either correct or incorrect, the test is considered to be
   a. projective.
   b. a behavioral assessment.
   c. a personality test.
   d. an aptitude or achievement test.

10. _____ tests were developed by psychoanalysts to assess unconscious motives by asking subjects to respond to ambiguous stimuli.
    a. Projective
    b. Objective
    c. Behavioral
    d. Intelligence

11. In the early 1900s, _____ developed a test to identify students who would not benefit from traditional schooling; these tests came to be called intelligence tests.
    a. psychoanalytic theorists
    b. Herman Rorschach
    c. Alfred Binet
    d. David Wechsler

12. Items on an intelligence test that should be answered correctly by children of a specific age are scored. The final score indicates a child's
    a. chronological age.
    b. IQ.
    c. mental age.
    d. performance IQ.

13. Which of the following formulas is used to determine IQ?
    a. $\dfrac{\text{Chronological age}}{\text{Mental age}} + 100 = \text{IQ}$
    b. $\dfrac{\text{Mental age}}{\text{Chronological age}} \times 100 = \text{IQ}$
    c. $\dfrac{\text{Performance IQ}}{\text{Verbal IQ}} \times 100 = \text{IQ}$
    d. $\dfrac{\text{Mental age} + \text{chronological age}}{100} = \text{IQ}$

14. Because it is inappropriate to use the concept of mental age when testing adults' intelligence, _____ are used instead.
    a. standard scores
    b. correlations
    c. chronological ages
    d. projective tests

15. Knowing that the distribution of scores on a test falls on the normal curve and knowing the standard deviation of the test allows us to
    a. tell whether the test has high validity.
    b. predict exactly what score an individual will receive.
    c. tell whether the test has high stability.
    d. judge what percentage of people taking it will get any particular score.

16. In Sternberg's definition, _____ comprises componential, experiential, and contextual skills.
    a. intelligence
    b. *g*
    c. inheritance
    d. test construction

17. Which statement about the inheritance of intelligence is accurate?
    a. The correlations for IQ scores between parents and children range from .05 to .20.
    b. The stronger the blood relationship between two people, the lower the correlation in IQ scores.
    c. The correlation in IQ scores is stronger between children and their adopted mothers than between children and their biological mothers.
    d. None of the above is accurate.

18. According to your textbook authors, when it comes to intelligence, genetics have nothing to do with _____ but can usefully predict _____ .
    a. performance IQ; verbal IQ
    b. black-white group differences; within-group differences
    c. identical-twin similarities; black-white group differences
    d. Asian intelligence; black-white differences

19. Which test has 556 true-false items that are divided into ten subscales designed to measure the existence of specific psychological disorders?
    a. the Rorschach
    b. the MMPI
    c. the Strong-Campbell Interest Inventory
    d. the Thematic Apperception Test

20. If an employer uses psychological tests in hiring decisions, he or she should
    a. avoid giving them in a battery of tests.
    b. use projective techniques.
    c. be able to demonstrate the tests' criterion validity.
    d. use tests that are suitable for clinical assessment.

Application Questions

1. In psychoanalytic theory, people who are fixated at the oral stage should be particularly interested in food, drink, and act in a dependent manner. These ideas illustrate
    a. a test without adequate reliability.
    b. a projective personality test.
    c. a theoretical construct.
    d. an untestable hypothesis.

2. Suppose we developed two different vocabulary tests and gave one test after the other to the same sample of people. If the correlation between scores on the two tests was high and positive, we could assume the test
   a. had good alternate-forms reliability.
   b. had good split-half reliability.
   c. was a projective test.
   d. was developed with a theoretical construct in mind.

3. Suppose a musical ability test accurately predicts those musicians who will be chosen for major symphony orchestras. What can we say about the test?
   a. It has high face validity.
   b. It has high construct validity.
   c. It has very good stability.
   d. It has high criterion validity.

4. In the assessment of her anxious clients, Dr. Taylor has their spouses or close friends count the number of times the client appears fearful and the places where this response occurs. This illustrates
   a. a projective technique.
   b. the use of construct validity.
   c. a behavioral assessment.
   d. the use of indirect interviewing.

5. A psychologist is considering using a projective test. In which of the following situations is it wise to use one?
   a. when you want to know what someone has the ability to perform
   b. when you want an indirect measure of motives and emotions
   c. when you want to predict a particular behavior in the future
   d. when you want to get the person's own view of his or her future success

6. Suppose a test shows a normal curve distribution, has a mean score of 50, and has a standard deviation of 10. Which of the following is an accurate statement?
   a. The test has strong internal consistency.
   b. The majority of people score below 50 on the test.
   c. About 68 percent of people score between 40 and 60.
   d. Less than 3 percent of people score above 60 on the test.

7. Jerald takes a psychological test that gives the following results: Performance IQ 120, Verbal IQ 109. What can we say about Jerald or the test he took?
   a. Jerald is mentally retarded.
   b. Jerald took the Stanford-Binet test.
   c. Jerald's mental age is below his chronological age.
   d. Jerald took a test developed by David Wechsler.

8. A psychologist says that some flower seeds that otherwise might grow into tall plants become dwarf plants if placed in poor soil and given too little water. When applied to intelligence,
    a. poor soil and too little water are genes that black children have.
    b. the tall plants are the genes that white children have.
    c. poor soil and too little water are the effects of culturally biased tests.
    d. poor soil and too little water are the social conditions black children face.

9. Wendy is shown pictures of people alone or in small groups and is asked to tell stories about the pictures. Wendy is
    a. taking the MMPI.
    b. taking a projective test.
    c. taking the Rorschach.
    d. Both *b* and *c*.

10. Dr. Lippert says, "Neither the theory behind them nor the measures themselves meet adequate standards of reliability. They may have moderately good stability and give us a window into underlying motives, but they should only be used as part of a battery of tests when doing clinical assessment." Dr. Lippert refers to
    a. projective tests.
    b. intelligence tests.
    c. objective personality tests.
    d. None of the above.

Fact and Concept Answers

1. * b. Mark Snyder developed the Self-Monitoring Scale to measure an individual's awareness of others' expectations and the tendency to adjust behavior to match those expectations. (p. 360)

    a. A person's ability to predict future behavior is called self-prediction.

    c. Self-monitoring is *not* concerned with introspection, the act in which one examines one's motives and feelings.

    d. Telling stories in response to ambiguous pictures is a task related to the Thematic Apperception Test but is unrelated to self-monitoring.

2. * d. The negative sign indicates a negative (inverse) relationship between variables, and since –.90 is close to the maximum correlation coefficient of –1.00, this is a very strong negative relationship. (pp. 362–363)

    a. A very weak negative correlation would be close to 0.00.

    b. Correlations show an association; they cannot indicate cause-and-effect relationships.

    c. If the two variables are completely unrelated, the correlation is 0.00 or a number close to that.

3. * a. Test-retest reliability indicates the consistency of measurement over time: the same test is given to the same people at two different times. (p. 362)

   b. In split-half reliability, the scores on two halves of a test are correlated to indicate the internal consistency of the test.

   c. Construct validity is developed in a gradual process of comparing test results with measures of theoretically relevant constructs.

   d. In alternate-forms reliability, scores on two equivalent versions of a test are correlated.

4. * c. Internal consistency is measured by correlating each item with every other item; if a test had perfect internal consistency, only one item would be necessary to measure the construct reliably. (p. 363)

   a. Validity involves the ability of a test to measure what it is designed to measure.

   b. Test-retest reliability examines the consistency of measurement over time, not internal consistency.

   d. Stability involves the maintenance of a particular score over time, not internal consistency.

5. * c. Criterion validity measures the ability of a test to predict observable outcomes that the test is designed to predict. (p. 364)

   a. When test items appear to measure what they are designed to measure, we say the test has face validity; it looks good.

   b. When a research program shows that a test correlates with other theoretical constructs, this indicates high construct validity.

   d. Tests with low reliability cannot possess high validity.

6. * a. The interview is the oldest and most commonly used assessment technique. (p. 367)

   b. The MMPI is the most commonly used *objective personality test*, but interviews are more widely used than tests.

   c. Ability tests are less commonly employed than interviews.

   d. Intelligence tests are less commonly employed than interviews.

7. * b. Because there is so much subjectivity and flexibility in both the administration and scoring of interviews, they have poor reliability. (p. 368)

   a. The flexibility and unstructured nature of interviews make them low in test-retest reliability: answers given at one time may be different at a second interview.

   c. There are no theoretical constructs that govern most interviews, so construct validity is irrelevant.

   d. Because *b* is correct, this cannot be the best answer.

8. * d. Self-predictions tend to be poor when people are asked to describe abstract aspects of themselves such as personality traits or when they might be inclined to answer dishonestly. (p. 369)

   a. The best predictor of success in smoking cessation programs is self-prediction, so this is one place where such assessments are useful.

   b. Self-prediction is defined as one's prediction of future behavior, so self-prediction may be helpful here.

   c. Self-prediction is most accurate when examining concrete behaviors such as school performance.

9. * d. Aptitude and achievement tests use set question-and-answer formats (objective tests) in which items are scored as correct or incorrect. (p. 370)

   a. Projective tests use responses to ambiguous stimuli to determine underlying motives and feelings.

   b. Behavioral assessment uses observations of actual behavior or self-reports of behavior.

   c. Personality test items are not scored as right or wrong.

10. * a. Projective techniques involve responses to ambiguous stimuli so that unconscious motives can be examined indirectly; such motives are major concerns for psychoanalysts. (pp. 370–371)

    b. Objective personality tests use fixed question-and-answer formats in written tests to assess personality.

    c. Behavioral assessments use observation of actual behavior or self-reports.

    d. Intelligence tests are objective measures: they use standard questions and fixed response formats.

11. * c. In 1904, Alfred Binet was asked by French educators to devise a test that would identify children who could and could not benefit from being schooled in traditional schools; his test was later used as a measure of intelligence. (p. 372)

    a. Psychoanalytic theorists are interested in unconscious motives, not school performance.

    b. Rorschach developed the inkblot test for personality assessment.

    d. After World War II David Wechsler developed intelligence tests that include performance and verbal IQ sections.

12. * c. Mental age on the Stanford-Binet intelligence test is based on the items that children of a particular age are able to answer correctly. (p. 373)

    a. Chronological age is simply one's age in years and months.

    b. IQ in the Stanford-Binet test is computed by dividing the mental age by the chronological age and multiplying the quotient by 100.

    d. Performance IQ is a subscale on Wechsler intelligence tests that measures nonverbal intelligence.

13. * b. On the Stanford-Binet, the intelligence quotient (IQ) is a ratio of mental age (cognitive ability) to chronological age, multiplied by 100; average IQ is, therefore, 100. (p. 373)

    a. This equation would mean that everyone would have an IQ over 100 and that as mental age (cognitive ability) increased, IQ would decrease.

    c. Performance and verbal IQ pertain only to Wechsler tests.

    d. This equation would mean that no one's IQ would be above 1, except those over 50 years old.

14. * a. Standard scores are the difference from the mean of a particular score, divided by the standard deviation; they allow comparison with thousands of others who took the test. (p. 374)

    b. Correlations are used to measure the direction and strength of an association between two measurements.

    c. Chronological ages are used only in forming a ratio with mental age, something that is not appropriate with adults, because mental age stops changing after puberty.

    d. Projective tests are used for personality assessment.

15. * d. On the normal curve, a particular score can be compared with performance of others taking the test; for instance, a score one standard deviation above the mean is better performance than that of 84 percent in the comparison sample. (p. 377)

    a. The normal curve does not reveal anything about validity.

    b. Nothing predicts an exact score.

    c. The normal curve does not reveal anything about stability, just the distribution of scores.

16. * a. Intelligence is commonly seen as a multifactor concept; Sternberg identifies three components involving analysis, creativity, and practicality. (p. 379)

    b. *g* stands for general intelligence and assumes that intelligence is comprised of only one overarching ability.

    c. Inheritance is unrelated to the components of intelligence.

    d. Test construction is based on reliability and validity, not intellectual skills.

17. * d. Neither *a* nor *b* nor *c* is an accurate statement. (p. 381)

    a. The range of parent-child correlations for IQ is .40–.60, an association roughly ten times stronger than .05–.20.

    b. Correlations increase as blood relationship (genetic similarity) increases.

    c. Child–adoptive mother correlations are about .15; child–biological mother correlations are about .32.

18. * b. Genetics do not account for group differences in races (particularly since race is not a biological reality); they do explain differences within groups. (p. 383)

   a. No separation is made between performance and verbal IQ when examining genetically related differences.

   c. Genetics do not account for group differences.

   d. There is no more reason to believe genetics account for Asian IQ scores than black IQ scores.

19. * b. The MMPI is the most commonly used objective personality test; it consists of 556 items chosen because they relate to psychological disorders. (p. 385)

   a. The Rorschach is a projective test, so there are no specific questions at all.

   c. The Strong-Campbell Interest Inventory is a test to determine suitability for various occupations.

   d. The Thematic Apperception Test (TAT) is a projective test, so there are no true-false items there either.

20. * c. The Equal Employment Opportunity Commission has regulations requiring employers to document the criterion validity of any test used in hiring decisions. (p. 390)

   a. Batteries of tests are advisable, especially in clinical assessments, since they give a broader picture of the individual.

   b. Projective techniques have low reliability and are inappropriate for making hiring decisions.

   d. The purpose of clinical assessments is to understand the psychological problems of individuals, not to decide who to hire for a job.

Application Answers

1. * c. A theoretical construct is an idea generated by a theory; psychoanalytic theory has produced the idea of orally fixated behavior. (p. 360)

   a. Reliability is unrelated to the fact that some ideas are based in theory.

   b. Although a psychoanalyst might study oral fixation with a projective test, this is not the only way it could be assessed.

   d. As long as an idea can be proven wrong (e.g., making clear predictions about the behavior of orally fixated people), it is testable.

2. * a. In alternate-forms reliability, two equivalent versions of a test produce similar results. (p. 363)

   b. Split-half reliability examines internal consistency by correlating each half of one test.

   c. Projective tests do not use specific items such as vocabulary words.

   d. Reliability reveals nothing about how test items were chosen.

3. * d. Criterion validity is high when there is a strong correlation between a test score and an observable, relevant outcome. (p. 364)

    a. We don't know what the test items included, so we cannot guess at the test's face validity.

    b. Until many research studies show that a test correlates with theoretically relevant constructs, we cannot comment on a test's construct validity.

    c. Nothing here suggests how long the time delay was between the test taking and selection to orchestras.

4. * c. A behavioral assessment involves recording specific behaviors, either through an observer or by oneself. (p. 370)

    a. A projective technique uses responses to ambiguous stimuli to reveal underlying motives.

    b. Construct validity builds gradually after many studies in which test results correlate with theoretically relevant constructs.

    d. Observation by others is quite direct and involves no interviewing.

5. * b. Projective tests get around the problem of faking and help uncover unconscious motives and emotions. (pp. 370–371)

    a. Ability tests are used to assess the ability to perform a task.

    c. Projective tests do not predict specific behaviors as much as one's current psychological state.

    d. Self-prediction is used to get an individual's view of future success.

6. * c. On the normal curve, scores ranging from 1 standard deviation below to 1 standard deviation above the mean comprise 68 percent of all scores. (p. 374)

    a. Reliability does not reveal anything about a test's normal distribution or standard scores.

    b. If the mean is 50 on a normal curve, half the people scored 50 or better on it.

    d. Less than 3 percent would score 2 standard deviations above the mean (70 or higher).

7. * d. Wechsler's intelligence tests have two subscales, one for performance IQ and the other for verbal IQ. (p. 375)

    a. Mental retardation involves test performance well below average; Jerald is above the average IQ of 100.

    b. If Jerald took the Stanford-Binet, there would be one score, not two.

    c. If Jerald's mental age were below his chronological age, his IQ would be less than 100.

8. * d. Poor education, employment, and housing conditions are more common for African Americans than for U.S. whites and are analogous to poor soil and water conditions for seeds. (pp. 382–383)

   a. Poor soil and little water represent environmental factors, not genetic ones.

   b. Children of any race have the capacity to have high IQs (be tall plants), but environmental conditions can "stunt" their growth.

   c. Cultural bias in tests reduces further the IQ performance of nonwhites in the United States, but environmental conditions are analogous to poor soil and little water.

9. * b. The projective test Wendy is taking is the Thematic Apperception Test, where the ambiguous stimuli are pictures of people and her stories about them reveal underlying motives about herself. (p. 388)

   a. The MMPI is comprised of over 500 true-false items.

   c. The Rorschach is also a projective test but uses inkblots as the ambiguous stimuli.

   d. Because Wendy is taking the TAT, this cannot be the best answer.

10. * a. Projective tests have poor reliability and little construct validity; they can, however, give a window into unconscious motives, a useful part of clinical assessment. (p. 389)

   b. Intelligence tests have strong reliability.

   c. Many objective personality tests have strong reliability.

   d. Because *a* is an accurate answer, this cannot be the best response.

CHAPTER 14

PERSONALITY

Learning Objectives

1. Define personality and describe the purpose of scientific personality study. (pp. 393–394)

2. Describe the central idea of psychodynamic theory. Discuss how hysteria and hypnosis played important parts in the origins of Freud's theory. (pp. 394–395)

3. Describe and discuss the structure of the psyche including the conscious, preconscious, and unconscious as well as the id, ego, and superego. (pp. 396–397)

4. Describe the libido and the five developmental stages: oral, anal, phallic, latent, and genital. Define fixation. Discuss how conflicts in the phallic stage are resolved and produce the superego. (pp. 398–399)

5. Discuss the role of defense mechanisms and describe the following: repression, reaction formation, isolation, intellectualization, projection, and sublimation. (pp. 400–402)

6. Describe the major concepts or contributions of Carl Jung, Alfred Adler, Erik Erikson, and Karen Horney. (pp. 402–404)

7. Describe the behavioral approach to personality, including the role of primary and secondary reinforcers. Discuss how shaping and superstitious behavior contribute to personality. (pp. 405–408)

8. Define the term *phenomenology*. Describe and discuss Abraham Maslow's phenomenological theory and concept of a hierarchy of needs. Describe and discuss Carl Rogers's theory, the idea of self-concepts, and conditions of worth. (pp. 408–410)

9. Explain what a trait theory of personality is. Discuss Sheldon's theory of body types and Allport's concepts of cardinal, central, and secondary traits. (pp. 410–411)

10. Discuss the history of testing personality theories and how research meant to study one thing evolved into something else. Describe how Jung's ideas about extraversion and introversion were studied by Eysenck. (pp. 412–415)

11. Describe and discuss the social learning concepts of observational learning, locus of control, and learned helplessness. (pp. 416–417)

12. Describe cognitive social learning theory and how it uses concepts from nonbehavioral approaches. (p. 417)

13. Explain how factor analysis is used to reveal the structure of personality. Discuss how Cattell and Eysenck used factor analysis. Describe the five basic personality dimensions. (pp. 418–421)

14. Discuss the controversy over the influence of traits and situations. Discuss Mischel's, Epstein's, and Bem and Allen's viewpoint on the controversy. Discuss what has happened to grand theories of personality. (pp. 421–423)

Chapter Outline

1. **Personality: the definition of the individual** (pp. 393–394)

   Personality consists of the longstanding patterns of behavior, thought, and emotion that make individuals unique. The purpose of personality psychology is to describe and understand what makes each person unique. There is a variety of broad theories to explain individual differences as well as research generated by those theories.

2. **Freud and the psychodynamic theories** (pp. 394–405)

   Sigmund Freud and psychologists who came after him developed a group of theories that assume that unconscious motives are the most important causes of behavior. These theories are grouped and called *psychodynamic theories*. Freud's belief in the unconscious came out of treating women suffering from hysteria with hypnosis. While in a trance state, the women reexperienced memories of which they were unaware and their symptoms changed. Freud came to believe that unconscious childhood memories and feelings shape our everyday lives.

   To Freud, the mind (psyche) was composed of the *unconscious mind*, the contents we are unaware of, and the *conscious mind*, the part we currently experience. The *preconscious mind* contains memories of which we are not currently aware but which could be made conscious if necessary. The functional parts of the psyche are the *id*, the *ego*, and the *superego*. The id is present from birth on. It seeks biological gratification and operates on the *pleasure principle*, the need for immediate satisfaction at any cost. The ego develops after birth and consists of those mental abilities that can satisfy id demands. It operates on the *reality principle*, satisfaction within the constraints of physical and social reality. The superego is the judgmental part of the psyche and defines right and wrong. Conflicts among these three parts of the psyche are entirely natural, according to Freud. The strength of the conflicts and their resolution determine how we act.

Freud believed that *libido*, the energy that moves people to seek pleasure, takes different forms at different ages. If needs are either oversatisfied or undersatisfied at each of these stages, personality is said to be fixated, meaning the person will continue to be driven by that kind of satisfaction later in life.

The *oral* stage of development (the first two years of life) is marked by libidinal drive centering on sucking. Adults who were fixated in the oral stage may be dependent and passive. At age two, the child's libidinal urges shift to the anus; during this *anal stage*, control becomes the major theme. Those fixated in the anal stage may either have too little self-control or be preoccupied with order. Around age five, the *phallic stage* occurs, a time during which the *Oedipus complex* is seen: the child's desire to possess the opposite-sexed parent. In boys, this leads to conflict with the father and *castration anxiety*, the boy's fear that his father will retaliate by castrating him. The child resolves this conflict through *identification*, by trying to be as much like the father as possible. As the conflict is resolved, the superego emerges. Freud believed that girls develop *penis envy* because they have nothing left to lose. The latency stage (ages 7 to 13) involves little change. Finally, in the genital stage, libidinal urges are expressed through adult sexual activity.

The ego has the task of controlling the id's impulses. *Sublimation*, when an unacceptable impulse is satisfied by an acceptable behavior, is an example of a *defense mechanism*, the ego's process of keeping impulses in the unconscious or transforming them so they are no longer threatening. The basic defense is *repression*, where impulses are pushed into the unconscious. *Denial* supports repression by consciously asserting the opposite of the unconscious feeling. In *reaction formation*, the impulse is converted into behaviors that are its complete opposite. In *isolation*, thoughts and feelings are separated, after which the feelings are repressed. If the thoughts are closely examined, *intellectualization* is said to take place. If an unconscious impulse is attributed to another person, *projection* occurs.

Carl Jung disagreed with Freud over the major motivating force. He expanded the idea of the unconscious to include a *collective unconscious*, the memories of all our ancestors. The contents of this unconscious are archetypes, innate images that make us understand the world in particular ways. Alfred Adler developed a different psychodynamic theory, one stressing the *inferiority complex*, the unconscious sense of being inferior. Erik Erikson argued that personality development continued throughout adulthood. Karen Horney stressed basic anxiety as the key motivational force and disputed the idea of penis envy.

3. **The behaviorist approach** (pp. 405–408)

The behaviorist approach uses principles of learning to explain individual differences. B. F. Skinner argued that behavior is maintained by reinforcers even if they are sometimes difficult to identify. Complex behaviors are learned through shaping. Random reinforcement can produce irrational or *superstitious behavior*.

4. **Humanistic/phenomenological theories** (pp. 408–410)

These theories argue that people are free to behave and that understanding humans requires the application of *phenomenology*, the study of experience. Abraham Maslow argued that healthy people should be the source of information about their own personalities and that a hierarchy of psychological needs rose to include self-actualization. Carl Rogers's theory also emphasized self-actualization as an innate tendency to develop our capacities. He suggested that *self-concepts*—ideas about the self—impair the self-actualization process. Parents and others impose *conditions of worth* that tell children that they are lovable only if they act in prescribed ways. These restraints on love distort the self-concept.

5. **Trait theories** (pp. 410–411)

A *trait* is a consistent way of behaving, thinking, and feeling that distinguishes the individual from others. Very broad traits can be considered types. One type theory, developed by William Sheldon, suggests that our physical body shape determines our temperament. Another trait theorist, Gordon Allport, suggested that *cardinal traits* control our behavior in most situations, *central traits* describe major portions of our lives, and *secondary traits* affect only small areas of behavior.

6. **Choosing among the theories** (p. 412)

Selecting a theory should be based on its accuracy, not personal preference. Research, over the years, has drifted away from testing the validity of theories and has focused more on specific behaviors of interest. No one theory is regarded as "true."

7. **Research in personality** (pp. 412–421)

Based on Jung's original ideas, research on *extraverts* (those who thrive on social occasions) and *introverts* (those who prefer to be alone) have found these traits to be a valuable way of distinguishing individuals. Hans Eysenck argues that these traits stem from biological differences in distractability.

The behaviorist perspective has been expanded to include reinforcement from social situations, ideas collectively called *social learning theory*. Albert Bandura developed the idea that complex learning occurred through observation of others. Julian Rotter noted that people have specific and generalized expectancies about whether reinforcement will follow after behavior. The generalized expectancy that we control our own reinforcement he called the *locus of control*, which can be internal or external. The importance of thoughts in learning is shown in *learned helplessness:* the expectation, based on experiences with failure, that one cannot succeed and so should not even try. *Cognitive social learning theory* (or social-cognitive theory) has combined research on observational learning, locus of control, learned helplessness, and other factors to expand behaviorism. Now social learning includes people's understandings of themselves and their world.

The phenomenological perspective has had little direct impact on research, although related work on how we view ourselves indicates that such perceptions strongly influence behavior.

Trait theories have stressed factor analysis, a statistical procedure for describing the structure of measurements such as traits. Raymond Cattell has used factor analysis to identify *surface traits* and the sixteen *source traits* he believes describe personality. Eysenck has used factor analysis, too, to identify three key dimensions of personality: introversion-extraversion, emotional stability-instability, and psychoticism. The analysis of many traits has boiled personality down to five basic dimensions: emotional stability, extraversion, openness to experience, agreeableness, and conscientiousness (the Big Five).

8. **Traits versus situations** (pp. 421–422)

In 1968, Walter Mischel argued that traits do not predict actual behavior very well and that behavior is strongly influenced by situations. Others have argued that traits need to be measured with several observations and that, for some people, only certain traits are consistent across situations. Both situations and traits shape behavior.

Grand personality theories are no longer relevant. Therapists and people in other fields tend to adopt ideas from one or more of the grand personality theories to apply to their work.

Fill-in-the-Blank Quiz

1. The defense mechanism in which the unconscious impulse is attributed to other people rather than to the self is called _____ .

2. In behaviorism, the kind of behavior caused by random reinforcement is called _____ .

3. The memories, feelings, and thoughts that one is not aware of but could become aware of if necessary is called the _____ .

4. In Freudian theory, the part of the psyche that satisfies id demands within the constraints of the physical and social world is called the _____ .

5. The system of ideas and feelings one has about oneself is called the _____ .

6. The longstanding patterns of thought, emotion, and action that distinguish one individual from others are called _____ .

7. The process by which an individual tries to be as much like someone else as possible is called _____ .

8. A consistent way of behaving, thinking, or feeling that distinguishes an individual from others is called a(n) _____ .

9. The defense mechanism in which an unacceptable impulse is satisfied by an acceptable behavior is called _____ .

10. The memories, feelings, and drives that we are not aware of are called the _____ .

11. The defense mechanism that bolsters repression with conscious efforts to ignore threatening impulses is called _____ .

12. In Adler's theory, the collection of unconscious feelings of inferiority stemming from childhood that shape adult behavior is called _____ .

13. In Freudian theory, the part of the psyche that demands the satisfaction of biological needs is called the _____ .

14. The defense mechanism that separates unconscious feelings from unconscious thoughts and then represses the feelings is called _____ .

15. In Freudian theory, the third stage of libidinal development, when satisfaction is focused on exclusive possession of the opposite-sexed parent, is called _____ .

16. In Freudian theory, the child's desire to possess the parent of the opposite sex is called the _____ .

17. The group of theories of personality that assumes that the most important causes of behavior are unconscious motives is called _____ .

18. In Rogers's theory, the constraints placed on individuals by parents and others that limit the individual's ability to develop an accurate self-concept are called _____ .

19. In Freudian theory, the part of the psyche that defines right and wrong and sets standards of behavior is called the _____ .

20. The study of experience is called _____ .

21. The memories, feelings, and drives that people are currently aware of is called the _____ .

22. In Allport's theory, a trait that describes most of the individual's behavior is called a(n) _____ .

23. In Freudian theory, the first libidinal stage, where satisfaction is focused on the mouth, is called the _____ .

24. A person who enjoys solitary activity is called a(n) _____ .

25. In Freudian theory, the principle under which the id operates is called the _____ .

26. The process that keeps impulses in the unconscious mind or transforms them so they are not threatening is called a(n) _____ .

27. A person who enjoys social activity is called a(n) _____ .

28. In Freudian theory, the principle under which the ego operates is called the _____ .

29. In Jungian theory, the unconscious memories of the ancestral past that provides the source of archetypes are called the _____ .

30. In Freudian theory, the energy that moves the individual to seek pleasure is called _____ .

31. According to Allport, a trait that describes only a small part of the person's behavior is called a(n) _____ .

32. In Freudian theory, the boy's fear that his father will castrate him in retaliation for the child's Oedipal feelings is called _____ .

33. According to Allport, a trait that describes a major portion of an individual's behavior, but not as much as a cardinal trait, is called a(n) _____ .

34. In Freudian theory, the second stage of libidinal development, when the focus of satisfaction is on the anus, is called _____ .

35. A new form of behaviorism that applies learning theory to complex human behavior is called _____ .

36. In Freudian theory, the envy girls feel in the phallic stage because their sexual anatomy is different than boys' is called _____ .

37. The defense mechanism that converts an impulse into a behavior that is diametrically opposed to that impulse is called _____ .

38. A generalized expectancy concerning one's ability to control the reinforcements one receives is called _____ .

39. The expectation, stemming from previous experiences of failure, that one cannot succeed and so should not even try is called _____ .

40. The defense mechanism that uses psychic energy to keep threatening impulses from reaching consciousness is called _____ .

41. The defense mechanism that represses feelings while closely examining related thoughts is called _____ .

42. The belief that behavior is the product of social learning and includes people's understanding of the world and themselves is called _____ .

43. According to Cattell, the kind of trait term we commonly use to describe personality is called a(n) _____ .

44. According to Cattell, one of the sixteen basic dimensions underlying surface traits is called a(n) _____ .

Fill-in-the-Blanks Answers

1. projection
2. superstitious behavior
3. preconscious mind
4. ego
5. self-concept
6. personality
7. identification
8. trait
9. sublimation
10. unconscious mind
11. denial
12. inferiority complex
13. id
14. isolation
15. phallic stage
16. Oedipus complex
17. psychodynamic theories
18. conditions of worth
19. superego
20. phenomenology
21. conscious mind
22. cardinal trait
23. oral stage
24. introvert
25. pleasure principle
26. defense mechanism
27. extravert
28. reality principle
29. collective unconscious
30. libido
31. secondary trait
32. castration anxiety
33. central trait
34. anal stage
35. social learning theory
36. penis envy
37. reaction formation
38. locus of control
39. learned helplessness
40. repression
41. intellectualization
42. cognitive social learning theory
43. surface traits
44. source traits

Fact and Concept Questions

1. He was a neurologist who developed the method of free association to treat women with hysteria. His ideas about unconscious motives gave rise to the psychodynamic theories of personality. Who was he?
   a. Carl Jung
   b. Sigmund Freud
   c. B. F. Skinner
   d. Erik Erikson

2. The part of psyche that is aware of current experience is the _____ ; the part that can be made aware of memories if necessary is the _____ .
   a. conscious mind; preconscious mind
   b. id; superego
   c. conscious mind; unconscious mind
   d. superego; preconscious mind

3. Which portion of the psyche operates on the reality principle and serves to satisfy id demands within the constraints of physical and social reality?
   a. the id
   b. the superego
   c. the libido
   d. the ego

4. If libidinal needs are left unsatisfied or are excessively satisfied during particular stages of childhood, a person is said to be experiencing _____ at that stage.
   a. identification
   b. internalization
   c. fixation
   d. isolation

5. When a boy has resolved the Oedipus complex, he has
   a. entered the genital stage of development.
   b. begun to experience castration anxiety.
   c. failed to identify with the same-sexed parent.
   d. begun to develop a superego.

6. Which statement about defense mechanisms is true?
   a. The purpose of defense mechanisms is to keep impulses in the unconscious mind or to distort them so they are no longer threatening.
   b. Defense mechanisms are controlled by the superego.
   c. The basic defense mechanism is identification: the need to be as much like the same-sexed parent as possible.
   d. Defense mechanisms are designed to help us become aware at a conscious level of the unacceptable impulses in the id.

7. The defense mechanism of _____ occurs when a person accuses others of having the feelings and motives that he actually has himself.
   a. repression
   b. projection
   c. intellectualization
   d. reaction formation

8. Archetype is to _____ as inferiority complex is to _____ .
   a. Karen Horney; Alfred Adler
   b. Carl Jung; Alfred Adler
   c. Erik Erikson; Carl Jung
   d. Alfred Adler; Erik Erikson

9. B. F. Skinner suggested that extremely complex human behaviors were created by
   a. random reinforcement.
   b. the development of generalized expectancies.
   c. a process he called "self-actualization."
   d. a lifetime of shaping.

10. A phenomenological approach to personality stresses
    a. the need to perform carefully controlled research.
    b. the unconscious motives that cause human behavior.
    c. the study of one's thoughts and feelings about oneself.
    d. the categorization of behavior into various types of traits.

11. According to Rogers,
    a. conditions of worth are helpful to children because they clarify what behaviors are expected.
    b. self-actualization is a nonsensical idea.
    c. self-concepts are distorted by conditions of worth.
    d. All of the above.

12. In William Sheldon's theory, traits are
    a. determined by one's body type.
    b. unimportant; only the situation shapes our behavior.
    c. either surface or source, and neither controls our temperament.
    d. considered cardinal when they define most of our behavior.

13. Which of the following is an accurate statement of your textbook authors' ideas on choosing a personality theory?
    a. It does not matter what theory one chooses because none does an adequate job of explaining individual differences.
    b. One should select a theory because it agrees with one's own personal preferences.
    c. Roughly fifty years of research have clearly shown which theories are accurate in predicting human behavior.
    d. Despite a great deal of research, we do not know which, if any, of the grand theories is true.

14. This concept was accepted by Carl Jung and Hans Eysenck. It is also included in the "big five" personality dimensions. What concept is being described?
    a. extraversion-introversion
    b. the preconscious and the unconscious
    c. locus of control
    d. self-actualization

15. Observational learning is part of the expanded version of the behavioral approach called
    a. expectancy theory.
    b. social learning theory.
    c. learned helplessness theory.
    d. humanistic/phenomenological theory.

16. People with _____ believe that if they work hard, they will be reinforced for their efforts.
    a. an extraverted personality
    b. an external locus of control
    c. emotional stability
    d. an internal locus of control

17. Which statement about learned helplessness is accurate?
    a. The idea of learned helplessness has been supported by both animal and human research.
    b. Learned helplessness had its origins in Freud's treatment of hysterical women.
    c. Learned helplessness demonstrates how unimportant cognitions are in influencing behavior.
    d. Behaviorists see learned helplessness as a genetically determined trait.

18. The fact that people who see themselves accurately—with all their shortcomings—are more prone to depression than those who have positive illusions about themselves illustrates the _____ approach to personality.
    a. behavioral
    b. trait
    c. phenomenological
    d. psychodynamic

19. Factor analysis is
    a. the method psychoanalysts use to bring unconscious impulses to the surface.
    b. how personality psychologists decide whether a trait is caused by genetics or environmental factors.
    c. the method Maslow used to determine basic human needs.
    d. a statistical procedure for organizing and structuring measurements.

20. Which statement about traits and situations is accurate?
    a. Walter Mischel argued that traits are the single best predictor of future behavior.
    b. Seymour Epstein showed that personality measures are good predictors of collections of behaviors.
    c. Bem and Allen proved that every trait shows consistency in behavior for every person.
    d. Buss and Craik argued that traits and behaviors are fundamentally unrelated to one another.

Application Questions

1. Psychiatrist to patient: "When I hypnotized you, you had unpleasant memories of childhood you had not been aware of. When you came out of the trance, some of your hysterical symptoms were gone." Who might have said this?
   a. B. F. Skinner
   b. Carl Rogers
   c. Sigmund Freud
   d. Hans J. Eysenck

2. Pat is an adult but acts like a young child. She wants immediate satisfaction of her needs at any cost and gives no thought to how those needs can be satisfied. Which part of Pat's psyche is most strongly expressed?
   a. her id
   b. her ego
   c. her superego
   d. her Oedipus complex

3. Harvey is always worried that he has done something wrong. He experiences tremendous guilt and is very rigid in his thinking. According to psychodynamic theory, Harvey
   a. was fixated at the oral stage.
   b. has too strong an ego.
   c. has too strong a superego.
   d. failed to resolve the Oedipus complex.

4. Jeffrey is five and a half years old. According to psychodynamic theorists, what should be happening in terms of his libidinal development?
   a. He should be in the latency stage, when the libido is inactive.
   b. He should be jealous and fearful of his father.
   c. He should hate and want to be rid of his mother.
   d. He should be in the genital stage, when he experiences penis envy.

5. "Women do not envy men's anatomy, they envy their power in society. Men and women alike are subject to the unconscious need to reduce the basic anxiety that stems from childhood." Which psychologist would most likely have said this?
   a. Alfred Adler
   b. Carl Jung
   c. Carl Rogers
   d. Karen Horney

6. Billie often picks fights with his younger brother, Bobbie. Billie gets Bobbie to cry and then gets scolded by his mother, but continues to pick on his younger brother. How would a behaviorist explain Billie's behavior?
   a. Billie is unconsciously motivated by a need to be with other people, even if it means fighting with them.
   b. Billie has a negative self-concept.
   c. Billie never developed self-control because he failed to resolve his castration anxiety.
   d. Billie gets attention from his mother, a secondary reinforcer.

7. Vera is no longer much concerned with meeting her physiological needs or even with being involved with other people. She is fully aware of the world and lives so she can fulfill her potential. Maslow might say she is
   a. a self-actualizing person.
   b. experiencing conditions of worth.
   c. Both *a* and *b*.
   d. Neither *a* nor *b*.

8. Wendy needs to live a quiet, uneventful life. She prefers to be alone and read books. According to Eysenck,
   a. Wendy is very easily distracted from performing tasks.
   b. Wendy is a classic extravert.
   c. Wendy needs a high level of stimulation to be happy.
   d. Wendy's brain is dominated by inhibitory processes.

9. Dr. Karlow says, "Human behavior is caused by a combination of positive and negative consequences and the thoughts we have before, during, and after we engage in behavior." Dr. Karlow's ideas are closest to that of
   a. psychodynamic personality theory.
   b. trait theory.
   c. cognitive social learning theory.
   d. humanistic personality theory.

10. Brian believes that there are sixteen basic dimensions or traits that define individual personality. Gretchen believes that there are only three basic dimensions. Brian's ideas are closest to _____'s theory; Gretchen's are closest to _____'s.
    a. Mischel; Eysenck
    b. Cattell; Eysenck
    c. Eysenck; Freud
    d. Cattell; Freud

Fact and Concept Answers

1. * b. Sigmund Freud was a neurologist before he was a psychiatrist and he developed his psychodynamic theory of personality by investigating the unconscious memories of women suffering from hysteria. (pp. 394–395)

   a. Carl Jung was not a neurologist; his contributions include the idea of the collective unconscious.

  c. B. F. Skinner was a founding figure in the behavioral approach.

  d. Erik Erikson was a follower of Freud and contributed the idea of personality development through life.

2. * a. The conscious mind is what you are aware of currently; the preconscious mind has memories you can be made aware of, such as the name of your second-grade teacher. (p. 396)

  b. the id is completely unconscious.

  c. the unconscious mind has memories that are unavailable to us.

  d. the superego is partially unconscious.

3. * d. The ego is the psychological problem solver and operates on the reality principle; it is aware of the hurdles in reality that must be negotiated so that id demands can be met. (pp. 396–397)

  a. The id demands immediate gratification and operates on the pleasure principle.

  b. The superego is concerned with morality, not problem solving.

  c. The libido is not a structure of the psyche; it is the force that drives behavior.

4. * c. Fixation occurs when libidinal development is stopped because satisfaction is either unmet or excessively met. (p. 398)

  a. Identification occurs when a child incorporates the ideas and feelings of the same-sexed parent in order to resolve conflicts in the phallic stage.

  b. Internalization is a made-up term.

  d. Isolation is a defense mechanism in which feelings are separated from thoughts and are repressed.

5. * d. The superego develops when the Oedipus complex is resolved through the process of identification. (p. 399)

  a. The genital stage begins at puberty (around age 12); the resolution of the Oedipus complex should occur at age seven.

  b. Castration anxiety is part of the Oedipus complex, so it is reduced when resolution of the conflict has occurred.

  c. Identification with the same-sexed parent is considered the resolution of the conflict.

6. * a. Defense mechanisms are an ego process by which threatening impulses from the unconscious are either kept there (repression) or distorted so that their impact is lessened (projection, intellectualization, and other mechanisms). (p. 400)

  b. The ego controls defense mechanisms.

  c. Identification is a key to resolving the Oedipus complex; repression is the basis of defense.

  d. Defense mechanisms do the opposite: they preserve us by keeping id impulses from reaching consciousness.

7. * b. In projection, an unacceptable impulse is attributed to other people: for example, a hostile person thinks that others are out to get him. (p. 402)

   a. Repression is the defense of motivated forgetting; threatening impulses are banished to the unconscious.

   c. In intellectualization, thoughts and feelings are separated and the thoughts are examined with great care. For example, a surgeon thinks about the color and shape of a heart valve and remains unaware of his/her feelings about the patient.

   d. In reaction formation, a person shows behavior that is diametrically opposed to the unacceptable impulse: a person with a fear of death drives his motorcycle at 100 miles per hour.

8. * b. Carl Jung developed the idea of the collective unconscious, the source of archetypes; Alfred Adler suggested that all people try to overcome feelings of inferiority they have as children. (pp. 403–404)

   a. Karen Horney was responsible for ideas concerning basic anxiety and the refutation of the concept of penis envy.

   c. Erik Erikson extended personality development to include the whole life span.

   d. Archetypes are Jung's idea; inferiority is Adler's.

9. * d. B. F. Skinner suggested that complex behaviors, such as how we have conversations with other people, are the result of years of shaping. (p. 405)

   a. Random reinforcement explains superstitious behavior.

   b. Generalized expectancies are concepts coined by Julian Rotter.

   c. Self-actualization is a humanistic/phenomenological concept.

10. * c. The phenomenological approach focuses on personal experience, and a major part of that is how we think and feel about ourselves. (p. 408)

    a. Phenomenological theory puts emphasis on how people view themselves; it downplays the value of scientific research.

    b. Unconscious motivation is central to psychodynamic theories.

    d. The trait approach seeks the appropriate categorization of traits.

11. * c. Rogers saw conditions of worth, the strings attached to love provided by parents, as the method by which self-concept is distorted and mental disturbance occurs. (pp. 409–410)

    a. Conditions of worth are harmful because they tell children that certain feelings are wrong.

    b. Self-actualization is a key force in Rogers's theory.

    d. Since *a* and *b* are incorrect, this cannot be the best choice.

12. * a. Sheldon's theory argues that body type determines one's temperament. (pp. 410–411)

    b. Sheldon is a trait theorist and gives little emphasis to the environment.

    c. The ideas of surface and source traits are Raymond Cattell's.

    d. Gordon Allport gave us the term *cardinal traits*.

13. * d. Research has spun off in many different directions; none of the grand theories has been shown to be completely false or completely true. (p. 412)

    a. All of the theories are helpful in explaining some of the individual differences, but none can explain everything.

    b. Personal preference is a poor reason for selecting a scientific theory; empirical evidence should guide decisions.

    c. Research has not shown which theories are best at predicting behavior.

14. * a. Jung was the first psychologist to discuss extraversion-introversion, Eysenck studied its causes, and it is now considered one of the five basic dimensions of personality after much factor analysis work. (pp. 413–415)

    b. The preconscious and the unconscious are solely psychodynamic ideas; they are not traits.

    c. Locus of control is a social learning theory term coined by Julian Rotter.

    d. Self-actualization is a humanistic term used by both Maslow and Rogers.

15. * b. Social learning theory adds observational learning to basic behavioral principles in order to explain complex social behavior (p. 415)

    a. Expectancies are part of social learning theory.

    c. Learned helplessness theory is another part of social learning theory.

    d. The humanistic/phenomenological theory does not include any types of learning.

16. * d. A person with an internal locus of control believes that the reinforcements she receives are caused by her own efforts, not by fate or other outside factors. (p. 416)

    a. An extravert prefers to be with other people.

    b. A person with an external locus of control believes that reinforcement comes because of luck or other external factors.

    c. Emotional stability is Eysenck's term for people who do not change moods very often or very much.

17. * a. Seligman began his work on learned helplessness with research on dogs; subsequent studies on humans supported the idea. (pp. 416–417)

    b. Learned helplessness had its origins in animal research.

    c. Learned helplessness points out how important beliefs that one cannot control situations are in influencing behavior.

    d. Learned helplessness is learned; it is not genetic.

18. * c. Phenomenological theories stress the self-concept—how we see ourselves. (p. 419)

    a. A purely behavioral approach, such as Skinner's, does not address thinking or self-concept.

    b. Trait theorists attempt to measure and describe the structure of personality traits.

    d. The psychodynamic theorists discount conscious awareness in favor of unconscious motives and impulses.

19. * d. Factor analysis uses correlation statistics to see how personality traits cluster as a means of organizing trait measurements. (pp. 418–419)

    a. Psychoanalysts may use free association or psychoanalysis to bring a person's unconscious impulses to consciousness.

    b. There is no one way psychologists determine whether genetic or environmental factors are the cause of traits.

    c. Maslow studied fully functioning humans to learn about self-actualization and the other human needs.

20. * b. Epstein found that by collecting behaviors, a process he called "aggregation," we could improve predictions based on personality measures. (p. 422)

    a. Mischel argued the reverse. He claimed that trait measurements were very poor predictors of specific behavior.

    c. Bem and Allen said the reverse. They feel that individuals differ as to the traits that are consistent for them.

    d. Buss and Craik suggest that traits are related to families of behaviors, not specific actions.

Application Answers

1. * c. Freud was a psychiatrist who first used hypnosis to study and treat hysteria. (p. 394)

    a. Skinner was a behavioral psychologist who did no treatment and was uninterested in childhood memories.

    b. Rogers was a psychologist who developed an important humanistic/phenomenological theory.

    d. Eysenck is a psychologist who does research on traits.

2. * a. The id is the inborn part of the psyche that demands instantaneous gratification without any thought about how it can be attained (the pleasure principle). (p. 396)

    b. The ego operates on the pleasure principle, so it *is* in tune with the practical issues in satisfying needs.

    c. The superego is focused on morality.

    d. The Oedipus complex is not a part of the psyche, it is an event that occurs during the phallic stage of development.

3. * c. Harvey has an overactive superego—the part of psyche that is concerned with morality and feels guilt. (p. 397)

   a. Fixation at the oral stage presumes highly dependent behaviors.

   b. A strong ego would mean Harvey functioned rationally and solved problems effectively.

   d. Failure to resolve the Oedipus complex might mean a lack of superego and the opposite of what Harvey shows.

4. * b. Jealousy and fear of father (castration anxiety) are all part of the Oedipus complex that occurs between ages five and seven. (p. 399)

   a. Latency occurs after fear and jealousy are resolved.

   c. While he experiences the Oedipus complex Jeffrey would want to possess and be close to his mother.

   d. The genital stage begins with puberty, about age twelve.

5. * d. Horney refuted the idea of penis envy and claimed that basic anxiety was the fundamental driving force in human behavior. (p. 404)

   a. Adler's main contribution was the inferiority complex.

   b. Jung's main contribution was the collective unconscious.

   c. Rogers's main contributions were self-actualization, conditions of worth, and the importance of self-concept.

6. * d. Behaviorists claim that all behavior is maintained by reinforcers. In Billie's case, scoldings are not punishments but secondary reinforcers because he gets attention. (p. 405)

   a. Behaviorists are uninterested in unconscious motives.

   b. Self-concept is a humanistic/phenomenological concept.

   c. Castration anxiety is a psychodynamic concept.

7. * a. Maslow saw self-actualizing persons as those who lived fully and had reduced need for other people's consent or admiration. (pp. 408–409)

   b. Conditions of worth are the negative strings attached to love that Rogers discussed in his theory.

   c. Because *b* pertains to Rogers, this cannot be the best choice.

   d. Because *a* is accurate, this cannot be the best choice.

8. * a. Introversion is believed to correspond to being easily distracted. (p. 415)

   b. Extraverts like to be with others and to be stimulated by change.

   c. Extraverts seem to have a need for increased stimulation not to be bored.

   d. High inhibitory processes make extraverts uncomfortable with a quiet world; they seek extra stimulation to offset this.

9. * c. Cognitive social learning theory is the idea that complex behavior can be understood by applying learning principles and including the person's cognitions about the world and themselves. (p. 417)

a. Psychodynamic theories put no emphasis on learning (positive and negative consequences).

b. Trait theories put little emphasis on cognitions.

d. Although humanistic theories are interested in cognitions about the self, they put little emphasis on positive and negative consequences (learning principles).

10. * b. Cattell used factor analysis to discover sixteen source traits; Eysenck used the same method to find three. (p. 420)

a. Mischel is an antitrait behaviorist.

c. Eysenck believes there are three basic dimensions, not sixteen.

d. Freud's three parts of the psyche—id, ego, and superego— are not traits.

CHAPTER 15

PSYCHOLOGICAL DISORDERS

Learning Objectives

1. Describe the Rosenhan study of pseudopatients in mental hospitals and its implications for abnormal psychology. (p. 425)

2. Discuss the problems in defining the term *psychological disorder*. (p. 426)

3. Describe and discuss the five axes of the DSM-III-R. Identify the most common forms of psychological disorder. Define and discuss intern's syndrome. (pp. 427–430)

4. Describe and discuss psychoactive substance abuse disorders and the anxiety disorders of simple phobia, social phobia, generalized anxiety, panic disorder, agoraphobia, and obsessive-compulsive disorder. (pp. 430–434)

5. Describe the symptoms of depression. Identify the myths surrounding suicide. Describe bipolar disorder. (pp. 434–436)

6. Describe the symptoms of the schizophrenic disorders including thought disturbances, affective disturbances, motor disturbances, and social isolation. Identify the subtypes of schizophrenia. (pp. 436–439)

7. Describe the symptoms of conversion disorders, somatization disorders, delusional disorders, and the dissociative disorders, including psychogenic amnesia, fugue, and multiple personality. (pp. 439–442)

8. Discuss how personality disorders are different from Axis I disorders. Describe the symptoms of antisocial personality disorder. (pp. 443–444)

9. Describe and discuss the sources of error in diagnosing psychological disorders. (pp. 444–445)

10. Identify the basic assumptions of the biological, psychodynamic, behaviorist, and social systems theories of psychological disorders. Define the diathesis-stress model. (pp. 445–447)

11. Discuss the evidence for psychological disorders stemming from genetics and the limitations of the evidence. Discuss what is known about the relation between disorders and brain function and anatomy. Discuss the effects of biological treatments. (pp. 448–453)

12. Discuss the role of such individual factors as the unconscious and learning on psychological disorders. Discuss how social factors provide the primary source of stress triggering psychological disorders. (pp. 453–456)

Chapter Outline

1. **Problems of definition and means of classification** (pp. 425–430)

   Research by Rosenhan (1973) in which "normal" people were admitted to mental hospitals points out how difficult it is to diagnose psychological disorders. It is difficult to define the term *psychological disorder*. One component of the definition is that the behavior is uncommon. Uncommon behavior that is either considered socially undesirable or irrational or causes distress to oneself or others, however, is more likely to be considered a sign of a psychological disorder.

   The *Diagnostic and Statistical Manual of Mental Disorders (DSM-III-R)* is a diagnostic tool that uses five dimensions or axes. Axis I is the psychological disorder, Axis II lists personality disorders, Axis III assesses relevant physical problems, Axis IV rates the stresses the person has experienced, and Axis V examines the person's functioning over the past year. Among the sixteen major categories of disorder, substance abuse, anxiety disorders, and mood disorders are the most commonly occurring in the United States.

   Students must be aware that *intern's syndrome,* the tendency to think one has a disease because one is learning about it, can occur among those learning about psychological disorders.

2. **Axis I disorders: psychoactive substance abuse, anxiety disorders, and mood disorders** (pp. 430–436)

   The most common disorders are psychoactive substance abuse disorders. Such abuse need not involve physical dependence: problems are signaled by impairment in work or personal relationships.

   Anxiety disorders have as their hallmark *anxiety,* the physical and emotional responses of fear to objects that are not sufficiently dangerous to warrant the responses. In simple phobias, the anxiety occurs in very specific situations that are carefully avoided. *Social phobias* are fears of social situations. In *generalized anxiety disorder* anxiety has no specific focus; dread and worry are fairly constant. The primary symptom of *panic disorder* is the *panic attack*—a sudden, unexpected, and intense experience of anxiety. Fear of experiencing repeated panic attacks may produce *agoraphobia,* a fear of having an attack in public places. Repeated thoughts to ward off anxiety are called *obsessions,* whereas repeated actions to so the same thing are *compulsions.* These are found together in obsessive-compulsive disorder.

The two main mood disorders are *depression* and *bipolar disorder.* Moods are out of control in both, but *mania* (undesirable optimism and energy) occurs only in bipolar disorder. In depression, everyday sadness becomes more intense and lasts longer. A common disorder, depression has as its major symptoms sadness, feelings of worthlessness, apathy, fatigue, sleep and eating disorders, and thoughts of suicide. Many misperceptions exist about suicide, including the idea that a previous attempt means a person is not serious about taking his or her life.

In bipolar disorder, mood swings from high to low. Manic states can be productive, but more often their irrationality disrupts family life. Mania is usually followed by intense depression.

3. **Axis I disorders: schizophrenic, somatoform, delusional and dissociative disorders** (pp. 436–442)

Schizophrenia is the most serious psychological disorder. Its symptoms lie outside ordinary experience and include thought disturbances such as *delusions* (false beliefs), hallucinations, and formal thought disturbances. In addition, people with schizophrenia show affective disturbances; motor disturbances, including *catatonic stupor;* and social isolation. The three main subtypes of schizophrenia are: disorganized, catatonic, and paranoid.

The central symptom of the *somatoform disorders* is a physical complaint having a psychological basis. In *conversion disorder,* there is a loss of movement or sensation that cannot be the result of neurological damage. In *somatization disorder,* people complain of vague physical symptoms although there is nothing physically wrong with them.

Delusional disorders are characterized by a single, well-organized delusion. The delusions can include ideas of reference or paranoid delusions that there is a conspiracy against the individual. These are less devastating disorders than paranoid schizophrenia.

Memory disturbance is the chief characteristic of the *dissociative disorders.* In *psychogenic amnesia,* psychological factors induce a specific and brief memory loss. A *fugue* is when people with amnesia leave their surroundings and start a new identity elsewhere. In *multiple personality disorder,* people have blackouts during which a new personality takes over. Usually some of the personalities are aware of one another, but the first is not aware of the others.

4. **Axis 2: personality disorders** (pp. 443–444)

Many personality disorders reflect symptoms in psychological disorders. Personality disorders, however, produce milder and more enduring forms of self-defeating behavior than psychological disorders do. In *antisocial personality disorder,* for example, there is a pervasive tendency to exploit others and feel no guilt or sympathy while doing it.

5. **A question of reliability** (pp. 444–445)

The diagnosis of disorders is made difficult by human complexity, clinician errors, and the distress that may accompany acknowledging a disorder's existence. There are also problems with the diagnostic tool, the DSM-III-R, a system influenced by politics as well as science.

6. **The origins of psychological disorders: traditional theories** (pp. 445–446)

Traditionally, psychologists have explained abnormal behavior in terms of biological, psychodynamic, behaviorist, and social systems theories.

7. **The diathesis-stress model: biological factors** (pp. 447–453)

An integrative approach, the *diathesis-stress model* argues that all disorders stem from a predisposition (*diathesis*) and a triggering factor (a *stressor*). Biological factors account for many of the preexisting vulnerabilities. Genetics is one such factor, as is seen in the greater likelihood of both identical twins being diagnosed with schizophrenia than both fraternal twins. Genes do not cause this and other disorders, but they do control factors that in turn make the person more vulnerable to developing the disorder.

One of those factors may be brain function or brain anatomy. In some forms of schizophrenia, the ventricles may be enlarged. Drugs such as phenothiazines and antidepressants alter neurotransmitters in the brain and reduce psychological symptoms. The diathesis for different disorders may stem from different neurotransmitter imbalances.

8. **The diathesis-stress model: individual and social factors** (pp. 453–457)

A diathesis may develop because of early childhood experiences and conflicts that affect the unconscious. Although treatment of unconscious conflicts can be successful, this outcome alone does not prove that the conflicts were the cause of the disorder. Similarly, behaviorists may assume incorrectly that learning is both the cause of the problem and the means of solving it. Cognitive theorists stress attention problems in schizophrenia and learned helplessness and emotion-driven remembering in depression.

Social factors may be the primary sources of stress that trigger disorders. The family system has a major impact, particularly when it has faulty communication patterns. In the United States, people in the lower socioeconomic classes face more extreme stressors and have fewer resources for coping than people in higher socioeconomic classes do.

Fill-in-the-Blank Questions

1. A more or less constant feeling of anxiety that is not attached to a specific situation is called _____ .

2. The tendency for people to believe incorrectly that they are suffering from diseases they are just learning about is called _____ .

3. A serious psychological disorder characterized by thought, emotional, motor, and social disturbances is called _____ .

4. Psychological disorders in which the major symptoms are physical complaints that have a psychological rather than physical basis are called _____ .

5. The psychological disorder in which a person loses personal memory and leaves his or her surroundings to live in a new place and with a new identity is called _____ .

6. An action that a person repeats again and again to ward off anxiety is called a(n) _____ .

7. A pattern of behavior, thought, or feeling that is abnormal, socially unacceptable, irrational, or painful to the individual or those around him or her is called a(n) _____ .

8. A state in which an individual is extravagantly, and often unrealistically, happy, optimistic, and energetic is called _____ .

9. The disorders in which the individual is unable to remember events, personal identity, or parts of his or her personality are called _____ .

10. The disorder in which an individual is afraid of panic attacks that occur in public places is called _____ .

11. The physical and emotional responses of fear to a situation that is not dangerous or not dangerous enough to warrant the responses are called, collectively, _____ .

12. The psychological disorder characterized by sadness and hopelessness is called _____ .

13. The motor disturbance in schizophrenia in which the individual does not move or speak for long periods is called _____ .

14. The dissociative disorder in which the individual seems to have more than one personality controlling his or her behavior at different times is called _____ .

15. An unreasonable fear of social situations that limits one's participation in those situations is called a(n) _____ .

16. Disorders in which the individual complains of vague physical symptoms that have no physical basis are called _____ .

17. The sudden, unexpected onset of the physical symptoms of anxiety is called a(n) _____ .

18. A false belief about the world is a(n) _____ .

19. Disorders in which the sufferer reports a loss of movement or sensation in the body for which there is no neurological basis are called _____ .

20. A thought that a person repeats again and again to ward off anxiety is called a(n) _____ .

21. The psychological disorder (once called manic-depressive disorder) in which the individual experiences episodes of both depression and mania is called _____ .

22. Psychological disorders in which individuals have a single, well-organized delusion are called _____ .

23. The belief that physical and mental disorders arise from both a predisposition and some triggering factor is called the _____ .

24. The personality disorder in which individuals have a moral deficiency, leaving them without sympathy for others and without guilt for their actions is called _____ .

25. A loss of memory arising from psychological rather than physical causes is called _____ .

Fill-in-the-Blank Answers

1. generalized anxiety
2. intern's syndrome
3. schizophrenia
4. somatoform disorders
5. fugue
6. compulsion
7. psychological disorder
8. mania
9. dissociative disorders
10. agoraphobia
11. anxiety
12. depression
13. catatonic stupor
14. multiple personality
15. social phobias
16. somatization disorders
17. panic attack
18. delusions
19. conversion disorders
20. obsession
21. bipolar disorder
22. delusional disorders
23. diathesis-stress model
24. psychogenic amnesia

Fact and Concept Questions

1. Which statement about the DSM-III-R is true?
   a. It has three dimensions or axes on which symptoms are recorded.
   b. It lists the environmental stresses that may have triggered the psychological problem.
   c. It indicates personality and psychological disorders on the same axis.
   d. It is a method of treating people with psychological and personality disorders.

2. The most common psychological disorders are
   a. psychoactive substance abuse disorders.
   b. anxiety disorders.
   c. schizophrenic disorders.
   d. mood disorders.

3. Unlike _____ , generalized anxiety disorders involve anxiety symptoms that _____ .
   a. dissociative disorders; occur in specific situations.
   b. simple phobias; occur in specific situations.
   c. simple phobias; occur in no particular situation.
   d. dissociative disorders; are mild and easily coped with.

4. A _____ is the sudden and unexpected onset of anxiety; it is related to the disorder called _____ .
   a. panic attack; multiple personality
   b. delusion; simple phobia
   c. panic attack; agoraphobia
   d. compulsion; antisocial personality disorder

5. Continually thinking about how germs can cause disease and repeatedly washing your hands to reduce anxiety about getting sick are characteristics of which disorder?
   a. generalized anxiety disorder
   b. conversion disorder
   c. somatization disorder
   d. obsessive-compulsive disorder

6. Which of the following is *not* a symptom of depression?
   a. feelings of worthlessness
   b. intense interest in pleasurable activities
   c. lack of energy and slowed movements or thoughts
   d. sleep disturbances

7. Which of the following is a myth about suicide?
   a. Many people who attempt suicide are not sure they want to die.
   b. The majority of people who are seriously depressed consider suicide.
   c. The majority of people who have attempted suicide tried to talk about it.
   d. Suicide attempts should not be taken seriously since they are usually attention-getting actions.

8. A person with schizophrenia who suffers from delusions
   a. is showing a common thought disturbance.
   b. is showing the affective disturbances common in the disorder.
   c. is very rare; delusions occur only in bipolar disorder.
   d. None of the above.

9. If an individual with schizophrenia stops moving, holds a bizarre position for hours, and ignores others, the symptom is called
   a. catatonic stupor.
   b. a hallucination.
   c. flattened affect.
   d. disorganized schizophrenia.

10. What is the major difference between paranoid schizophrenia and delusional disorders?
    a. Only in paranoid schizophrenia does one see ideas of reference.
    b. People with delusional disorders usually function better.
    c. People with delusional disorders have motor and social disturbances.
    d. Paranoid schizophrenia develops later in life.

11. In conversion disorders,
    a. there is real physical damage to the body caused by psychological stress.
    b. there is a loss of memory for recent events.
    c. people complain of vague physical complaints.
    d. people report a loss of sensation even though they show no neurological damage.

12. Which statement about psychogenic amnesia is true?
    a. It is the most common symptom in schizophrenia.
    b. It always results in a person's moving to another area and developing a new identity.
    c. It is caused by biological damage to the brain.
    d. It is very uncommon and memory loss is usually brief.

13. In multiple personality
    a. the person acts schizophrenic some of the time and normal the rest of the time.
    b. people have uncontrollable thoughts and repeated actions that are designed to ward off anxiety.
    c. alternate personalities exist to act in ways the first personality cannot.
    d. dissociation makes the person move to a new area and develop a new identity.

14. Lying, exploiting others, and feeling neither guilt nor sympathy about doing this are characteristics of
    a. people with bipolar disorder.
    b. the dissociative disorders.
    c. the antisocial personality.
    d. conversion disorders.

15. When two clinicians use the DSM-III-R system to assign diagnoses to the same individuals, the percent of time they agree when the diagnosis falls within the sixteen major categories is about
    a. 15 percent.
    b. 40 percent.
    c. 60 percent.
    d. 80 percent.

16. The traditional approach to psychological disorders that stresses the impact of family relationships on the individual's behavior is called the _____ approach.
    a. behaviorist
    b. social systems
    c. diathesis-stress
    d. biological

17. In the diathesis-stress model, poverty is to _____ as genetics are to _____ .
    a. stress; diathesis
    b. individual factors; social factors
    c. predisposition; triggering factors
    d. personality disorders; psychological disorders

18. Evidence from identical and fraternal twins indicates that there is a genetic predisposition for
    a. schizophrenia.
    b. bipolar disorder.
    c. Both *a* and *b*.
    d. Neither *a* nor *b*.

19. The fact that phenothiazines reduce dopamine levels in people with schizophrenia
    a. shows that schizophrenia must be caused by biological abnormalities.
    b. fails to prove that schizophrenia is caused by biological abnormalities.
    c. rejects the idea that they also have enlarged ventricles.
    d. suggests that, for schizophrenia, there is no diathesis.

20. Loss of positive reinforcement and learned helplessness are both _____ .
    a. cognitive and learning factors in depression.
    b. social triggering mechanisms in schizophrenia.
    c. cognitive and learning factors in schizophrenia.
    d. biological factors in depression.

Application Questions

1. Dr. Jenkins defines it this way: "A person who acts in an unusual and irrational manner and whose actions cause the individual great personal discomfort." What is "it"?
   a. personality disorder
   b. formal thought disturbance
   c. schizophrenia
   d. psychological disorder

2. Jeffrey has just started reading about abnormal behavior and is convinced that he shows the symptoms of bipolar disorder, generalized anxiety disorder, and fugue. What Jeffrey is really showing is called
   a. antisocial personality disorder.
   b. intern's syndrome.
   c. Axis II disorder.
   d. All of the above.

3. Marta is so fearful of situations such as parties, sporting events, and classrooms that she avoids them at all costs. Marta's behavior best illustrates
   a. antisocial personality disorder.
   b. multiple personality.
   c. simple phobia.
   d. social phobia.

4. Norma has periods of wild energy and enthusiasm. She makes irrational plans that involve spending great amounts of money. Afterward, she "crashes" into an intense depression. What is the best diagnosis for Norma?
   a. paranoid schizophrenia
   b. obsessive-compulsive disorder
   c. delusional disorder
   d. bipolar disorder

5. Bill's thinking is severely impaired. His emotions are uncontrolled and he completely neglects both hygiene and appearance. Of the three forms of schizophrenia, Bill is most likely to be diagnosed with
   a. paranoid schizophrenia.
   b. catatonic schizophrenia.
   c. disorganized schizophrenia.
   d. somatoform schizophrenia.

6. Lana complains of vague back and shoulder aches. She is always saying she is tired and dizzy. Thorough physical examinations show no signs of physical problems. A reasonable diagnosis for Lana's condition is
   a. somatization disorder.
   b. obsessive-compulsive disorder.
   c. delusional disorder.
   d. intern's syndrome.

7. Brenda "woke up" in a small town in Nebraska and began to develop a new identity because she had no memory of her "old self." If the memory loss was psychological, what is the best diagnosis for Brenda?
   a. catatonic schizophrenia
   b. fugue
   c. conversion disorder
   d. multiple personality

8. Dr. Martinez is a psychiatrist who believes that psychological disorders occur because unconscious conflicts generate anxiety *and* because of neurotransmitter imbalances that make coping with this anxiety very difficult. Dr. Martinez's approach to disorder combines
   a. diathesis and stress.
   b. traditional psychodynamic and biological approaches.
   c. traditional psychodynamic and social systems approaches.
   d. diathesis-stress and psychodynamic approaches.

9. Herman is diagnosed as having schizophrenia. When he walks into a room where his mother is seated, she says, "Herman, come over here and give me a hug." But when he tries to hug her, she yells, "Not in public, you silly boy." This incident would illustrate what family systems theorists call
   a. a paranoid delusion.
   b. a loss of positive reinforcement.
   c. a double bind.
   d. a diathesis.

10. Dr. Richmond says, "The diathesis-stress model assumes that a combination of factors causes both psychological and physical disorders. Social factors are the primary source of stress, but biological factors tend to activate the diathesis." Which of the doctor's statements is wrong?
    a. Diathesis-stress assumes a combination of factors is involved.
    b. Both psychological and physical disorders are explained.
    c. Social factors are the primary source of stress.
    d. Biological factors activate the diathesis.

Fact and Concept Answers

1. * b. On Axis IV of the DSM-III-R, diagnosticians indicate whether an environmental stressor such as divorce or job loss occurred. (p. 427)

   a. There are five axes or dimensions to the DSM-III-R.

   c. Psychological disorders are listed on Axis I; personality disorders are on Axis II.

   d. The DSM-III-R is a diagnostic tool; it does not help treat people.

2. * a. In a study of several cities in the United States, alcohol and drug abuse accounted for more than half of all diagnoses. (p. 430)

   b. Anxiety disorders are the second most common disorders.

   c. Schizophrenic disorders are the most serious disorders, but not the most common.

   d. Mood disorders are the third most common disorders.

3. * c. Generalized anxiety disorders, as the name implies, occur in a wide range of situations, unlike simple phobias, which are fear and avoidance responses to specific objects or settings. (p. 432)

   a. Generalized anxiety disorders show anxiety symptoms in a wide range of situations.

   b. Generalized anxiety disorders show anxiety symptoms in a wide range of situations.

   d. Dissociative disorders entail memory loss; generalized anxiety disorders involve intense anxiety and are not easy to cope with.

4. * c. When sudden, unexpected anxiety strikes (a panic attack), people may avoid any public place where it might occur again. When that kind of avoidance is persistent, the diagnosis is agoraphobia. (pp. 432–433)

   a. Multiple personality is unrelated to panic attack.

   b. A delusion is a false belief about the world.

   d. A compulsion is the ritualistic performance of an act to reduce anxiety; antisocial personality disorder involves lying and remorselessness, not avoidance of others.

5. * d. Obsessive-compulsive disorder is diagnosed when a person engages in obsessions such as persistent thinking about germs and compulsions such as repetitive hand washing. (pp. 433–434)

   a. In generalized anxiety disorder, people worry about everything but rarely have any compulsive rituals.

   b. Conversion disorder involves specific movement or sensation impairments without any neurological cause.

   c. In somatization disorder, people show vague physical complaints without any physical cause.

6. * b. In depression, people lose all interest in activities, even ones that used to be highly pleasurable. (p. 435)

   a. Feelings of worthlessness are a central feature of depression.

   c. Lack of energy and slowed movements and thoughts are common in depression.

   d. Depressed people either sleep a great deal or have trouble staying asleep.

7. * d. Suicide attempts are a signal that a person is in great distress; they should be taken seriously. (pp. 435–436)

   a. The majority of people who attempt suicide are unsure they want to die.

   b. As many as 80 percent of depressed persons have considered suicide.

   c. One study showed that 70 percent of people who attempted suicide tried to talk about it.

8. * a. False beliefs, such as thinking that relatives want to poison you, are a common thought disturbance in schizophrenia. (p. 437)

   b. The affective, or mood, disturbances in schizophrenia are flat affect (lack of expression) or inappropriate expression.

   c. Delusions are quite common in schizophrenia.

   d. Because *a* is an accurate response, this cannot be the best choice.

9. * a. People in a catatonic stupor withdraw so completely from others that they stop moving and responding. (p. 439)

   b. A hallucination is a false perception, such as hearing voices that are not there.

   c. Flattened affect has to do with lack of facial response, not lack of movement or speech.

   d. In disorganized schizophrenia, a person shows profound thought disturbance but is not motionless or unresponsive.

10. * b. People with delusional disorders have only a specific false belief as their symptom. Unburdened by the additional disturbances of schizophrenia, they function better. (pp. 439–440)

   a. Ideas of reference is one of the delusions found in delusional disorders.

   c. There are no motor or social disturbances in the delusional disorders, just delusions.

   d. Paranoid schizophrenia develops earlier.

11. * d. Conversion disorders involve loss of movement or sensation even though neurologically everything seems fine. (p. 440)

   a. In conversion disorder, there is no actual tissue damage; many physical illnesses can be related to psychological stress, however.

   b. Memory loss is a symptom of psychogenic amnesia.

    c. Vague physical complaints occur in somatization disorder as opposed to the specific complaints of sensory or motor loss in conversion disorder.

12. * d. Psychogenic amnesia is a rare occurrence and its duration is usually short. (p. 441)

    a. The most common symptom of schizophrenia is thought disturbance, not memory loss.

    b. Only in fugue is there such movement.

    c. It is called "psychogenic" because it is caused by psychological, rather than biological, factors.

13. * c. The first personality is usually timid and unable to be as assertive and protective as the alternate personalities. (pp. 441–442)

    a. Schizophrenia and multiple personality have nothing to do with one another.

    b. Uncontrolled thoughts and actions related to anxiety are signs of obsessive-compulsive disorder.

    d. Movement to a new region after psychogenic amnesia is the central feature of fugue.

14. * c. The antisocial personality uses other people without guilt or sympathy; they are often charming liars. (p. 443)

    a. People with bipolar disorder have uncontrolled mood swings.

    b. Dissociative disorders are characterized by memory impairments caused by psychological stress.

    d. Conversion disorders involve the loss of movement or sensation in a body part in the absence of a neurological cause.

15. * d. Research by Robins and Helzer (1986) shows an 80 percent level of agreement on diagnosis within the sixteen categories of Axis I. (p. 444)

    a. Agreement is more than five times better than this.

    b. Agreement is twice as good as this.

    c. Research shows the agreement level as 80 percent.

16. * b. The social systems approach views disorder as stemming from such systems as the family and the broader community and culture. (p. 446)

    a. A behaviorist approach stresses learning.

    c. The diathesis-stress approach gives equal emphasis to preexisting vulnerabilities (biological or psychological) and individual and social factors that trigger the disorder.

    d. A biological approach stresses internal abnormalities.

17. * a. Poverty is a socioeconomic condition that generates stress and reduces one's ability to cope with it; a diathesis is a predisposing factor such as genetic vulnerability. (pp. 447, 455)

b. Poverty is a social factor, not an individual one.

c. Genetics are predisposing factors; poverty is a social factor that triggers disorder.

d. The diathesis-stress model is equally appropriate for personality, psychological, and physical disorders.

18. * c. The concordance ratio for schizophrenia in identical twins is nearly 50 percent, but only about 15 percent in fraternals. For bipolar disorder, the numbers are 70 and 30 percent. Both are strong evidence for genetic predisposition. (pp. 449–450)

a. This is true, but so is *b*.

b. This is true, but so is *a*.

d. Because both *a* and *b* are true, this cannot be the best choice.

19. * b. Just because a certain factor is effective in treating a disease does not mean that it is implicated in the cause. (p. 453)

a. Schizophrenia is probably caused by multiple factors including genetics, learning, and social factors.

c. Enlarged ventricles are unrelated to neurotransmitter imbalance.

d. On the contrary, it suggests that a dopamine imbalance may be a portion of the diathesis.

20. * a. Depressed people may learn to perform fewer behaviors because of the loss of positive reinforcement; they may give up in situations where they can be effective because of learned helplessness beliefs. (p. 454)

b. Loss of positive reinforcement and learned helplessness are individual factors.

c. These factors are not crucial to schizophrenia.

d. Both of these factors are nonbiological.

Application Answers

1. * d. Your text defines psychological disorder as an uncommon behavior that is irrational or socially unacceptable or that causes distress to the person doing the behavior or others. (p. 426)

a. A personality disorder is a long-lasting pattern of self-defeating action.

b. A formal thought disturbance is the inability to think coherently; associations between thoughts are loose and disconnected.

c. Schizophrenia is a very severe psychological disorder with specific symptoms such as thought disturbance and social isolation.

2. * b. Intern's syndrome occurs when people who are learning about disorders believe incorrectly that they have them. (p. 429)

a. Antisocial personality involves exploitation of others without guilt.

    c. Axis II disorders are personality disorders.

    d. Because *a* and *c* are incorrect, this is not the best choice.

3. * d. In a social phobia, a person is so fearful of social activities that he or she avoids any potentially social situation. (p. 422)

    a. Antisocial personality has to do with exploiting others and lying, not staying away from others.

    b. Multiple personality involves the dissociation of separate personalities.

    c. Simple phobia is diagnosed when fear and avoidance are the response to specific objects such as elevators or snakes.

4. * d. Bipolar disorder gets its name from the swing in moods from one pole (elation and mania) to the other (depression). (p. 434)

    a. Paranoid schizophrenia is a thought disorder marked by paranoid delusions.

    b. Obsessive-compulsive disorder's chief symptoms are persistent, unwanted thoughts and ritualistic actions.

    c. The only symptom of delusional disorders is delusions.

5. * c. Disorganized schizophrenia is diagnosed when there is profound thought disturbance, lack of self-care, and uncontrolled emotions. (p. 439)

    a. Paranoid schizophrenia is characterized by delusions about persecution and grandeur.

    b. Catatonic stupor is the primary symptom in catatonic schizophrenia.

    d. This is a made-up term.

6. * a. In somatization disorder, people complain of vague physical problems for which there is no biological explanation. (p. 440)

    b. In obsessive-compulsive disorder, people have persistent, unwanted thoughts and engage in ritualistic acts to ward off anxiety.

    c. The chief symptom of delusional disorders is a delusion.

    d. Intern's syndrome occurs when people who are learning about disorders come to believe they have them.

7. * b. In fugue, people have psychogenic amnesia and then move to a new region where they adopt a new identity. (p. 441)

    a. Catatonic schizophrenia is marked by thought disturbances and profound motor disturbances.

    c. In conversion, there are specific physical complaints that cannot be explained neurologically.

    d. Multiple personality does not usually involve movement to a new region; one personality "takes over" when life becomes stressful.

8. * b. Dr. Martinez is merging a traditional biological approach (neurotransmitter imbalance) with traditional psychodynamic thinking about the unconscious. (p. 446)

    a. A diathesis-stress approach would explicitly discuss predisposing factors, such as genetics, and current triggering factors, such as stress.

    c. A social systems approach includes family and community life, topics Dr. Martinez does not mention.

    d. Although psychodynamic concepts are presented (the unconscious), the predisposition-and-stress notions of diathesis-stress theory are absent.

9. * c. A double bind is a family communication pattern in which contradictory messages are given. (p. 455)

    a. A paranoid delusion is a false belief that others are out to get you.

    b. Loss of positive reinforcement is more relevant to depression.

    d. A diathesis is a predisposing factor such as genetic vulnerability or neurotransmitter imbalance.

10. * d. Social factors such as stress seem to activate the diathesis; biological factors are more likely to cause the diathesis itself. (p. 454)

    a. Diathesis-stress theory, as the name implies, assumes a combination of factors.

    b. Diathesis-stress is intended to explain both.

    c. Social factors are the primary sources of stress.

CHAPTER 16

TREATMENT OF PSYCHOLOGICAL DISORDERS

Learning Objectives

1. Define and give an example of therapeutic insight. Name the four groups of treatments; define psychotherapy. Discuss whether different treatments can be combined. (pp. 459–461)

2. Discuss the basis of psychoanalysis. Describe and discuss free association, interpretation, resistance, and transference as means of gaining insight. Describe what occurs when a person is working through conflicts. Describe variations on classical psychoanalysis. (pp. 461–464)

3. Discuss the basis of humanistic therapies. Discuss the goals and methods of Rogers's person-centered therapy. Describe the goals of Frankl and Perls's existential therapies. Discuss the advantages of group therapy. (pp. 464–467)

4. Discuss the basis of behavioral therapies. Describe and discuss systematic desensitization and flooding. (pp. 467–469)

5. Describe and discuss the operant techniques of time out, token economy, and punishment. (pp. 469–470)

6. Describe and discuss the cognitive-behavioral techniques of modeling and cognitive restructuring (in the form of Ellis's rational-emotive therapy and Beck's therapy for depression). Discuss how cognitive-behavioral therapies are similar but different from insight-oriented ones. (pp. 470–472)

7. Describe a systems approach. Discuss the basic assumptions of family systems therapies. Explain how family boundaries affect family system functions and produce psychological symptoms. (pp. 473–474)

8. Describe the community mental health movement, including the goals and methods of deinstitutionalization and its aftermath. Discuss why the community mental health movement was unsuccessful. (pp. 474–477)

9. Discuss the value of biological therapies. Describe the major drug treatments and the disorders for which they are typically prescribed, including tranquilizers, antidepressants, lithium, antipsychotic drugs, and the stimulant Ritalin. (pp. 477–480)

10. Describe electroconvulsive therapy (ECT), its appropriate uses and side effects. Discuss prefrontal lobotomy and why it is no longer performed. (pp. 480–482)

11. Describe the problems in evaluating the effectiveness of therapies. Describe a meta-analysis and the general conclusions reached by Smith, Glass, and Miller (1980). Discuss why all therapies appear to be equal in effectiveness. (pp. 483–485)

12. Describe the five main types of mental health professionals. Discuss what one should look for in a therapist. Discuss the ethical considerations in using biological treatments against a client's will. Discuss the ethics and role of the legal system in involuntary treatment. (pp. 486–489)

Chapter Outline

1. **The techniques and variety of therapy** (pp. 460–461)

   Some therapies rely on therapeutic insight, the recognition and understanding of unconscious thoughts and feelings, to help people to change. There are four groups of treatments: insight-oriented and behavioral therapies (which compose the two main forms of *psychotherapy*), and systems approaches and biological therapies. Treatments are not rivals; they can and are used in combination.

2. **Insight-oriented therapies** (pp. 461–467)

   Insight-oriented therapies emphasize self-understanding. Therapies based on Freud's ideas about intrapsychic conflict are called *psychodynamic therapies*. Freud's original therapy is called *psychoanalysis*. It involves two steps: helping clients gain insight and working through conflicts.

   Clients gain insight through saying whatever comes to mind (*free association*) and receiving *interpretations* from the analyst. When clients evade insight by showing *resistance*, additional clues to unconscious impulses are revealed. Additional information is provided when clients play out unresolved conflicts with the analyst in a process called *transference*. Once insight is gained, behavior change occurs in the process called "working through the conflicts." Other psychoanalytic theorists have modified psychoanalysis, and modern treatment is briefer than classical psychoanalysis.

Humanistic therapies give greater importance to the client's responsibility and control. In Carl Rogers's person-centered therapy, the tendency to actualize is strengthened as the self and self-concept are brought into congruence. Therapists assist this process by providing unconditional positive regard, genuineness, and accurate empathy through the reflection of feelings. Existential therapies emphasize personal meaning and personal awareness and include those developed by Viktor Frankl and Fritz Perls.

Both psychodynamic and humanistic therapies have been adapted for groups. Group therapy is different from systems approaches because it regards the individual as an independent unit, not part of a system. Groups have the advantages of providing more help and increasing feedback from others.

3. **Behavioral therapies** (pp. 467–473)

Behavioral therapies are based on classical and operant conditioning as well as on cognitive-behavioral principles. Behavioral therapists consider symptoms to be learned behaviors that can be modified using learning theory. Anxiety disorders can be treated using therapies based on classical conditioning. In one, *systematic desensitization*, the client and therapist construct a hierarchy of feared situations. Afterward, the client learns how to relax and then pairs relaxation with scenes imagined from the hierarchy of fears. In the other, *flooding*, clients image or actually visit the most terrifying scenes of anxiety and, after repeated presentation, see their fear subside.

Operant techniques include *time out*, in which the person is prevented from receiving reinforcement, and *token economies*, in which behaviors are rewarded with tokens that can be exchanged for privileges. Punishment, a rarely used behavioral technique, can weaken a response.

Cognitive-behavioral therapies have become quite popular. *Modeling*, the strengthening or weakening of a response by demonstration, has been used to reduce fears and to teach social skills. Cognitive restructuring alters the way people think. In Ellis's rational-emotive therapy, clients' irrational beliefs are attacked. Aaron Beck's treatment of depression also focuses on self-talk. With the inclusion of thoughts in cognitive-behavioral therapies, the distinctions between behavioral and insight-oriented therapies have begun to blur. Cognitive-behavior approaches, however, focus on current problems and rely on research evidence for their underpinnings.

4. **Systems approaches** (pp. 472–477)

Systems approaches emphasize the impact of the groups to which we belong, our systems, on individual behavior. A most important group is the *family system*, the people, relationships, and expectations that constitute a family. Rather than focusing on the problems of an individual, family systems therapists examine the purpose one member's symptoms serve for the family as a whole. Basic assumptions in this approach are: the interrelatedness of the family parts, the inability to understand one person in isolation from the family, the need to understand the entire family's functioning, that family structure affects behavior, and that patterns of interaction shape behavior. Salvador Minuchin's structural family therapy stresses the need for boundaries that leave members neither disengaged from nor enmeshed with one another.

The community mental health movement also works with larger structures than individuals, in this case, communities. In an effort to reduce suffering in mental hospitals, the movement urged *deinstitutionalization* in the 1960s and 1970s. Federally funded mental health centers were to expand services provided and reduce the need for prolonged mental hospitalization. Inpatient numbers were drastically reduced, but deinstitutionalized patients failed to get adequate postdischarge help because insufficient resources were committed to their care.

5. **Biological approaches** (pp. 477–483)

Biological treatments are not "cures," nor have the reasons they may influence behavior been clearly explained. However, one method, drug treatment, is the most common form of treating psychological disorders. *Tranquilizers* such as Valium and Librium are anti-anxiety drugs; they are prescribed for anxiety symptoms but have addicting properties. Depression can be treated with *antidepressants* such as MAO inhibitors and tricyclics. These drugs have side effects, too, particularly MAO inhibitors when certain foods are eaten. Lithium is a drug that is frequently effective in the treatment of bipolar disorder. *Antipsychotic drugs* are effective in treating the symptoms of schizophrenia but have side effects including tardive dyskinesia. Ritalin, a stimulant, has been used to treat attention-deficit hyperactivity disorder.

In *electroconvulsive therapy* (ECT), a brief electric current causes a seizure. This is an effective treatment for severe depression, but the reasons for its effectiveness are unknown. The most serious side effects of ECT are memory impairments. Surgery on the brain to change behavior, *psychosurgery*, was once commonly performed in the form of prefrontal lobotomy.

6. **Evaluation of therapies** (pp. 483–486)

Insight-oriented therapies are frequently used for anxiety, somatoform, and dissociative disorders. Behavioral therapies are particularly effective with anxiety disorders; cognitive-behavior therapies have been designed with chronic depression in mind. Family systems therapies are often used to treat eating disorders and adjustment problems. Drug treatments may be more effective with schizophrenia than psychotherapy or systems approaches.

It is difficult to evaluate therapies because clinicians differ in identifying criteria for success. Eysenck's early attacks on therapy effectiveness have largely been reversed. *Meta-analysis*, a statistical technique that pools the results of many studies, has shown that people receiving psychotherapy are helped more than those who are not, regardless of the type of psychotherapy. There seem to be no differences in effectiveness between drug and psychotherapy and between therapies of different lengths. The "active ingredient" of successful treatment appears to be the therapist's support.

7. **Finding a therapist** (pp. 486–487)

With one in five Americans having a diagnosable disorder, it is likely that many people will seek out a therapist. The five major categories of mental health professionals—psychiatrists, clinical psychologists, social workers, counselors, and psychiatric nurses—have different training backgrounds and may have different focuses in treatment. When therapist and client are compatible, regardless of ethnic or gender similarity, the chances of success increase.

8. **Ethics (pp. 487–489)**

It is wise to remember that Benjamin Rush thought he was serving his patients when he took what we now see as unethical and ineffective actions. Consent for treatment is a thorny ethical issue that crops up with schizophrenic patients. Involuntary treatment is preceded by the legal procedure of civil commitment.

Fill-in-the-Blank Quiz

1. The client's projection of unresolved conflicts onto his or her relationship with the psychoanalyst is called _____ .

2. The two-part behavioral therapy developed by Joseph Wolpe and based on classical conditioning that is used to treat phobias is called _____ .

3. The recognition of underlying conflicts thoughts and feelings is called _____ .

4. In behavioral therapy, the demonstration of behavior and its consequences either to strengthen a desired or to weaken an unwanted response is called _____ .

5. The people, relationships, expectations, and traditions that constitute a family are called a(n) _____ .

6. Medications including the benzodiazepines that are used to alleviate anxiety symptoms are called _____ .

7. Any primarily verbal system for treating psychological disorders that focuses on an individual's thoughts, feelings, and behaviors is called a(n) _____ .

8. The statistical technique that combines the results of many studies to form a single set of conclusions is called _____ .

9. The medications, including MAO inhibitors and tricyclics, used to treat chronic depression are called _____ .

10. In psychoanalysis, the explanation a therapist gives a patient to help the patient understand his or her own feelings is called a(n) _____ .

11. In behavioral therapy, the prevention of reinforcement by removing an individual from the social situation after he or she makes an unwanted response is called _____ .

12. The community mental health practice of releasing mental patients from large hospitals to transitional facilities in order to reintegrate them in the community is called _____ .

13. A therapy based on the idea that symptoms of disorders can be alleviated by resolving intrapsychic conflicts is called a(n) _____ .

14. The medication, made from a mineral salt, that is highly successful in treating bipolar disorder is called _____ .

15. The behavioral therapy that has clients imagine being in their most terrifying situation or places them there so their fear can diminish is called _____ .

16. In psychoanalysis, the process of saying whatever comes to mind is called _____ .

17. The treatment that uses electric current to produce a kind of seizure and that alleviates some of the symptoms of chronic depression is called _____ .

18. In psychoanalysis, the client's evasion of insight when it is close at hand is called _____ .

19. The treatment method developed by Freud of having patients achieve insight into and working through their intrapsychic conflicts is called _____ .

20. The group of medications that reduce or stop many of the symptoms of schizophrenia is called _____ .

21. An operation performed on the brain to alter a patient's behavior or experience is called _____ .

Fill-in-the-Blank Answers

1. transference
2. systematic desensitization
3. therapeutic insight
4. modeling
5. family system
6. tranquilizers
7. psychotherapy
8. meta-analysis
9. antidepressants
10. interpretation
11. time out
12. deinstitutionalization
13. psychodynamic therapy
14. lithium
15. flooding
16. free association
17. electroconvulsive therapy (ECT)
18. resistance
19. psychoanalysis
20. antipsychotic drugs
21. psychosurgery

Fact and Concept Questions

1. What is the chief characteristic of all the forms of psychotherapy?
   a. They use talking as the primary method of helping.
   b. They focus on the family or larger groups.
   c. They help by changing the biology of the person in need.
   d. They require the individual to develop insight into his or her problems.

2. Sigmund Freud developed a form of treatment he called _____, which is one form of _____ therapy.
   a. meta-analysis; insight-oriented
   b. psychoanalysis; humanistic
   c. person-centered; insight-oriented
   d. psychoanalysis; psychodynamic

3. In psychoanalysis, when a patient engages in free association,
   a. he or she is projecting unconscious impulses onto the relationship with the therapist.
   b. the therapist tries to stop this because it interferes with therapy.
   c. he or she says everything that comes to mind.
   d. the therapist projects his or her unconscious impulses onto the relationship with the patient.

4. Resistance and transference are
   a. steps in working through the conflicts.
   b. sources of information that help clients gain insight.
   c. elements of psychoanalysis that therapists try to avoid or reduce.
   d. components of psychoanalysis developed by Jung and Adler.

5. According to Rogers, three elements must be present in the therapist-client relationship for therapy to be successful. One is unconditional positive regard. What are the other two?
   a. modeling and reinforcement
   b. genuineness and accurate empathy
   c. accurate interpretation and transference
   d. awareness of self as integrated and personal meaning

6. Viktor Frankl and Fritz Perls were therapists who took a(n) _____ approach to treatment.
   a. family systems
   b. operant
   c. psychodynamic
   d. existential

7. Behavioral therapists believe that psychological symptoms
   a. are signs of underlying conflicts.
   b. are caused by biological abnormalities.
   c. can be changed using the principles of learning.
   d. must be understood in the context of the family.

8. In what form of therapy is a hierarchy of feared situations paired with relaxation so that anxiety is reduced?
   a. systematic desensitization
   b. token economy
   c. classical psychoanalysis
   d. cognitive restructuring

9. Which treatment is most likely to be found in mental hospitals, where it is important to increase the frequency of self-care behaviors such as feeding and using the toilet?
   a. systematic desensitization
   b. flooding
   c. token economy
   d. time out

10. Which of the following is a cognitive-behavioral form of treatment?
    a. punishment
    b. modeling
    c. time out
    d. flooding

11. One difference between rational-emotive therapy and token economies is that rational-emotive therapy
    a. is an insight-oriented treatment.
    b. emphasizes the client's thinking.
    c. is done in groups.
    d. assumes that people think rationally.

12. If a therapist sees a child's bedwetting as a symptom that keeps mother and father from having arguments over sex, the therapist probably takes a _____ approach to treatment.
    a. family systems
    b. behavioral
    c. cognitive restructuring
    d. biological

13. Which statement about Salvador Minuchin's structural family therapy is accurate?
    a. It seeks to change the individual rather than the family.
    b. It assumes that families have irrational beliefs that must be attacked and changed.
    c. It argues that families have unconscious impulses and conflicts, just as individuals do.
    d. It tries to establish clearly defined and healthy boundaries for family members.

14. Deinstitutionalization was successful in that it
    a. reduced the number of homeless people in the United States.
    b. increased the number of people who were involuntarily committed to hospitals.
    c. successfully reintegrated discharged patients into the community.
    d. dramatically reduced the number of people in mental hospitals.

15. The most common form of treatment for all psychological disorders is
    a. insight-oriented psychotherapy.
    b. electroconvulsive therapy (ECT).
    c. drug treatment.
    d. behavioral therapy.

16. For which form of drug treatment must a patient be very careful not to eat cheese or other aged foods or drink wine?
    a. antipsychotic drugs such as chlorpromazine
    b. antianxiety drugs such as Valium
    c. antidepressant drugs called MAO inhibitors
    d. stimulant drugs called Ritalin

17. A person who develops tardive dyskinesia has probably been taking _____ drugs.
    a. illegal
    b. antipsychotic
    c. antianxiety
    d. antimanic

18. Some of the _____ therapies were designed especially for treating chronic depression.
    a. cognitive-behavioral
    b. family systems
    c. community mental health
    d. psychodynamic

19. The results of Smith, Glass, and Miller's (1980) meta-analysis of therapy effectiveness show that
    a. psychotherapy is effective.
    b. insight-oriented therapies are more effective than behavioral therapies.
    c. psychotherapy is more effective than drug therapies.
    d. the longer one is in therapy, the better the outcome.

20. Research indicates that success in therapy is based on
    a. how many years of training the therapist had before receiving a professional degree.
    b. the match between the client's gender and ethnicity and that of the therapist.
    c. how compatible the client is with the therapist.
    d. the degree to which the therapy emphasizes insight.

Application Questions

1. Hannah sees her therapist five times a week. She describes her dreams and allows herself to say anything that comes to mind. Hannah is a patient in what form of therapy?
   a. person-centered psychotherapy
   b. cognitive restructuring
   c. classical psychoanalysis
   d. meta-analysis

2. George has developed therapeutic insight into his symptoms and problems. If he continues in psychodynamic therapy we can expect that
   a. he will use this understanding to work through his conflicts.
   b. he will develop unconditional positive regard for his therapist.
   c. his therapist will use modeling to show him appropriate behaviors.
   d. None of the above.

3. Dr. Quinn says, "Individuals are not controlled by unconscious forces or the outside environment. People have the capacity to solve their own problems because every person is ultimately responsible for his or her behavior." Dr. Quinn most agrees with the _____ approach to treatment.
   a. psychodynamic
   b. behavioral
   c. family systems
   d. humanistic

4. Client: "I am so tired and lonely. I feel like no one is out there for me."
   Therapist: "You feel tired and separate from others, almost like there is no one to provide support."
   This exchange best illustrates _____ therapy.
   a. social skills training
   b. person-centered
   c. structured family
   d. Gestalt

5. Norm is terribly frightened of public speaking. His therapist has him imagine giving a speech in front of thousands of people so that he can feel the intense anxiety this situation provokes. Over time Norm's fear diminishes. What therapy is being described?
   a. flooding
   b. punishment
   c. systematic desensitization
   d. time out

6. Laura's therapist believes that psychological disorders are the result of irrational beliefs. Her therapist challenges her foolish beliefs and points out how they cause her to act in self-defeating ways. Laura's therapist is probably
   a. an insight-oriented therapist
   b. a family systems therapist
   c. an operant conditioning therapist
   d. a rational-emotive therapist

7. Dr. Elsworth says, "The idea was correct: we needed to increase the connections between people and their home community. A lack of federal funding reduced its effectiveness, not a lack of thinking." What is Dr. Elsworth referring to?
   a. prefrontal lobotomies
   b. family systems therapy
   c. the community mental health movement
   d. civil commitment of psychotic patients

8. Dr. McGill says, "I will prescribe them for people going through short-term crises. They are effective for reducing nervousness, but the potential for addiction is too great to allow continued use." What medications are being discussed?
   a. antipsychotic drugs
   b. antianxiety drugs
   c. antidepressant drugs
   d. stimulants

9. Dr. Stanski is a clinical psychologist. Which of the following is undoubtedly untrue of Dr. Stanski?
   a. She has either a Ph.D. or a Psy.D.
   b. She got her graduate degree after four or five years.
   c. She was trained to do diagnostic work as well as therapy.
   d. She can perform ECT.

10. A psychologist says, "Civil commitment is a legal procedure that makes it happen less often. But the ethics are complex: many people needing help don't get it and wind up homeless." What is the psychologist talking about?
    a. informed consent for family systems therapy
    b. involuntary treatment for schizophrenics
    c. deinstitutionalization
    d. cognitive restructuring for schizophrenics

Fact and Concept Answers

1. * a. All forms of psychotherapy use talking as the primary means of increasing understanding and behavior change. (p. 460)

   b. Only systems-oriented therapies focus on the family or other groups in which individuals are embedded.

    c. Biological approaches focus on biology.

    d. Insight-oriented psychotherapies do emphasize insight, but they are only one portion of a large category called psychotherapy.

2. * d. Freud developed classical psychoanalysis, in which the intrapsychic conflicts of individuals are made conscious; psychoanalysis was the first form of psychodynamic therapy. (p. 461)

    a. Meta-analysis is a statistical technique for combining the results of many studies.

    b. Freud had a psychodynamic theory, not a humanistic one.

    c. Rogers was responsible for person-centered therapy.

3. * c. The psychoanalytic technique of free association asks the individual to say whatever comes to mind as a way of relaxing the censor on normally suppressed thoughts. (p. 462)

    a. Transference is the term used when patients project their past experiences and impulses on the therapist.

    b. Psychoanalysts encourage free association so they can gain more information about the patient.

    d. Although not covered in the text, this phenomenon occurs. Psychoanalysts call it countertransference, not free association.

4. * b. When and how patients resist insight and the ways they project conflicts onto the therapist are both sources of information used to gain insight. (p. 462)

    a. Resistance and transference are part of gaining insight, not working through the conflicts.

    c. Psychoanalysts encourage transference and accept the inevitability of resistance.

    d. Freud is responsible for both concepts; Jung and Adler developed the ideas of archetype and inferiority complex.

5. * b. Rogers said that the necessary conditions for success in treatment was a therapist-client relationship based on unconditional positive regard, genuineness, and accurate empathy. (pp. 464–465)

    a. Modeling and reinforcement are behavioral concepts.

    c. Interpretation and transference are psychodynamic concepts.

    d. Awareness of an integrated self is a Gestalt concept; personal meaning is central to Frankl's therapy.

6. * d. Frankl and Perls were existential therapists. (pp. 465–466)

    a. The only family systems therapist noted in the text is Salvador Minuchin.

    b. Neither Frankl nor Perls would accept the idea that reinforcement causes behavior.

    c. Neither Frankl nor Perls emphasized the need for unconscious impulses to be brought to the surface.

7. * c. Behavioral therapies make use of learning principles and assume that symptoms are behaviors that were learned inappropriately. (p. 467)

    a. Behavioral therapists differ with psychodynamic therapists because they do not see symptoms as signs of underlying conflicts.

    b. Biological approaches stress this.

    d. Family systems therapists see symptoms as coming from family structures or traditions.

8. * a. Systematic desensitization is a two-part therapy in which a hierarchy of fears is developed, followed by the pairing of relaxation with each fearful situation (least fear-inducing first). (p. 468)

    b. In token economy, tokens or points are awarded for desirable behavior and are later exchanged for privileges.

    c. Classical psychoanalysis uses insight rather than relaxation or any other behavioral technique.

    d. Cognitive restructuring focuses on one's thinking.

9. * c. In a token economy, desirable behaviors are rewarded with points or tokens that are later exchanged for privileges; this requires the kind of structured environment one finds in a mental hospital. (p. 470)

    a. Systematic desensitization is useful in anxiety disorders and uses relaxation skills.

    b. Flooding is a classical conditioning method that repeatedly presents a fear-inducing situation until the fear diminishes.

    d. Time out involves removing a person from reinforcement so that an undesirable behavior is weakened.

10. * b. Modeling requires the observation of behavior and memory for it; it is a form of cognitive-behavioral treatment. (p. 471)

    a. Punishment is an operant technique requiring no cognitions.

    c. Time out is an operant technique requiring no cognitions.

    d. Flooding is a classical conditioning technique rather than a cognitive-behavioral one.

11. * b. Rational-emotive therapy challenges the irrational beliefs of clients, whereas token economies deal with observable behavior only. (p. 471)

    a. Rational-emotive therapy does not require the kind of self-understanding that is characteristic of insight therapies.

    c. Rational-emotive therapy is usually an individual form of treatment.

    d. Rational-emotive therapy assumes that patients think irrationally and that the goal of therapy is greater rationality.

12. * a. Family systems therapists see one person's symptoms as influenced by other relationships in the family. (p. 473)

    b. Behavioral treatment looks at the current reinforcers that maintain a symptom.

    c. Cognitive restructuring alters the way one thinks about one's own behavior and that of others.

    d. Biological treatments seek to change behavior by altering the chemistry or structure of the brain.

13. * d. Family boundaries that are either enmeshed or disengaged are unhealthy, according to structural family therapy's founder, Salvador Minuchin. (p. 474)

    a. All family systems therapists seek to change family patterns so that individuals can improve.

    b. Irrational beliefs are the central theme of rational-emotive therapy.

    c. Unconscious impulses are important in psychodynamic therapies.

14. * d. Deinstitutionalization more than reached its goal of halving the number of psychiatric inpatients: from 469,000 in 1969 to 211,000 in 1981. (p. 475)

    a. Discharged patients who have not been cared for in the community have become part of the large number of homeless people in the United States.

    b. Deinstitutionalization sought to reduce the number of people in hospitals, whether they were there voluntarily or not.

    c. Deinstitutionalization failed to reintegrate former patients into the community.

15. * c. Drug treatment is more often used than any other treatment method. (p. 478)

    a. Insight-oriented therapy is not as common as drug treatment.

    b. ECT is not a common treatment at all.

    d. Behavioral therapy is not as common as drug treatment.

16. * c. If people taking MAO inhibitors eat cheese or drink wine, they can suffer a fatal drop in blood pressure. (p. 479)

    a. Although chlorpromazine has serious side effects, none of them involves food interactions.

    b. Although people can become addicted to Valium, this effect has no relation to a food interaction.

    d. Stimulants do not have any food interaction effects.

17. * b. Antipsychotic drugs such as chlorpromazine can produce tardive dyskinesia if given over a long period of time. (p. 480)

    a. Illegal drugs cannot produce tardive dyskinesia.

    c. Antianxiety drugs cannot produce tardive dyskinesia.

    d. Antimanic drugs such as lithium do not produce tardive dyskinesia.

18. * a. Aaron Beck's form of cognitive restructuring was specifically designed as a treatment for depression. (p. 483)

      b. Family systems therapies may be designed with psychosomatic and eating disorders in mind, but not depression.

      c. Community mental health was not targeted at a specific disorder when it was formulated.

      d. Psychodynamic therapy is intended for all nonpsychotic conditions.

19. * a. Meta-analysis as developed by Smith et al. showed that therapy is effective, but that different forms of treatment are all equivalent in their effectiveness. (pp. 483–484)

      b. There was no difference in the effectiveness of one therapy over another.

      c. Psychotherapy and drug treatment were found to be equally effective.

      d. Length of time in treatment proved to have no effect on success.

20. * c. Studies show that therapist-client compatibility is the key to success. (p. 486)

      a. Amount of training is not related to success.

      b. Gender and ethnicity need not be matched.

      d. Type of therapy is unrelated to success.

Application Answers

1. * c. In classical psychoanalysis, the patient sees the therapist five or six times per week and gains insight by reporting dreams and free associating. (p. 462)

      a. In person-centered psychotherapy, the therapist reflects the feelings of the client.

      b. In cognitive restructuring, the therapist actively counters the patient's way of thinking.

      d. Meta-analysis is a statistical technique, not a form of therapy.

2. * a. After gaining insight, the psychoanalytic client works through conflicts by using those insights to change behavior. (p. 462)

      b. Unconditional positive regard is a concept associated with person-centered therapy.

      c. Modeling is associated with cognitive-behavior therapies.

      d. Because *a* is an accurate answer, this cannot be the best choice.

3. * d. Humanistic therapists consider their clients capable of making responsible decisions; they stress the need to recognize the integrity and wholeness of the person. (p. 464)

      a. Psychodynamic therapists believe that unconscious forces do control their patients.

b. Behavioral therapists believe that environmental forces strongly influence their clients.

c. Family systems therapists emphasize the power of family relationships over individuals.

4. * b. This sounds like a fragment of person-centered therapy because the therapist is reflecting the feelings of the client and providing little if any guidance. (p. 465)

a. In social skills training, the therapist would actively show the client new ways of behaving.

c. In structured family therapy, the therapist would point out unhealthy relationships in the family.

d. Gestalt therapists would emphasize the unity of the person having these feelings.

5. * a. In flooding, a person either imagines or actually experiences what he or she most fears so that, after repeated exposures, the fear diminishes. (p. 469)

b. Punishment is an operant process by which undesired behavior is weakened by supplying some negative consequence.

c. In systematic desensitization, the least feared situation would be paired with relaxation.

d. Time out means removal from social reinforcement.

6. * d. A rational-emotive therapist attacks irrational beliefs and pushes the client to think rationally so that self-defeating behaviors diminish. (p. 471)

a. Insight-oriented therapists presume that self-understanding comes from within the client and cannot be obtained through the therapist's efforts to change beliefs.

b. Family systems therapists emphasize family interactions.

c. Operant conditioning focuses on observable behaviors and consequences, not irrational beliefs.

7. * c. The community mental health movement had the goals of reducing the psychiatric inpatient population while integrating troubled people in the community; a lack of monetary resources (among other reasons) impeded its attainment of the second goal. (pp. 474–475)

a. Prefrontal lobotomies were popular operations before psychoactive drugs came on the market.

b. Family systems therapy is unrelated to federal funding and community integration.

d. The aim of deinstitutionalization was exactly the opposite; it sought to reduce involuntary hospitalizations.

8. * b. Antianxiety drugs have considerable addiction potential when used over a period of time. (p. 479)

a. Antipsychotic drugs are not known to be addicting.

    c. Antidepressant drugs are not known to be addicting.

    d. Stimulants may be addicting, but they certainly do not reduce nervousness.

9. * d. Only psychiatrists, who have medical degrees, can perform electroconvulsive therapy (ECT), a biological form of treatment. (p. 480)

    a. Clinical psychologists have either a Ph.D. or a Psy.D. degree.

    b. Clinical psychologists usually require four or five years (or more) to receive their graduate degree.

    c. Clinical psychologists are trained in diagnostics as well as the major forms of therapy.

10. * b. Treating schizophrenics (or others) against their will requires a legal proceeding called civil commitment. (p. 489)

    a. Informed consent for most nonbiological forms of therapy involves nonpsychotic individuals who will not need civil commitment.

    c. Deinstitutionalization sought to reduce hospitalizations, voluntary and involuntary.

    d. Cognitive restructuring cannot be done against the will of the patient.

CHAPTER 17

RELATIONS BETWEEN INDIVIDUALS

Learning Objectives

1. Define social psychology. Define attribution theory and describe how we use Kelley's three dimensions of consistency, distinctiveness, and consensus to explain the behavior of other people. Discuss how self-attributions work. (pp. 491–494)

2. Describe and discuss the fundamental attribution error and why it occurs. Discuss how and why actor and observer attributions differ. Discuss self-serving bias and the dangers of first impressions. (pp. 494–497)

3. Discuss how impressions are organized into person schemas. Describe how the balance principle helps people organize conflicting impressions. Discuss when we use stereotypes and the role of physical attractiveness in person perception. (pp. 498–500)

4. Discuss how first impressions bias the ways in which we interpret later information and influence others' behavior. (pp. 500–502)

5. Explain how nearness (propinquity), similarity, and reciprocity influence whom we like. Discuss the order in which these factors affect liking. Define and distinguish between passionate and companionate love. (pp. 503–506)

6. Define prejudice and discuss its social-motivational origins. Discuss how ingroup-outgroup differences foster prejudice. Describe the just-world phenomenon and how it influences prejudice. (pp. 507–509)

7. Describe Sherif and colleagues' study to reduce prejudice and competition. Discuss the jigsaw classroom method of combating prejudice. (pp. 509–510)

8. Define attitudes. Discuss the circumstances when attitudes are good predictors of behavior. Describe cognitive dissonance theory and how behaviors produce attitude change. (pp. 511–514)

9. Describe self-perception theory and differentiate it from cognitive dissonance theory. Discuss the evidence for both ideas. (pp. 514–515)

10. Differentiate persuasion that involves a central route from one that uses a peripheral route. Describe audience, message, and communicator effects on the persuasion process, and which effects are central and which are peripheral. Distinguish between the foot-in-the-door and the door-in-the-face techniques. (pp. 515–517)

11. Define aggression. Review the evidence that aggression is innate. Discuss evidence that aggression is learned through direct experience or exposure to aggressive models. Discuss the role of the environment in aggressive behavior. (pp. 518–520)

12. Define altruism and discuss such explanations as social pressure, empathy, and the "selfish gene." Discuss the factors in the environment that increase helping in everyday situations. Describe the factors that influence helping in an emergency. Discuss the problems of reproducing real-life situations in the social psychology laboratory. (pp. 520–524)

Chapter Outline

1. **Social psychology and interpersonal perception** (pp. 491–503)

   Social psychology is the scientific study of how people think, feel, and act in relation to other people. One important area of social psychology examines how we form impressions of other people. *Attribution theory* involves explaining others' behaviors in terms of properties either within or outside the individual. In Harold Kelley's attribution theory, behavior is examined according to consistency, consensus, and distinctiveness. For behavior to be explained as coming from within the person (a trait) it must be consistent, low in consensus (others do not do it), and low in distinctiveness (the individual does it in other situations). We also explain our own behavior through self-attributions.

   In the absence of complete information, we often make biased attributions. The most common error is the *fundamental attribution error*, the tendency to underestimate the role of the situation in determining behavior. This error occurs because we focus our attention on people rather than other factors; we automatically attribute behavior to traits and only afterwards look to see if situational factors could change this explanation. As actors, we see our behavior as situationally determined, but as observers we think there are trait explanations. A related issue is *self-serving bias,* the attribution of our successes to our ability or effort but the attribution of our failures to situational pressures.

   Impressions of others are organized into *person schemas*, systems of ideas about people's attributes that help us understand behavior and remember experiences. Heider suggested that the *balance principle* (good things belong with other good things) helps people resolve inconsistencies in schemas. Preconceived generalizations about the traits of people in a social group are called *stereotypes*. Stereotypes are usually negative and are used when we are not thinking carefully about individuals. They may simplify complex impressions, but they lead to errors in memory. Physical attractiveness leads to stereotypes that are usually positive: we think that what is beautiful is good.

First impressions influence later information. They can make changes in impressions more difficult because all contradictory information is screened through them. First impressions also affect the behavior of the person with whom one interacts. They create self-fulfilling prophesies.

2. **Interpersonal attraction** (pp. 503–506)

We tend to like and become friends with others who are physically near us (propinquity). This may be because we like anything that is familiar, although there are limits to this idea. We tend to become friends with people who are similar to ourselves, another example of the balance principle at work. Finally, we tend to like others because of *reciprocity:* we like people who like us. Although propinquity may start a relationship, it is similarity and reciprocity that maintain it.

Romantic love seems to have two components: *passionate love* (the intense emotional condition where even the thought of the loved one produces arousal) and *companionate love* (intense liking based on two people's similarities). Passionate love may help people become intimate so that they will explore their similarities.

3. **Prejudice** (pp. 507–511)

Prejudice is a strong negative belief about another person based solely on that individual's membership in a social or other group. Prejudice may arise out of the need to blame some group for difficulties (a scapegoat) or a need to maintain one's status at someone else's expense. The tendency to form *ingroups* and *outgroups* tends to exaggerate group differences and fosters prejudice. This is another expression of the balance principle: we assume that our membership in a good ingroup makes the outgroup bad. Another process that contributes to prejudice is the *just-world phenomenon*, the belief that bad things happen only to bad people. This view makes it easy for us to blame victims and see the powerless as deserving their misfortune.

To combat prejudice, social contact between groups is not enough. We must undercut negative stereotypes by having different groups work collaboratively. Aronson's jigsaw classroom technique, for example, helps children work toward shared goals.

4. **Attitudes and persuasion** (pp. 511–518)

An *attitude* is a feeling of liking or disliking that involves the way people think about and behave toward an object. The ability to predict our behavior on the basis of our attitudes is increased when we appreciate whether an attitude is considered socially appropriate, when our action is clearly linked to an attitude, when practical factors do not interfere, and when we think about the attitude at the time we act.

Behaviors can alter attitudes. *Cognitive dissonance* theory argues that people feel uncomfortable when their attitudes and actions are inconsistent. The discomfort produces attitude change. Festinger and Carlsmith's study (and nearly a thousand studies conducted afterwards) showed that when people are induced to act in ways contradictory to their attitudes, they tend to change their attitudes. Daryl Bem's *self-perception theory* explains this attitude change in terms of the attributions we use when observing our own actions. If we act as though we believe in A, we interpret ourselves as believing in A. In some cases, cognitive dissonance theory, which involves remembering past attitude positions, is supported by evidence; in others, self-perception theory's simpler formulation is supported.

Attitudes can be changed through messages—the process of *persuasion*. Persuasion may occur through a central route (when we consciously process information about the message and the communicator) or a more peripheral route (when we don't pay such close attention to the process). If the audience has a need for cognition—a desire to think about problem solving—it will tend to process persuasive messages through the central route. Two-sided messages are persuasive when the audience is intelligent and initially opposed to your position. Emotional appeals can work if they generate strong arousal and are followed by information about how to avoid feared outcomes. Persuasive communicators are expert, attractive, and credible. Whether the arena is politics or advertising, central factors in persuasion are the quality of the argument and the credibility of the communicator; all the rest are peripheral factors.

Manipulation can also change attitudes. Two manipulation tactics are the foot-in-the-door technique (a small request is followed by a larger one) and the door-in-the-face technique (a large request is followed by a smaller one you are likely to agree to).

5. Aggression (pp. 519–520)

Behavior that is intended to hurt another person is considered *aggression*. Freud believed that aggression is an innate drive that builds up unless it is relieved through *catharsis*. Konrad Lorenz also saw aggression as a biologically based behavior to defend territory and preserve resources. Considerable indirect evidence links aggression to genetics and biochemistry.

Aggression is learned through direct experience and models of aggression. Exposure to violent pornography, for example, increases men's acceptance of rape myths. Such environmental factors as temperature, overcrowding, and economic hard times also influence aggressiveness.

6. Altruism and helping (pp. 520–525)

Altruism is helping another person without the expectation that one will be rewarded. People may be motivated to perform acts of altruism because societies disapprove of not helping or because they wish to avoid negative feelings. Empathy is associated with helping. Ethologists argue that helping stems from a species instinct to preserve genes, the so-called selfish gene concept.

Helping in everyday situations is increased by situational factors such as models for helping and positive mood. Diffusion of responsibility reduces helping in an emergency: as the number of potential helpers increases, the *bystander effect* occurs and individual acts of helping become less likely.

Social psychological research has the difficult task of trying to match in the laboratory the complexity of real-life situations. It also takes theories worked out in the laboratory and tests them in the real world.

Among the steps involved in helping in an emergency is recognizing that an emergency exists. The presence of others influences this recognition process.

Fill-in-the-Blank Quiz

1. Behavior that is intended to hurt another person is called _____ .

2. An organized system of ideas about a person's attributes is called a(n) _____ .

3. Helping another without any expectation of a reward is called _____ .

4. The theory that people come to know their own attitudes by unconsciously observing and interpreting their behavior and the situation in which it occurs is called _____ .

5. The form of romantic love that is based on lovers' similarities is called _____ .

6. Any group to which an individual belongs is called a(n) _____ .

7. A theory of how people understand the behaviors of others by ascribing those behaviors to properties of the individuals or the situation is called a(n) _____ .

8. The tendency to attribute successful behaviors to oneself and unsuccessful behaviors to situational pressures is called _____ .

9. The phenomenon of decreased helping when the number of potential helpers increases is called the _____ .

10. A generalization about the traits of people in a social group is called a(n) _____ .

11. Attempts to change someone's attitudes or beliefs through verbal messages are called _____ .

12. The intense form of romantic love in which the presence or even the thought of the loved one produces physiological arousal is called _____ .

13. A feeling of liking or disliking that involves the way people think about and behave toward the object of their feeling is called a(n) _____ .

14. The tendency to underestimate the role of the situation in determining behavior is called the _____ .

15. The concept that organizes impressions of people and events by assuming that good things belong with other good things and bad things with other bad things is called the _____ .

16. Any group an individual is not a member of or is unaware of membership in is called a(n) _____ .

17. The process of relieving an unconscious impulse by expressing it directly or indirectly is called _____ .

18. The tendency for people to like those who like them is called _____ .

19. The discomfort produced by acting in a way that is inconsistent with one's attitudes is called _____ .

20. The belief that the world is just and that therefore bad things happen only to bad people is called the _____ .

21. A strong negative belief about another person based only on that individual's membership in a social group is called _____ .

22. The scientific study of how people think, feel, and act in relation to other people is called _____ .

Fill-in-the-Blank Answers

1. aggression
2. person schema
3. altruism
4. self-perception theory
5. companionate love
6. ingroup
7. attribution theory
8. self-serving bias
9. bystander effect
10. stereotype
11. persuasion
12. passionate love
13. attitude
14. fundamental attribution error
15. balance principle
16. outgroup
17. catharsis
18. reciprocity
19. cognitive dissonance
20. just-world phenomenon
21. prejudice
22. social psychology

Fact and Concept Questions

1. Suppose we know that many people stutter when they are in front of a crowd and that Jim, who stutters in front of a crowd, never stutters when he is with friends and relatives. We would attribute Jim's stuttering to
   a. the consensus of the group.
   b. stereotyping and prejudice.
   c. some characteristic of crowds, not Jim.
   d. some characteristic of Jim, not crowds.

2. The tendency to underestimate the importance of situational factors in causing behavior is sometimes called
   a. self-serving bias.
   b. the fundamental attribution error.
   c. the just-world phenomenon.
   d. stereotyping.

3. Which of the following is an example of self-serving bias?
   a. A professor claims that students sleep in her class because they must live in noisy dormitories.
   b. Computer analysts who make mistakes volunteer for extra training.
   c. People who watch soap operas believe the actors are as nasty as the characters they portray.
   d. Olympic champions explain their success in terms of ability and effort.

4. If you see a person wearing glasses and assume that the person is intelligent, conscientious, thoughtful, and serious, you are organizing your impressions by using
   a. actor-observer differences.
   b. a person schema.
   c. physical attractiveness bias.
   d. prejudice.

5. Research shows that subjects who are presented with both positive and negative descriptions of a person
   a. tend to change the information so that it seems more consistent.
   b. tend to believe the positive and ignore the negative.
   c. explain the negative descriptions in terms of situational pressures.
   d. use the balance principle and remember one good trait for every bad trait.

6. Information that conforms to a stereotype
   a. is remembered better than information that does not.
   b. tends to undercut people's prejudices.
   c. makes the balance principle more difficult to use.
   d. tends to destroy the person schema one is using.

7. First impressions have all of the following effects except one. Which one?
   a. They make it harder to change one's impression.
   b. They tend to reduce stereotyping.
   c. They influence the behavior of the person being observed.
   d. They affect how well you can remember information about the person being observed.

8. Propinquity, similarity, and reciprocity all increase the likelihood that
   a. a person will make biased attributions.
   b. two people will experience passionate love.
   c. stereotypes will lead to prejudiced behavior.
   d. two people will become friends.

9. Which factor in interpersonal attraction is most effective early in the relationship but has the least power over a long period of time?
   a. altruism
   b. similarity
   c. propinquity
   d. reciprocity

10. _____ love is characterized by intimacy, trust, and intense liking.
   a. Romantic
   b. Passionate
   c. Companionate
   d. Altruistic

11. The fact that lynchings of blacks in the American South were most common in years when cotton prices were lowest supports the idea that prejudice is
   a. caused by internal traits.
   b. the same thing as ingroup-outgroup cognitions.
   c. best combatted using the jigsaw approach.
   d. related to blaming a scapegoat.

12. How is the balance principle applied to ingroup-outgroup differences?
   a. Ingroups are seen as having all good qualities.
   b. Outgroups are seen as having all good qualities.
   c. Ingroups are seen as having a balance of both positive and negative qualities.
   d. None of the above.

13. According to the just-world phenomenon,
   a. prejudice and stereotyping should never exist.
   b. crime victims and unemployed people must have done something wrong to experience their problems.
   c. for every good thing a person does, there is a bad event that will balance it out.
   d. people in the outgroup have just as much right to resources as those in the ingroup.

14. The ability to predict a person's behavior on the basis of his or her attitudes has been found to be
    a. almost perfect, as long as the attitude being measured is very general.
    b. quite good, as long as the attitude is not remembered when the person takes action.
    c. poor if the action is not clearly linked to the attitude.
    d. poor if the attitude is socially acceptable.

15. _____ theory assumes that people will change their attitudes when their actions and attitudes are inconsistent.
    a. Cognitive dissonance
    b. Self-perception
    c. Attribution
    d. Persuasion

16. Persuasion involves the changing of attitudes through
    a. two processes: a central route and a peripheral route.
    b. verbal messages.
    c. Both *a* and *b*.
    d. Neither *a* nor *b*.

17. Physical attractiveness in a communicator
    a. tends to reduce the persuasiveness of the message.
    b. is considered a peripheral attitude change process.
    c. associates the message with the negative stereotypes we have concerning attractive individuals.
    d. is important only in using a two-sided message.

18. When multiple requests are made of an individual and the first request is unacceptably large, the manipulation technique being used is called
    a. the foot-in-the-door technique.
    b. the jigsaw method.
    c. the diffusion of responsibility tactic.
    d. the door-in-the-face technique.

19. Increased temperature, overcrowding, and economic difficulties are all associated with
    a. lower crime rates.
    b. the acceptability of violent pornography.
    c. increased altruism.
    d. greater aggression.

20. According to the concept of diffusion of responsibility,
    a. the greater the number of people witnessing an emergency, the lower the chances that any individual will help.
    b. the greater the number of people witnessing an emergency, the higher the chances that an individual will help.
    c. the better the mood a person is in, the more likely it is that he or she will help.
    d. the less clear it is to people that an emergency exists, the greater the chances that someone will offer help.

Application Questions

1. Margaret was pulled over by a state trooper when she was driving 60 miles per hour on a 55-mile-per-hour section of road. She automatically thinks the trooper did this because he is mean, unfeeling, and sexist. Margaret's attributions
    a. illustrate the fundamental attribution error.
    b. illustrate the use of Kelley's three-dimension concept.
    c. stem from the just-world phenomenon.
    d. reject the assumptions of actor-observer differences.

2. Arnie likes Bill but hates Charlie. David likes Charlie but hates Bill. According to _____ , how does Arnie feel about David?
    a. self-serving bias; he likes him.
    b. the balance principle; he hates him.
    c. attribution theory; he likes him.
    d. the fundamental attribution error; he hates him.

3. Before she ever met Timothy Jones, Mrs. Torrez, a first-grade teacher, was told that Timothy was very artistic but terrible at math. In actuality, Timothy is average in both. In Mrs. Torrez' class, however, he showed great ability in drawing but little interest or ability in math. This illustrates
    a. the effect of the just-world phenomenon.
    b. the problem of self-attribution.
    c. the impact of self-fulfilling prophecies.
    d. prejudice in the classroom.

4. Which of the following sayings is best supported by research on interpersonal attraction?
    a. "Absence makes the heart grow fonder."
    b. "Opposites attract."
    c. "Birds of a feather flock together."
    d. "Beauty is in the eye of the beholder."

5. At Plastic University, freshmen, as a group, are seen by others as stupid, immature, and shallow. Sophomores, more than juniors or seniors, have this view of freshmen. This phenomenon illustrates
   a. the tendency for prejudice to stem from people's need to reassert their status.
   b. the tendency to be prejudiced against young people.
   c. the just-world phenomenon's way of blaming the victim.
   d. Kelley's use of consistency, consensus, and distinctiveness to make attributions.

6. In an elementary school, Hispanic children and Anglo children have hostile impressions of each other. Research suggests that one of the following actions will be effective in reducing these prejudices. Which?
   a. Separate the children so they can feel good about themselves.
   b. Increase the amount of casual contact the children have with one another.
   c. Use the just-world concept to reduce their incorrect beliefs.
   d. Have them work on tasks that force them to cooperate.

7. Delta Upsilon Mu selects its fraternity brothers after a physically and emotionally draining initiation. Anyone can join Nu Alpha Chi. According to cognitive dissonance theory, what are member attitudes among the Delts?
   a. They like their fraternity more than the Nus like theirs.
   b. They like their fraternity less than the Nus like theirs.
   c. They like their fraternity the same amount as the Nus like theirs.
   d. They like the Nu fraternity more than they like their own.

8. Dr. Peters says, "Freud believed that aggression was innate, an animal instinct to preserve territory. Since his time evidence has grown that aggression is related to genetics and biochemistry." Dr. Peters is incorrect when he says that:
   a. Freud believed aggression was innate.
   b. Freud thought the instinct was related to preserving territory.
   c. evidence indicates that genetics are related to aggression.
   d. evidence indicates that biochemistry is related to aggression.

9. Sharon thinks that helping is based on the evolutionary principle that species want their genes to survive and so individuals may sacrifice themselves for the greater good of their kind. Sharon's ideas mirror
   a. Lorenz' ideas concerning aggression.
   b. the concept that empathy moves us to be altruistic.
   c. the concept of diffusion of responsibility.
   d. the selfish-gene concept of ethologists.

10. John is alone on the train platform. He sees an older woman sitting on a bench at the other end of the station. She shudders, closes her eyes, and drops her head. John is unlikely to help the woman because
    a. altruism does not actually exist.
    b. he is a victim of the bystander effect.
    c. there is diffusion of responsibility.
    d. it is not clear if an emergency exists.

Fact and Concept Answers

1. * c. What is described here shows high consensus and high distinctiveness (in Kelley's attribution model), both of which point toward situational causes, not trait causes. (p. 493)

    a. Consensus examines only whether others engage in the same behavior; it is a way of making an attribution and not an attribution itself.

    b. Stereotypes and prejudice are negative beliefs about members of a group. There are no negative beliefs expressed here.

    d. Trait attributions are made when there is no consensus and distinctiveness is low; the opposite is true here.

2. * b. The fundamental attribution error is the tendency to underestimate the importance of situational factors in explaining behavior. (p. 494)

    a. Self-serving bias is the tendency to take credit for our successes and blame others for our failures.

    c. The just-world phenomenon is the belief that bad things happen to bad people.

    d. Stereotypes are preconceived generalizations about the traits of people in social groups.

3. * d. Self-serving bias is the tendency to explain our successes in terms of effort and ability (internal traits) rather than situational pressures. (p. 497)

    a. Noisy dormitories are situational forces; according to the fundamental attribution error, we are more prone to use trait explanations for others such as the laziness of the students.

    b. Self-serving bias would be illustrated if the mistakes were explained in terms of situational pressures, not personal failings.

    c. This illustrates a form of the balance principle, where good or bad actions are linked to good or bad people.

4. * b. A person schema helps us organize our perceptions of others, often by taking one trait and linking it to others we suspect are similar. (p. 498)

    a. Actor-observer differences influence the attributions we make. We think actors (ourselves) are more influenced by situations than those we observe.

    c. Wearing glasses is not thought by most to be a sign of physical attractiveness.

    d. Prejudice would involve sweeping, negative judgments about all individuals in a group; the traits listed here are neither negative nor based on group membership.

5. * a. The balance principle works to smooth out inconsistencies in our impressions of others. (p. 498)

    b. We do not seem to be especially prone to believing the positive about others, we simply want consistency.

    c.   The fundamental attribution error applies when forming impressions of strangers, so we would stress traits, not situational forces.

    d.   The balance principle does *not* offset the bad with the good, it seeks to find consistency in impressions.

6. * a.   Research by O'Sullivan and Durso (1984) shows that we have a better memory for information conforming to our stereotypes because it represents a "chunk" rather than separate, inconsistent details. (p. 499)

    b.   When stereotypes are confirmed, prejudices are strengthened.

    c.   This would agree with the balance principle since the stereotyping trait (good or bad) would be linked to similar information.

    d.   This would strengthen the person's system for organizing an impression of the other person, and that is what a person schema does.

7. * b.   First impressions examine only the superficial aspects of a person and therefore make stereotyping easier and more probable. (pp. 500–501)

    a.   First impressions make change unlikely because all later information is filtered through them.

    c.   First impressions create self-fulfilling prophecies, altered behavior caused by expectations.

    d.   We remember behavior that confirms our first impressions better than we do behavior that unconfirms them.

8. * d.   Friendship, a form of interpersonal attraction, is influenced by physical nearness (propinquity), similarity in attitudes and interest, and reciprocity. (pp. 503–504)

    a.   Biased attributions stem from the fundamental attribution error, actor-observer differences, self-serving bias, and other cognitive errors.

    b.   Propinquity, similarity, and reciprocity are determinants of liking.

    c.   These three factors are involved in interpersonal attraction, not in attributions or person perception.

9. * c.   Being physically near someone else makes the start of a relationship more likely, but similarity and reciprocity are more powerful in determining liking over the long haul. (p. 504)

    a.   Propinquity is more clearly associated with interpersonal attraction than altruism.

    b.   Similarity is crucial for maintaining a friendship.

    c.   Reciprocity is crucial for maintaining a friendship.

10. * c.   Companionate love, an intense form of liking, is based on intimacy and trust. (p. 506)

    a.   Romantic love is based on two components: passionate and companionate love.

  b. Passionate love involves excitement and arousal at the mere thought of the loved one.

  d. Altruistic love is a made-up term.

11. * d. Finding a scapegoat is one explanation for prejudice. In the American South of sixty to one hundred years ago, low cotton prices were an economic hardship that led to blaming the powerless—blacks. (p. 507)

  a. Prejudice is not based on an individual's traits but on group motivational and cognitive factors.

  b. Ingroup-outgroup thoughts are not social-motivational origins.

  c. The jigsaw approach is appropriate for combatting prejudice in the elementary school classroom.

12. * a. The balance principle is applied as follows: we are members of the ingroup, we are good, therefore the whole ingroup is good, too. (p. 508)

  b. We are not members of the outgroup, so we see them as worse than we.

  c. The balance principle clusters good things with other good things; it does not balance good with bad.

  d. Since *a* is a correct answer, this cannot be the best choice.

13. * b. According to just-world thinking, bad events like crime and unemployment happen to bad people. (p. 508)

  a. The just-world phenomenon is unrelated to issues of tolerance.

  c. The just-world phenomenon assumes that good things happen to good people.

  d. The just-world phenomenon is unrelated to ingroup-outgroup differences.

14. * c. Predicting actions on the basis of attitudes is quite imprecise but is improved when the attitude is specific enough to be clearly linked to the action. (p. 511)

  a. The more general the attitude, the lower the ability to predict behavior.

  b. Predicting behavior on the basis of attitudes is improved when the person was thinking about his or her attitudes at the time of acting.

  d. Social acceptability helps us hide our true feelings and beliefs, making the prediction of behavior much harder.

15. * a. Cognitive dissonance says that attitudes change when the inconsistency between our beliefs and actions make us uncomfortable. (p. 512)

  b. Self-perception theory explains attitude change without including the idea of discomfort brought on by inconsistency.

  c. Attribution theory is unrelated to attitude change.

  d. Persuasion is the active effort to change attitudes through verbal messages.

16. * c. Persuasion, according to Petty and Cacioppo (1986) can take a central (conscious) route or a peripheral route. It is also based on verbal message designed to change our attitudes. Since both *a* and *b* are correct, this is the best answer. (p. 515)

   a. This is correct, but so is *b*.

   b. This is correct, but so is *a*.

   d. Because *a* and *b* are correct, this cannot be the best choice.

17. * b. Physical attractiveness is not central to the argument; it is therefore a peripheral route to persuading an individual. (p. 516)

   a. Physically attractive communicators tend to be more persuasive than unattractive ones.

   c. The stereotypes associated with physically attractive people are almost universally positive.

   d. Physical attractiveness is unrelated to one- or two-sided messages.

18. * d. In the door-in-the-face technique, an unacceptably large request is made first so that a more reasonable position will be accepted later. (p. 517)

   a. In the foot-in-the-door technique, small requests are made first, leading to increased compliance with the requester.

   b. The jigsaw method uses cooperative tasks to combat prejudice.

   c. Diffusion of responsibility relates to helping.

19. * d. As temperature and crowding increase and the economy declines, aggressive actions such as violent crime increase. (p. 520)

   a. Crime rates go up in hot weather, in high-density areas, and when the economy is weak.

   b. Violent pornography is unrelated to temperature, overcrowding, and economic hardship.

   c. Altruism probably decreases in such conditions.

20. * a. Because other people are observing a situation in which help is needed, each person is thinking that someone else will take action. (p. 522)

   b. As there are more witnesses, the responsibility for acting is diffused even more; the chances of anyone helping go down.

   c. This is a true statement but is unrelated to diffusion of responsibility.

   d. When it is not clear that an emergency is occurring, people are less likely to initiate helping.

Application Answers

1. * a. By assuming that the trooper's actions were caused by his personality traits, Margaret is underestimating the situational forces (the fact that the trooper has a job to do) and illustrates the fundamental attribution error. (p. 494)

   b. If she thought about the trooper's behavior in terms of consistency, consensus, and distinctiveness, she would be applying Kelley's model.

   c. The just-world phenomenon would apply if she thought she was a bad person (bad things happen to bad people).

   d. She is making trait attributions about a person she observes; this is consistent with actor-observer differences.

2. * b. The balance principle says that bad things (and people) belong with other bad things (and people). In this case, the friend of my enemy is my enemy. (p. 498)

   a. Self-serving bias pertains to self-attributions only when one either succeeds or fails.

   c. Attribution theory only pertains to the explanation of others' behavior.

   d. The fundamental attribution error involves the underestimation of situational factors.

3. * c. When expectations alter the behavior of others, we see the impact of self-fulfilling prophecies (p. 502)

   a. The just-world phenomenon assumes that bad things happen only to bad people.

   b. Self-attribution would apply if Mrs. Torrez explained why she acted the way she did.

   d. There is no information to make us believe she saw Timothy as weak in math because of group membership.

4. * c. Birds of a feather are similar, and similarity is an important factor in friendship formation. (p. 503)

   a. Physical closeness is associated with liking.

   b. Opposites rarely attract and usually do not stay attracted for long.

   d. Physical attractiveness is important in interpersonal attraction, but the subjective nature of beauty is not relevant.

5. * a. Only freshmen are lower on the ladder than sophomores, so sophomores may need to reassert their status by having prejudicial attitudes toward the freshmen. (p. 507)

   b. The prejudice is greatest in those who have to reassert their status.

   c. There is no mention of blaming the freshmen for their misfortune.

   d. Kelley's model is used to determine whether behavior stems from situational or trait factors.

6. * d. Research by Sherif and colleagues (1961) and Aronson (1978) shows that prejudice is reduced by forcing people of equal status to work collaboratively on a shared goal. (p. 510)

   a. Increased contact on a cooperative task is necessary, not separation.

   b. Contact alone does not combat prejudice.

   c. Just-world thinking would make it easier to believe that each outgroup deserved its mistreatment.

7. * a. Cognitive dissonance research confirms the idea that the harder the initiation, the more positive the attitude toward the group. (p. 512)

   b. Because they have an initiation, they will like their fraternity more than the group that had none.

   c. Attitudes are changed by the inconsistency between wanting to join and having to endure the initiation.

   d. Positive attitudes are increased because of cognitive dissonance.

8. * b. Konrad Lorenz believed that human aggression had its origins in animal instincts to preserve territory and fight for resources; Freud did not. (p. 518)

   a. Freud saw aggression and sex as the innate drives that shape personality.

   c. Certain genetic strains of animals show much more aggressiveness than other strains.

   d. Testosterone is a chemical that is associated with aggression.

9. * d. The selfish-gene concept was developed by ethologists to explain altruism; they see individual sacrifice as based on the species' need to have genes survive. (p. 520)

   a. Lorenz suggested that aggression was the result of territoriality and the fight for resources; he did not discuss altruism.

   b. Empathy is unrelated to genetics or evolution.

   c. Diffusion of responsibility is associated with failing to help when many observers are present at an emergency.

10. * d. When it is not clear that an emergency exists, we tend not to help because we don't want to act foolishly or intrude in another person's life. (p. 523)

   a. Altruism—offering help with no expectation of reward—does, indeed, exist.

   b. Bystander effects occur only if other people observe the same incident.

   c. There cannot be diffusion of responsibility if John is alone.

CHAPTER 18

THE INDIVIDUAL AND THE SOCIAL GROUP

Learning Objectives

1. Define conformity. Describe and give examples of explicit norms and norms that are more covert. (pp. 528–529)

2. Discuss how informational social influences define what is proper and affect our behavior. Describe the impact of normative social influences on behavior. Discuss the Asch perception study and differentiate compliance from conformity. (pp. 529–532)

3. Discuss the balance between the confidence of the individual and the power of the group. Explain how a group's attractiveness, size, apparent independence of members, and unanimity affect individual conformity. Discuss whether a minority in a group can affect the majority. (pp. 532–534)

4. Differentiate obedience from conformity. Describe in detail the method used in the Milgram shock experiment and its results. Discuss reasons why the results are not believed to be caused by personality factors. (pp. 534–537)

5. Discuss the roles of distance between teacher and learner, the gradual evolution of a moral dilemma, the authority of the experimenter, and the presence of an ally in explaining Milgram's results. Describe the lessons to be learned from Milgram's work and the ethical concerns it presents. (pp. 538–542)

6. Define and give an example of a social role. Describe the method, results, and conclusions of the Stanford prison experiment. Discuss the similarities and differences between the prison experiment and the Milgram experiment. (pp. 542–544)

7. Describe deindividuation and its effects on behavior. Explain why deindividuation occurs. Discuss the frequency of conflicts between social forces and individual values. Discuss how social psychological principles help explain cult behavior. (pp. 544–547)

8. Describe social facilitation and social interference effects on behavior. Evaluate the arousal, evaluation apprehension, and self-consciousness explanations for social facilitation and interference. Describe social loafing and discuss explanations for it. (pp. 548–552)

9. Describe the phenomenon of groupthink and the circumstances in which it occurs. Discuss group polarization and the reasons that the thinking of individual members moves in the direction of the group. (pp. 552–555)

10. Give an example of a social dilemma. Describe the "tragedy of the commons." Discuss the factors that can stop this social dilemma. (pp. 555–557)

11. Describe the Prisoner's Dilemma game, and discuss how rational, competitive choices lead to irrational consequences. Examine the Prisoner's Dilemma game in international relations in the form of "tit for tat" and GRIT. (pp. 557–560)

12. Discuss how knowledge about social forces on the individual can alter human behavior. (pp. 560–561)

Chapter Outline

1. **Conformity** (pp. 528–534)

   Conformity occurs when people change their behavior, feelings, or beliefs to match the expectations of the group. Some of these expectations are standards of behavior that group members share, or *norms*. Norms can be extremely clear or more difficult to recognize. One such covert norm is that which governs how far from one another we are expected to be when having conversations. Norms can influence people through information that defines reality, a process called *informational social influence*. For example, Newcomb (1943) reported that, over four years at Bennington College, students gained information from older students and faculty and became more politically liberal. By disapproving of deviant behavior, *normative social influence* can also produce conformity. The Asch (1956) study involving the perception of different-sized lines illustrates this process. Asch's subjects showed *compliance*—a change in behavior without a change in beliefs—rather than conformity.

   The influence process is affected both by the individual's confidence and by the group's power. When people are low in confidence, they are more likely to conform. Groups that are attractive, large, unanimous, or whose members appear to be making independent judgments exert stronger influence over individuals than those that are not.

Although we do not know all the reasons for it, a minority portion of a group can influence the majority.

2. Obedience (pp. 534–542)

A person who complies with the direct order of another person is showing *obedience*. Stanley Milgram performed a series of studies to understand obedience. In each experiment, the subject was led to believe that he or she was a teacher in a memory study and that electric shocks had to be given to the learner (a confederate of the experimenter) when errors were made. The shocks increased in intensity with each error until, at 450 volts, the learner appears to shriek in agony. Unexpectedly, 62 percent of subjects in the original study went all the way to 450 volts in response to the experimenters' commands that they continue. No personality characteristics explain the results, nor are they the result of experimental error. There is a strong willingness to obey those in authority when there is distance between the subject and the victim, when the moral dilemma gradually evolves, and when there are no others rejecting the demands of the authority. The lessons of the Milgram experiments are that we all have the potential to be led astray by authorities and that even one dissenter can impede blind obedience. Milgram's research came under attack for ethical reasons, but he argued in return that no objections would have been raised if the results had not been so upsetting. A balance must be struck between the costs of research to subjects and the benefits to science; this is a difficult balance to assess.

3. Social roles (pp. 542–548)

Individuals in groups are assigned an organized system of norms called, collectively, *social roles*. "Student" is an example of one. Zimbardo's Stanford Prison Experiment illustrated the power of the guard and prisoner social roles over individual behavior. At the other extreme is *deindividuation*—the loss of one's sense of individual identity that increases the power of the situation over behavior. Deindividuation lets people step out of typical roles and may lead to increased or decreased aggression, depending on situational cues. Typically, people act in accord with society's expectations.

Cults represent social groups in which attitude-changing techniques such as the foot-in-the-door occur and norms influence individuals to conform. The sacrifices members make for the group leader increase their liking of the group whether this effect happens through cognitive dissonance or self-perception.

4. The effects of others on performance (pp. 548–552)

The presence of others can improve individual performance, an effect called *social facilitation*. The presence of others, however, can also impair performance—*social interference*. Robert Zajonc (pronounced "ZY-ence") suggested that both processes stem from physiological arousal. Arousal improves performance on simple tasks but inhibits performance on complex tasks. A second explanation is that audiences have their effect because they can create evaluation apprehension in the performer. Audiences can also force the performer to pay more attention to his or her actions and increase self-consciousness.

Individuals often show reduced effort in group tasks compared to the effort they make on their own. This is called *social loafing*, and it seems to occur when individual contributions cannot be identified and feedback is not given to individuals.

5. **Group decisions** (pp. 552–555)

Group decision making is prone to problems. One is *groupthink*, the tendency for groups to reduce their consideration and critical evaluation of alternatives. Groupthink was illustrated in John F. Kennedy's decision to invade Cuba in 1961. It is most likely to occur in cohesive groups where there is a strong leader. Groups also have the problem of making more extreme decisions than the average member would alone, a process called *group polarization*. It may occur because arguments favor movement in one direction or its opposite; a second is that people want to be different—but not too different—from others.

6. **Cooperation and conflict** (pp. 555–561)

Social dilemmas are situations in which the rational behavior of individuals produces a cumulative negative and often conflictual effect on both the individuals and those around them. A good example of these dilemmas is the *tragedy of the commons*. This is a situation in which each individual's use of a resource benefits the individual and has little impact; with more and more individuals using it, however, the resource diminishes until everyone suffers. The solution to this dilemma is difficult: to keep groups small, to invent formal procedures to conserve resources, or to make large users pay more.

The *prisoner's dilemma* is a model of the real world in which two competing individuals produce a worse outcome than if they had cooperated; the rational choice for each individual leads to an irrational outcome for both. Personality does not affect how people play the game as much as the payoff for the competitive choice. The prisoner's dilemma model can be applied to international relations. A "tit-for-tat" strategy, in which one player copies the other's move, promotes cooperation. Osgood has developed this idea into *graduated reciprocal initiatives for tension reduction* (GRIT), a strategy that can be applied for achieving world peace.

Social psychology teaches us about powerful forces in situations that affect individual and group behavior. As we become more knowledgeable about them, we free ourselves from their dominance.

Fill-in-the-Blank Quiz

1. The model of real-world situations in which two competing rational decisions produce a worse outcome than two cooperative decisions is called the _____ .

2. A situation in which the rational behavior of individuals has negative cumulative effects on both the individuals and those around them is called a(n) _____ .

3. The tendency for a group's decisions to be more extreme than the average decision of individuals in the group is called _____ .

4. The pattern of group decision making that limits the consideration of alternatives and the critical evaluation of them is called _____ .

5. The tendency to work less hard when other people are sharing the work is called _____ .

6. The negative effect of the presence of other people on individual performance is called _____ .

7. The positive effect of the presence of other people on individual performance is called _____ .

8. The loss of a sense of personal identity that increases the impact of situational factors on behavior is called _____ .

9. An organized system of norms assigned to one or more individuals in a group is called a(n) _____ .

10. Complying with the direct request of another person is called _____ .

11. Changing one's external behavior while maintaining one's personal beliefs is called _____ .

12. The capacity of a group to influence its members by threatening its disapproval is called _____ .

13. The capacity of a group to influence behaviors and attitudes by defining what is true or correct is called _____ .

14. A pattern of behavior shared by members of a group is called a(n) _____ .

15. Changing one's behavior, feelings, or beliefs to match the expectations of a group is called _____ .

Fill-in-the-Blank Answers

1. prisoner's dilemma
2. social dilemma
3. group polarization
4. groupthink
5. social loafing
6. social interference
7. social facilitation
8. deindividuation

9. social role
10. obedience
11. compliance
12. normative social influence
13. informational social influence
14. norm
15. conformity

Fact and Concept Questions

1. When a norm sets proper behavior for individuals, such as when to applaud a performer, behavior is shaped because of
   a. informational social influence.
   b. compliance to direct demands.
   c. obedience to authority.
   d. normative social influence.

2. In Asch's (1956) study, subjects were asked to judge a line of the same length as another in the presence of people who gave incorrect answers. The results showed that
   a. people with high self-esteem refused to go along with the group.
   b. there was true conformity based on informational social influence.
   c. there was compliance based on normative social influence.
   d. normative social influence was less powerful than informational social influence.

3. Which of the following factors *increases* the likelihood of conformity to group norms?
   a. The group is not highly respected.
   b. The group is small and tightly knit.
   c. The group is large and members seem to make independent judgments.
   d. The group is evenly split about the norms it chooses to use.

4. Stanley Milgram's series of studies discovered disturbing information about
   a. how groups make irrational decisions.
   b. how deindividuation increases the likelihood of aggression.
   c. social norms and their effect on conformity.
   d. individual obedience to authority.

5. Which statement about the results of Milgram's experiments is true?
   a. Fewer than 50 percent of subjects gave 450 volt shocks.
   b. The subjects firmly believed they were harming the other volunteer.
   c. Most of the subjects that gave 450 volt shocks were weak willed and morally deficient.
   d. Fewer subjects gave painful shocks than psychiatrists had predicted they would.

6. What relationship was found between distance between teacher and learner and rates of compliance in the Milgram experiments?
   a. The greater the distance, the greater the compliance.
   b. The greater the distance, the less the compliance.
   c. Compliance was greatest at a middle range of distance, but it was minimal at either extreme of distance.
   d. Distance was found to have no relationship to compliance.

7. The most powerful factor in reducing obedience to authority seems to be
   a. a situation in which the authority has a poor reputation.
   b. the presence of a dissenting ally.
   c. having a large audience for the act of obedience.
   d. making the moral dilemma a gradually increasing one.

8. Concerning the ethics of the Milgram experiments, which statement is true?
   a. Milgram apologized for putting his subjects through the unnecessary pain they endured.
   b. More than 50 percent of the experimental subjects regretted having been in the study.
   c. Roughly 20 percent of the experimental subjects had long-term emotional disorders stemming directly from the research.
   d. Many of the ethical objections were related to the fact that the results of the study were upsetting.

9. Funeral directors are expected to wear dark suits, speak quietly, have great patience, and never laugh while working. These prescriptions for behavior are called
   a. social dilemmas.
   b. deindividuation.
   c. social roles.
   d. social facilitation.

10. What do *both* the Milgram and Zimbardo experiments illustrate?
    a. The innate violence in the human spirit.
    b. The willingness for people to comply but never to conform.
    c. The power of individual personality over behavior.
    d. The power of norms and roles over individual behavior.

11. Deindividuation is likely to be greatest when
    a. no one can determine the identity of the individuals in a large group.
    b. a small group works together on a task requiring cooperation.
    c. rational decisions made by individuals lead to irrational outcomes for the group.
    d. None of the above.

12. Behavior in cults can illustrate which of the following social psychological processes?
    a. use of the "foot-in-the-door" technique for attitude change
    b. deindividuation of cult group members
    c. attitude change based on cognitive dissonance
    d. All of the above.

13. According to the concept of social facilitation,
    a. individuals work less hard when they work on a group task than they would as individuals.
    b. the presence of others has a positive effect on individual performance.
    c. people like other people who share the same norms and roles.
    d. the more difficult the task, the more the presence of others improves performance.

14. What is Robert Zajonc's explanation for social facilitation and social interference effects?
    a. inheritance
    b. physiological arousal
    c. social norms and roles
    d. deindividuation

15. How are social loafing and social facilitation the opposite of each other?
    a. In social loafing, people work without an audience; in social facilitation, they have an audience.
    b. In social loafing, performance is improved; in social facilitation, it is reduced.
    c. In social loafing, others do not know the individual's performance; in social facilitation, they do.
    d. In social loafing, the group makes moderate decisions; in social facilitation, they make extreme decisions.

16. When a cohesive group makes decisions without adequately considering or evaluating all the alternatives, we can say that there is
    a. groupthink.
    b. social loafing.
    c. group polarization.
    d. the tragedy of the commons.

17. Group polarization is increased if
    a. every argument for one position is balanced by an argument against it.
    b. the social norm is for people to disagree.
    c. everyone in the group feels he/she must make the same judgment as all the others.
    d. individuals want to be somewhat different from others.

18. The tragedy of the commons is an example of
    a. a social dilemma.
    b. group polarization that produces groupthink.
    c. aggression that stems from deindividuation.
    d. the prisoner's dilemma.

19. Creating smaller communities, inventing formal regulations to protect resources, and forcing the largest user to pay the greatest cost are all measures designed to
    a. increase social facilitation.
    b. solve the prisoner's dilemma.
    c. stop the tragedy of the commons.
    d. improve international relations.

20. Osgood's graduated reciprocated initiatives in tension reduction (GRIT) are best seen as
    a. an ineffective way of reducing social loafing.
    b. an application of the "tit-for-tat" strategy in the search for world peace.
    c. an irrational set of decisions that have a rational outcome.
    d. a form of the prisoner's dilemma game in which competition is the path to world peace.

Application Questions

1. At Barnes Junior High, all the seventh-grade girls wear their sunglasses on the top of their heads and put hot pink polish on their nails. This illustrates _____ and _____ .
   a. deindividuation; explicit social norms
   b. conformity; norms
   c. social facilitation; social roles
   d. conformity; obedience to authority

2. After playing a round of golf, Judd, a new member of the country club, joked about the putts he had blown on the final three holes. The stares and sneers he received from other members told him never to joke about his poor golfing again. Judd's behavior was altered by
   a. deindividuation in the group.
   b. informational social influence.
   c. his desire to conform to group roles.
   d. normative social influence.

3. Milgram's experimental findings help us explain why
   a. it is easier to obey orders to bomb a hospital from 20,000 feet than it is to blow it up from a tank 50 feet away.
   b. there are so few empathic and sensitive people who take jobs as prison guards.
   c. a few dissidents in a military unit make the rest of the soldiers so willing to obey orders from a cruel officer.
   d. cult leaders encourage the members of their group to examine the ethical consequences of the actions they take.

4. A social psychologist proposes a study on overcrowding in which subjects are forced to live in overcrowded circumstances without the option to leave. The ethics of this study
   a. would be evaluated by a review committee that ensures the safety of subjects.
   b. would be evaluated in terms of the benefits of knowledge balanced against the cost to the people involved.
   c. Both *a* and *b*.
   d. Neither *a* nor *b*.

5. If we apply the knowledge gained from Zimbardo's Stanford prison experiment to actual prisons, we would anticipate that
   a. the prisoners tend to become brutal while the guards become passive.
   b. prisoners and guards would have different personality styles in their childhoods.
   c. prisoners would obey guards because they represent unconscious authority figures.
   d. the job description of "guard" would generate cruelty.

6. It is a hot summer night and there is an electric blackout. Crowds of people break into grocery and appliance stores and steal as much as they can carry away because no one can identify who committed the crimes. This incident best illustrates
   a. informational social influence.
   b. deindividuation.
   c. social facilitation.
   d. group polarization.

7. An Olympic gymnastics coach walks into the gym. Under which circumstance is the presence of this person going to *improve* the performance of a young gymnast who is practicing there?
   a. The coach never even looks at the gymnast.
   b. The gymnast performs an old and well-practiced routine.
   c. The gymnast performs a new and difficult routine.
   d. The coach tells the gymnast that performance on that one routine determines whether the person has a future in the sport.

8. Under which of the following circumstances is groupthink most likely to occur?
   a. a cohesive group in which the leader is not highly respected
   b. a cohesive group that has many contacts with opposing positions outside the group
   c. a noncohesive group with a highly respected leader
   d. a cohesive group that is isolated from outside opinions

9. Only a limited number of fish are left in the Atlantic Ocean. Each Atlantic fisherman cheats a little so he can make more money than his competition. Since everyone cheats, however, all the fish are caught and eventually the fishermen go broke and their customers go hungry. This chain of events best illustrates
   a. the tragedy of the commons.
   b. social interference effects.
   c. the power of the personality over the situation.
   d. the GRIT approach to conflict resolution.

10. The Lout Corporation is in conflict with the Union of American Widgetmakers. If the union negotiator competes whenever the Lout president competes, but cooperates whenever the president cooperates, the union negotiator would be using
   a. the process called group polarization.
   b. informational social influence.
   c. the "tit for tat" strategy in the prisoner's dilemma game.
   d. the GRIT approach to the commons game.

Fact and Concept Answers

1. * a. Informational social influence occurs when norms tell people what is proper or correct behavior. (p. 529)

   b. Compliance to direct demands or requests is considered obedience.

   c. Unlike the subtle norms for knowing when to applaud, obedience to authority involves direct demands.

   d. Normative social influence occurs when deviance from norms leads to disapproval.

2. * c. No one in the Asch experiment described proper behavior, they simply threatened to disapprove of perceptions that were different from the others. (p. 53)

   a. Personality factors had no impact on the behavior of subjects in the Asch study.

   b. Rather than actually changing their beliefs (conformity), Asch's subjects only altered their behavior; they complied.

   d. Normative social influence was more powerful than informational.

3. * c. Conformity is more likely when groups are attractive, large, unanimous, and members seem to be making independent judgments. (p. 532)

   a. Conformity increases as the group's attractiveness and expertise increase.

   b. The larger the group, the more the conformity.

   d. Conformity increases when norms are unanimous.

4. * d. Milgram's studies were designed to understand the factors affecting obedience to authority (the experimenter). (p. 534)

   a. Irrational decision making in groups was the focus of Irving Janis's work on groupthink.

   b. Deindividuation is the thrust of Philip Zimbardo's work.

   c. Norms and conformity were more involved in Asch's study.

5. * b. Films show that Milgram's subjects were extremely upset because they thought they were harming, even killing, the other volunteer. (p. 536)

   a. More than 60 percent of the subjects in the first experiment went all the way to 450 volts.

   c. Personality factors played no role in who showed total obedience.

   d. Psychiatrists predicted that only one person in a thousand would go all the way, not more than one person in two.

6. * a. When teachers and learners were separated by a greater distance, they were more inclined to obey and harm the volunteer than when they were physically closer. (p. 538)

   b. Compliance is more difficult when the teacher and learner are close to each other.

c. As distance increases, compliance increases.

d. Distance has a strong relationship to compliance.

7. * b. When one person disobeys the experimenter, obedience is reduced greatly. (p. 540)

    a. Even when Milgram changed the location of the experiment from Yale University to a more disreputable place, there was a substantial degree of obedience.

    c. Audience effects were not a part of the Milgram studies.

    d. The fact that the moral dilemma was a gradually increasing one made obedience more likely.

8. * d. Milgram argued (and subsequent research found) that ethical objections to the study were strong because the results painted an unflattering picture of our willingness to obey authority. (p. 541)

    a. Milgram never apologized for his work.

    b. A little over 1 percent expressed regrets for being in the study.

    c. None of the subjects had emotional scars and over 80 percent said they were either somewhat or very glad to have participated.

9. * c. Social roles are the organized set of prescriptions for behavior we give to people; funeral directors act a certain way because of their social roles. (p. 542)

    a. Social dilemmas are situations in which individuals' choices of behavior may be rational but cumulatively they lead to irrational outcomes for the group.

    b. Deindividuation occurs when personal identity and responsibility for action is reduced and the power of situations over behavior is increased.

    d. Social facilitation occurs when the presence of others improves the individual's performance.

10. * d. In both experiments, norms (for obeying those in authority) and roles (guards or prisoners) controlled individual behavior. (p. 544)

    a. Both studies pointed out the situational factors in generating violence, not anything that is innate or inherited.

    b. Particularly in the Zimbardo prison experiment, individuals conformed their behavior to fit social roles; they did not pretend to be guards and prisoners, they became them.

    c. In neither experiment did the personalities of subjects predict behavior.

11. * a. Deindividuation occurs when people's individual identity and responsibility for actions are reduced; this effect is more likely in a large mob than in a small group. (p. 544)

    b. Large groups foster deindividuation.

    c. Rational decisions by individuals leading to irrational outcomes produce a social dilemma.

    d. Since *a* is an accurate answer, this cannot be the best choice.

12. * d. Cult leaders at first make small requests and gradually increase their demands ("foot in the door"); they cut off members from outside contacts and reduce their personal sense of identity (deindividuation); and they make members sacrifice so that staying in the organization creates cognitive dissonance, which leads to increased liking of the group. (p. 547)

   a. This is correct, but so are *b* and *c*.

   b. This is correct, but so are *a* and *c*.

   c. This is correct, but so are *a* and *b*.

13. * b. Social facilitation occurs when the presence of others improves the individual's performance. (p. 548)

   a. Social loafing occurs when individuals work less hard on a group collaborative task than they would if alone.

   c. Similarity of attitudes is unrelated to social facilitation.

   d. The simpler the task, the more the presence of others improves performance.

14. * b. Zajonc proposes physiological arousal caused by the presence of an audience as the explanation for improved performance on simple tasks but impaired performance on difficult tasks. (p. 549)

   a. Zajonc does not suggest that inheritance or any other internal factor influences a person's social facilitation.

   c. Social norms and roles are not relevant to social facilitation effects since they seem to occur with cockroaches.

   d. Deindividuation pertains to lost personal identity, not audience effects.

15. * c. Individual effort drops off in the phenomenon of social loafing because no one knows how much each individual is exerting himself or herself; in social facilitation, the entire audience can see the individual's effort and results. (p. 550)

   a. Social loafing involves a kind of audience because others in the group are working on the task.

   b. The reverse of this is true.

   d. Social loafing and facilitation are unrelated to group decision making.

16. * a. Irving Janis says that groupthink occurs in cohesive groups in which there is a strong leader and little contact with opposing points of view outside the group. (p. 552)

   b. Social loafing occurs when individual effort drops off because there is no feedback on performance in a group task.

   c. Group polarization is the tendency for groups to make more extreme decisions than the average individual in the group would make.

   d. The tragedy of the commons is a type of social dilemma.

17. * d. Social comparison—the desire to be different from others, but not too much—is a partial explanation for group polarization effects. (p. 553)

  a. Polarization is increased when only one argument is repeated and embellished.

  b. Polarization is increased when people are *not* expected to disagree.

  c. Polarization is linked to social comparison: the desire to be somewhat different from others.

18. * a. The tragedy of the commons occurs when individuals use a resource for their own good (a rational decision) but end up destroying the resource so that both the individuals and the group suffer. This is a type of social dilemma. (p. 556)

  b. The tragedy of the commons involves individual decision making, not group decision making.

  c. The tragedy of the commons is unrelated to aggression.

  d. The prisoner's dilemma involves choices in competitive or cooperative behavior and does not necessarily relate to the use of resources as the tragedy of the commons does.

19. * c. Steps for solving the tragedy of the commons are decreasing the size of the community (so there is greater communication and individual responsibility), setting formal regulations on resource use, and imposing punishments for excessive use. (p. 557)

  a. Social facilitation is related only to audiences and task difficulty.

  b. The prisoner's dilemma is not a problem to be solved; it is a model for cooperative and competitive behaviors.

  d. GRIT is more appropriately used to solve international conflicts.

20. * b. GRIT is a strategy for reducing international conflict by cooperating with an opponent or competing with the opponent in a gradually increasing fashion; it is based on the "tit-for-tat" tactic of the prisoner's dilemma. (p. 560)

  a. GRIT is unrelated to social loafing.

  c. The prisoner's dilemma is a model of behavior in which rational individual actions lead to irrational outcomes.

  d. GRIT does make use of the prisoner's dilemma game, but it suggests that matching the opponent's last move increases cooperation.

Application Answers

1. * b. When everyone matches the behavior of others we see conformity; in this case there is a norm for wearing sunglasses and nail polish that all seventh graders (notorious for conformity) adhere to. (p. 528)

  a. Nothing indicates that the seventh graders are not identified personally; the norms are probably subtle rather than explicit.

   c. Social facilitation occurs when audiences improve the performance of simple tasks.

   d. There is no authority figure who demands that the seventh graders wear their sunglasses in the same manner or buy the same color nail polish.

2. * d. Normative social influence occurs when deviance is threatened with group disapproval; this is what Judd got from the other golfers for his behavior. (p. 531)

   a. Deindividuation occurs when personal identities and responsibilities are removed from individuals.

   b. This kind of social influence would occur if the country club had a clear policy about the way one can discuss one's golf performance.

   c. Individual differences are not relevant to this example.

3. * a. As the distance between the persecutor and the victim increases, obedience to authority (and the willingness to carry out unethical behaviors) increases. (p. 538)

   b. Zimbardo's work, not Milgram's, had to do with prisons.

   c. When there are dissidents, the chances of complete obedience are greatly reduced.

   d. Cult leaders expect blind obedience and no consideration of ethics.

4. * c. Social psychological research is evaluated by a review committee before it is done so that the safety of subjects is insured. The evaluation process examines the potential of the study to advance scientific knowledge against the physical or psychological costs to participants. (p. 541)

   a. This is true, but so is *b*.

   b. This is true, but so is *a*.

   d. Because both *a* and *b* are correct, this cannot be the best choice.

5. * d. Zimbardo argues that the social role, not personality, sets in motion behaviors and responses that promote cruel behavior. (p. 543)

   a. Prisoners tend to become passive, whereas guards dominate.

   b. Personality styles were not predictive of Zimbardo's results.

   c. Nothing in Zimbardo's work indicates that psychoanalytic theory explains the results.

6. * b. When the lights go out, personal identity is lost and the social trigger of seeing others looting stores increases aggressive behavior. (p. 544)

   a. Informational social influence occurs when culture teaches us what is proper behavior.

   c. Social facilitation occurs when individual performance is improved by the presence of an audience.

   d. Group polarization is the tendency for groups to make more extreme decisions than the average individual in the group.

7. * b. Because physiological arousal is not pushed to too high a level when the individual performs a well-learned or simple task, audiences tend to improve a person's performance on those tasks; we can assume the gymnast can perform the routine with "her eyes closed." (p. 549)

   a. If the coach does not look, there is no audience effect.

   c. Performance on a difficult or poorly learned task is impaired by an audience because arousal goes too high.

   d. High evaluation apprehension will probably push arousal too high and reduce performance.

8. * d. Cohesive groups that have little contact with opposing outside views are more inclined to make the unwise decisions seen in groupthink. (p. 553)

   a. Groupthink is most likely when a cohesive group has a strong, highly respected leader.

   b. Reducing contacts with outsiders makes the group's appraisal of a limited number of alternatives seem reasonable.

   c. Groupthink can occur only in cohesive groups.

9. * a. The tragedy of the commons involves the exploitation of a group's resource (fish) so that individuals prosper for a time; eventually, however, all individuals suffer because the resource is destroyed. (p. 556)

   b. Social interference occurs when audiences reduce individual performance.

   c. All of social psychology teaches the power of the situation over the power of personality.

   d. GRIT involves conflict reduction for two parties and may have nothing to do with the use of a common resource.

10. * c. "Tit for tat" is a strategy for improving cooperation in which one party begins by cooperating with and then matching the response of the opponent. (p. 559)

    a. Group polarization involves group decisions that are more extreme than those of the average group participant.

    b. Information social influence occurs when a group provides information that defines proper conduct in specific situations.

    d. There is no such thing as the commons game.

STATISTICS IN PSYCHOLOGICAL RESEARCH

Learning Objectives

1. Define the term *data*. Discuss the null hypothesis. Describe and discuss the uses of a frequency histogram. (A1–A2)

2. Discuss the value of descriptive statistics. Define N in a research study. Describe, discuss, and distinguish among the mode, median, and mean as measures of central tendency. Discuss why the median can be a more effective measure of central tendency than the mean. (A2–A4)

3. Describe the variability measures called the range and the standard deviation. Explain how two groups can have identical means but different standard deviations. (A4–A5)

4. Describe the characteristics of the normal distribution and how it is related to percentile scores. Define the term *standard score*. (A5–A6)

5. Discuss how the correlation coefficient is calculated. (A6–A7)

6. Discuss the value of inferential statistics. Describe the t test and the meaning of the term *statistical significance*. List the factors that are included in the calculation of the t statistic. (A8–A9)

7. Discuss how degrees of freedom and p values are used to determine statistical significance. (A10)

8. Discuss how analysis of variance is used when more than two groups are compared. (A11)

Appendix Outline

1. **Describing data** (A1–A2)

Psychological research generates *data,* numbers that represent findings and are the sources of conclusions. In experiments, researchers test the *null hypothesis*—the idea that the independent variable will have no effect on the dependent variable.

After data are collected, they can be depicted as a *frequency histogram,* a bar graph showing the number of cases for each score in the data set. Histograms are useful in giving a picture of results, but *descriptive statistics* can be more precise.

2. **Descriptive statistics** (A2–A8)

The goal of descriptive statistics is to summarize data with numbers. One such number is N, the designation for the number of subjects in a study. Measures of central tendency indicate the typical performance of the group. The *mode* is the most commonly occurring score. The *median* is the middlemost score in the data set. Half the scores are above the median, half below. The mean is the arithmetic average and is a preferred measure of central tendency. The mean, however, is more sensitive to extreme scores than the median.

Variability is the scatter in a set of scores. The *range* is a simple reflection of variability: it is the difference between the highest and lowest scores in the data set. More useful is the *standard deviation (SD),* which measures the average difference of each score from the mean. Whereas two groups can have identical means, one group can have a large standard deviation, showing considerable scatter in scores, and another a small standard deviation with most of the scores bunched around the mean.

Often the distribution of scores resembles a bell-shaped curve called the *normal distribution.* When a distribution is truly normal, the mean, median, and mode all have the same value. Further, the standard deviation can be used to determine what percentage of the whole population scored above or below a certain score. *Percentile scores* indicate each 10 percent of the distribution. *Standard scores* indicate how far from the mean a score is in terms of standard deviations.

The correlation coefficient describes the direction and strength of a relationship. It is calculated by summing together the difference of each score on one variable from its general mean times the difference of each score on the other variable from its general mean. This number is divided by a denominator that ensures the coefficient ranges from −1.00 to +1.00.

3. **Inferential statistics** (A9–A11)

Descriptive statistics can indicate that groups of scores differ, but *inferential statistics* indicate whether the difference is large enough to be important, whether it was the result of chance or not. One of the most important tools of inferential statistics is the *t test,* used to determine whether the differences in two groups' scores are statistically significant. The calculation of t requires subtracting the mean scores of one group from another. This number is divided by a number estimating the standard deviation of the differences between group means. When *degrees of freedom* are factored in, the resulting t value can be compared with a number on a special t table. Numbers larger than those corresponding to *p* values of .05 indicate that such differences are the result of chance only five times out of 100. When *t* values obtained are less than the *t* values in the table under the .05 column, differences are not considered statistically significant.

Other statistical tests exist, including an analysis of variance, a way of determining if there are statistically significant differences in more than two groups.

Fill-in-the-Blank Quiz

1. The difference between the highest and lowest score in a data set is the variability statistic called the _____ .

2. The expression of how far a score is located from the mean in terms of standard deviations is called a(n) _____ .

3. The measure of central tendency that indicates the middlemost score in a distribution is called the _____ .

4. The average difference between each score and the mean of the data set is called the _____ .

5. Numbers that summarize a pool of data are called _____ .

6. The idea that the independent variable has no effect on the dependent variable is called the _____ .

7. The percentage of items that fall below a given score on the normal distribution is called a(n) _____ .

8. The numbers that represent a researcher's findings are called _____ .

9. The arithmetic average of a group of scores is called the _____ .

10. The measure of central tendency that uses the most commonly occurring score is called the _____ .

11. The numbers psychologists use to decide if research results are the result of chance or if the same experiment would yield similar or stronger effects are called _____ .

12. The inferential statistic used to decide if the difference in means between two groups is statistically significant is called the _____ .

13. The notation to indicate the number of subjects in a study is _____ .

14. A picturelike graph that shows how many cases received various categories of scores is called a(n) _____ .

15. The bell-shaped curve that is frequently found in recording psychological events is called the _____ .

16. Descriptive statistics that indicate the dispersion or spread of scores in a data set are called measures of _____ .

17. The sample size or number of scores in a data set minus the number of experimental groups that are used to decide if a *t* value is statistically significant are called _____ .

Fill-in-the-Blank Answers

1. range
2. standard score
3. mode
4. standard deviation
5. descriptive statistics
6. null hypothesis
7. percentile score
8. data
9. mean
10. mode
11. inferential statistics
12. *t* test
13. *N*
14. frequency histogram
15. normal distribution
16. variability
17. degrees of freedom

Fact and Concept Questions

1. A psychologist has done a study comparing the reading scores of children who were taught in a traditional classroom with the reading scores of children taught in an open floor plan classroom. The psychologist will use statistics to test a null hypothesis. What is the null hypothesis in this study?
   a. Open floor plan children will read better.
   b. Open floor plan children will read worse.
   c. Floor plan will make no difference in the reading scores.
   d. None of the children will learn to read.

2. In an experiment, a psychologist reports that the *N* was 38. This means that
   a. the average score for the subjects was 38.
   b. the difference between the highest and the lowest score was 38.
   c. there were 38 categories of scores used in giving the descriptive statistics.
   d. there were 38 subjects in the study.

3. In the following group of scores, what is the mode?

   0, 0, 0, 4, 7, 10, 21

   a. 0
   b. 3
   c. 4
   d. 6

4. The _____ is the measure of central tendency that is most sensitive to extreme scores. It is usually thought of as the average.
   a. median
   b. range
   c. standard deviation
   d. mean

5. The range and the standard deviation are both
   a. inferential statistics
   b. measures of central tendency
   c. ways of measuring the null hypothesis
   d. measures of variability

6. When a sample of scores forms the normal distribution, we know that
   a. the mean and the mode are the same score.
   b. 68 percent of the scores are one standard deviation above and below the mean.
   c. the curve is bell shaped.
   d. All of the above.

7. What is a standard score?
   a. The difference between the mean and a particular score measured in terms of standard deviations.
   b. The average difference between each score and the mean of the whole sample.
   c. The number of subjects in the study.
   d. A way of determining if the differences between the means of two groups are caused by chance.

8. Unlike descriptive statistics, inferential statistics are designed to
   a. summarize the data in terms of central tendency.
   b. summarize the data in terms of variability.
   c. determine whether differences or correlations are genuine and stable.
   d. prove that the null hypothesis is better than the experimental hypothesis.

9. A psychologist would correctly use a *t* test
   a. if it were unclear whether the study was an experiment or a correlation.
   b. when she/he wanted to know if the difference in mean scores for two groups was statistically significant.
   c. if there were only one subject in the study.
   d. when she/he wanted to know if three or more groups' mean scores were correlated.

10. An analysis of variance is
    a. a measure of the standard deviation.
    b. an inferential statistic used to analyze more than two groups.
    c. a way of comparing the scores of one person against those of the entire sample.
    d. considered statistically significant if differences would occur 20 out of 100 times by chance.

Application Questions

1. A psychologist is reporting the descriptive statistics for a study. We would expect which of the following information?
    a. the N for the study
    b. the results of the t test
    c. Both a and b.
    d. Neither a nor b.

2. On a 60-point test, five students get the following scores: 10, 10, 20, 50, 60. What is the median score for the students?
    a. 10
    b. 20
    c. 30
    d. 50

3. Dr. Kim says, "In my study the means of the two groups were the same as the modes. The range was 50, but the standard deviation was only 2.5. The difference in the means was 10.5." Which of Kim's statistics is impossible?
    a. It is impossible for the means to be the same as the modes.
    b. It is impossible for the range to be greater than the standard deviation.
    c. It is impossible for the difference in the means to be greater than the standard deviation.
    d. There is nothing impossible in the statistics being reported.

4. Dr. Gartner has performed an experiment in which there are two groups. To determine whether differences in the means of the two groups are genuine and stable, she would use
    a. a correlation coefficient.
    b. an analysis of variance.
    c. a t test.
    d. a measure of central tendency.

5. Jill is getting ready to perform a *t* test on the data she collected for her senior honors project. What statistics does she need in order to do the computations?
   a. the number of people in each group
   b. the standard deviation for each group
   c. Both *a* and *b*.
   d. Neither *a* nor *b*.

Fact and Concept Answers

1. * c. The null hypothesis asserts that the independent variable has no effect on the dependent variable; in this study, floor plan would have no effect on reading scores. (A1, A8)

   a. The null hypothesis says that the independent variable has no effect.

   b. The null hypothesis says that the independent variable has no effect.

   d. The idea that children will fail to learn to read is not a part of this study.

2. * d. *N* is the notation used as a descriptive statistic for the number of subjects or cases in a research study. (A2)

   a. The average score is the mean.

   b. The difference between the highest and lowest scores is the range.

   c. *N* refers to the number of subjects, not the number of categories.

3. * a. The most commonly occurring score was 0, and the mode is the measure of central tendency reflecting the most commonly occurring score. (A3)

   b. The mode does not reflect how many people got the same score.

   c. The median is the middle-most score.

   d. The mean is the arithmetic average.

4. * d. The mean is most representative of the value of all the data, but it is greatly influenced by extreme scores. (A5)

   a. The median is the middle-most score and is largely unaffected by extreme scores.

   b. The range is a measure of variability.

   c. The standard deviation is a measure of variability.

5. * d. The range and standard deviation are descriptive statistics that summarize information about the spread or dispersion of scores. (A4)

   a. The range and standard deviation are descriptive statistics.

   b. The mean, median, and mode are measures of central tendency.

   c. Inferential statistics are needed to test the null hypothesis.

6. * d. The normal curve is bell shaped, with the mean, median, and mode at the same point (the top of the curve); it is also a curve that permits precise estimates of the distribution of scores, such as knowing that 68 percent of scores fall one standard deviation above and below the mean. (A5)

   a. This is correct, but so are *b* and *c*.

   b. This is correct, but so are *a* and *c*.

   c. This is correct, but so are *a* and *b*.

7. * a. Standard scores measure the distance between a specific score and the mean in terms of standard deviations. (A6)

   b. The standard deviation is the averaged difference of scores from the mean.

   c. *N* refers to the number of cases or subjects in a study.

   d. The *t* test is an inferential statistic that determines whether group differences are due to chance.

8. * c. Descriptive statistics summarize and describe; inferential statistics make judgments about the stability of results and their likelihood of having happened because of chance. (A2, A8)

   a. Descriptive statistics summarize information about central tendency in terms of the mean, median, and mode.

   b. Descriptive statistics summarize information about variability in terms of the range and the standard deviation.

   d. Inferential statistics cannot prove that one hypothesis is better than another, just the likelihood that results are caused by chance.

9. * b. The *t* test is an inferential statistic designed to determine if the difference between two groups' means are caused by chance or not. (A9)

   a. There is no statistic that can make this determination; the design of the study indicates this.

   c. A *t* test makes sense only if there are two groups of subjects.

   d. Analysis of variance must be used to determine if group differences for more than two groups are caused by chance alone.

10. * b. Analysis of variance is an inferential statistical method used to determine if differences in means of more than two groups are the result of chance or a genuine effect. (A11)

   a. Analysis of variance is an inferential statistical method, not a descriptive statistic.

   c. Percentile and standard scores are methods of comparing individual scores with group population scores.

   d. Psychologists typically consider results statistically significant if they might be caused by chance in *five* out of 100 cases.

Application Answers

1. * a. Descriptive statistics include the number of subjects studied (N), measures of central tendency, measures of variability, and correlation coefficients. (A2–A3)

   b. The t test is an inferential statistic because it estimates the likelihood that results were the result of chance.

   c. Because b is not accurate, this cannot be the best choice.

   d. Because a is accurate, this is not the right answer.

2. * b. This score is halfway through the distribution of scores, two are below it and two above. The median is the middlemost score. (A3)

   a. This score is the most frequently occurring score, the mode.

   c. This score represents the arithmetic average for the data set, the mean.

   d. Check your arithmetic: this score represents neither the mean, the median, nor the mode.

3. * d. There is nothing wrong or impossible in what Dr. Kim says. (A4)

   a. The mean and the mode can be the same; in fact, in normal distributions they always are.

   b. The range must be larger than the standard deviation because it is the maximum separation of scores; the standard deviation is the average difference from the mean.

   c. Differences in means are unrelated to standard deviation scores; one deals with central tendency, the other with variability.

4. * c. The t test is the inferential statistic to use when determining whether the difference between two means is due to chance or some genuine effect. (A9)

   a. A correlation coefficient indicates the direction and strength of association between two groups of scores; it is not used for difference scores.

   b. Analysis of variance is used when there are more than two groups.

   d. Measures of central tendency such as the median and mean are descriptive; they do not indicate the genuineness or stability of results.

5. * c. The calculation of the t statistic requires the means of the two groups, the number of subjects in each group, and the standard deviation for each group. (A9)

   a. This is true, but so is b.

   b. This is true, but so is a.

   d. If a and b are accurate, why would you choose this?